ALIAS

S. S. VAN DINE

ALIAS

S. S. VAN DINE

JOHN LOUGHERY

CHARLES SCRIBNER'S SONS
New York

MAXWELL MACMILLAN CANADA
Toronto

MAXWELL MACMILLAN INTERNATIONAL
New York Oxford Singapore Sydney

Charles Scribner's Sons   Maxwell Macmillan Canada, Inc.
Macmillan Publishing Company   1200 Eglinton Avenue East, Suite 200
866 Third Avenue   Don Mills, Ontario M3C 3N1
New York, NY 10022

Library of Congress Cataloging-in-Publication Data
Loughery, John.
Alias S. S. Van Dine / John Loughery.
p.   cm.
Includes bibliographical references and index.
ISBN 0-684-19358-2
1. Van Dine, S. S.   2. Novelists, American—20th century—
Biography.   3. Detective and mystery stories, American—History and
criticism.   I. Title.
PS3545.R846Z75   1992   91-32328   CIP
813'.52—dc20
[B]

Macmillan books are available at special discounts for bulk purchases for sales promotions, premiums, fund-raising, or educational use. For details, contact:

Special Sales Director
Macmillan Publishing Company
866 Third Avenue
New York, NY 10022

10 9 8 7 6 5 4 3 2 1
Printed in the United States of America

FOR VIRGINIA AND EDWARD LOUGHERY

WILLARD HUNTINGTON WRIGHT (AND PHILO VANCE)

"... probably the biggest liar in Christendom ... but nevertheless an amusing fellow."
—*H. L. Mencken*

"Under Wright *The Smart Set* reflected a shameless blood-lust, too fulgurous and unrelieved to suit me entirely, but still forceful and convincing."
—*Theodore Dreiser*

"Wright thinks me a bit cracked and regards himself as the sane and normal and practical male."
—*Ezra Pound to James Joyce*

"... the most interesting and attractive unlikable man I have ever known."
—*Ernest Boyd*

"Handsome, arrogant, erudite, and corrupt ..."
—*Odell Shepard*

"A serious and discerning critic ... reckless ... his views on modern art were more daring than any that had yet been expressed."
—*Sam Hunter*

"Philo Vance was the form under which a gallant, gentle man concealed a spirit almost too delicate and sensitive for an age so turbulent and crude as this."
—*Maxwell Perkins*

"Philo Vance/Needs a kick in the pance."
—*Ogden Nash*

CONTENTS

ACKNOWLEDGMENTS

The research needed to complete a biography necessarily leads a writer in directions, both geographical and intellectual, that he never anticipated traveling. In fact, the very lack of a clear-cut path is a biographer's incentive, and the unforeseen travels, new relationships, and odd readings that forge the path are what makes such work as pleasurable as it is. Certainly the subject of this book—called by his friend H. L. Mencken "the biggest liar in Christendom"—did nothing to expedite the process; Willard Huntington Wright destroyed more letters and released more false information about himself than I ever imagined possible when I began my research. So it is a particularly satisfying task to acknowledge those individuals and institutions that were helpful in my attempt to tell the story of this singular life and career.

My principal archival sources of information for this book have been the Willard Huntington Wright Scrapbooks (sixty-eight volumes containing Wright memorabilia and most of the newspaper articles written by and about Wright) at the Princeton University Library, the Willard Huntington Wright Collection (over 1,200 family letters) at the Alderman Library at the University of Virginia, and the Wright letters to Alfred Stieglitz, H. L. Mencken, James Gibbons Huneker, and others at the Beinecke Library at Yale University. The librarians at those institutions were unfailingly helpful, most especially Ann Van Arsdale at Princeton.

I have also consulted Wright materials, principally correspondence, in the following collections and universities: the Theodore Dreiser Collection and the Burton Rascoe Collection at the Van Pelt Library of the University of Pennsylvania; the William Stanley Braithwaite Collection at the Alderman Library of the University of Virginia; the Scribner Archive at the Princeton University Library; the Jack London Collection at the Huntington Library in San Marino, California; the Ben Huebsch Papers at the Library of Congress in Washington, D.C.; the Local History Collection of the Jones Memorial Library in Lynchburg, Virginia. My visits to the Historical Society of Albemarle County in Charlottesville, Virginia, the Huntington Memorial Library in Oneonta, New York, and the Santa Monica Public Library in Santa Monica, California, were also vital to my research. I am pleased to acknowledge the personal and courteous assistance the staff members at those places gave me. The registrars and librarians at Harvard University, Loyola-Marymount College, Pomona College, Syracuse University, and the University of Southern California answered my many questions about their schools and Wright's college days with patience and promptness.

My knowledge of Wright's working life and its social context owes much to the resources of the Archives of American Art, the Library of Congress, the Los Angeles Public Library, the *Los Angeles Times* Archives, the New York Public Library, the San Francisco Public Library, the New Britain Institute, and the libraries of the Metropolitan Museum of Art, the Museum of Modern Art, and the Whitney Museum of American Art. Without access to the books, periodicals, newspapers, correspondence, and journals housed at those libraries, my work would have been greatly impeded.

A secondary benefit of this undertaking has been the chance to learn more about Willard Huntington Wright's brother, Stanton Macdonald-Wright, a talented painter and remarkable man.

Mrs. Macdonald-Wright of Beverly Hills kindly shared with me some information about her late husband and his brother, for which I am grateful. Jon Tuska's correspondence with, and recollections of, Stanton Macdonald-Wright also provided many interesting facts and insights about the Wrights and aided my research immeasurably. (Film and detective-fiction students know Mr. Tuska's work.) As the author and editor of an informative chapbook on S. S. Van Dine, Jon Tuska had a lively interest in this biography, and I appreciated the opportunity to visit him in Oregon and discuss Wright's career and strange relationship to his brother. The Carl Dolmetsch/Macdonald-Wright letters at the Swett Library of William and Mary College were also useful sources of information, and of course Dr. Dolmetsch's book on *The Smart Set* advanced my labors in countless ways.

Acknowledgment must be made to a fair number of individuals. I am particularly grateful for various services, information, and thoughtful suggestions provided by William C. Agee, Dr. Joseph Baird, Marilyn Baker, Fred Basten, William T. Beatty II, A. Scott Berg, Carl Bode, James Butcher, Philip Butcher, Marie Bruni, Anne Caiger, Eugenie Candau, Anne Chamberlain, Joseph Chowning, Paul Christopher, Allen Churchill, Walter Crawford, Calvin Fenton, Angie Florie, Franklin Gilliam, the late Lloyd Goodrich, Anne Harrell, Robert Hull, Christopher Knight, Gail Levin, Richard Lingeman, Honor Lister, Richard Ludwig, Elizabeth Marsh, Tim Mason, Sandy McAdams, Dorothy Mongam, Nancy Moure, Francis Naumann, Tom Owen, Barry Parris, Otto Penzler, Mary Pratt, Henry Reed, Kathleen Reed, John Rewald, Thomas Riggio, Tanya Rizzo, John Robinson, Millard Sheets, Arnold Schwab, Midori Scott, Craig St. Clair, Carolyn Strickler, Richard Terry, Judith Throm, the Rev. Richard Trame, S. J., Dori Boynton Watson, and Dr. Joseph Youngerman.

At Scribners I was well served by the editorial skill of Ned Chase, Bill Goldstein, and Hamilton Cain and the superb copyediting of Fred Sawyer and Andrew Attaway.

My thanks to Richard Martin, former editor of *Arts Magazine*, and Michael Seidman, former editor of *The Armchair Detective*, for publishing excerpts from the manuscript in years past.

Three people—friends—deserve special mention. David R.

Smith, archivist at Disney Studios, graciously shared with me his vast collection of S. S. Van Dine materials and screened his rare print of *The "Canary" Murder Case* for me at his home in Burbank. Robert O. Davis, a friend of Willard Wright's cousin, Marguerite Beatrice Child, was bequeathed the Wright family scrapbook, and to his kindness and care of those photographs I owe most of the illustrations in this book. And Dr. Michael Robertson of Lafayette College has been both an intellectual ally and a bountiful source of literary and bibliographic information. In his time at Princeton, he was my "academic world" contact and an invaluable guide through the stacks and mss. catalogues.

My mother in Connecticut was encouraging (and diligent in her proofreading), and my good friends there and in New York—Ty and Angie Florie, Tom Gatch, Cindy Kane, Kevin Lally, Helen Malinowski, and Stewart Galanor—supplied me with much-needed confidence and assistance.

Maria Soares went well beyond the bounds of friendship with her goodwill, enthusiasm, and much-needed prodding. Her faith in me was vital.

Last but certainly not least: Thomas Orefice has lived the experience with me. After so many years, he knows my gratitude and regard.

John Loughery
1991

PREFACE

In the early autumn of 1938, in what had become a seasonal ritual of therapy, Willard Huntington Wright met his editor, Max Perkins, for "tea." A few doors down the street from Perkins' office on Fifth Avenue, over snifters of Courvoisier, the two old friends talked about the book business and the state of the world. For Willard, who usually did most of the talking, these were equally painful topics of conversation.

Throughout the late Twenties, Willard Huntington Wright had been one of Scribners' best-selling authors. His detective novels, translated into eleven languages, had sold more than a million copies by the end of the decade. With his Van Dyke beard and pearl-handled cane, he was a striking (if enigmatic) figure in New York society, a man who had appeared out of nowhere, it seemed, to become the famous mystery novelist "S. S. Van Dine." As Van Dine, Willard had enjoyed all the rewards of a formidable success. Even by the standards of the Jazz Age, his penthouse was palatial, and his spending sprees were notorious. The modern paintings and the Chinese ceramics, the private kennels and the specially bred dogs, the fantastic aquaria and the exotic fish (more than two thousand of them)—it had all been photographed and written about, endlessly. In those lavish years Willard could have been a character in a Fitzgerald short story, a performer in a magical, unreal world, dazzled by his own good fortune.

No one, least of all Willard himself, had ever expected his novels to create much of a stir. When Willard had shown his first plot outlines to Max Perkins, he had merely hoped someday to get out from under a mountain of debt. Yet, within a few weeks of the publication of his first novel in 1926, the phenomenon of S. S. Van Dine had taken on a life of its own. So strong was the appeal of Willard's sleuth Philo Vance by 1930 that Perkins could credit the Van Dine murder mysteries with seeing Scribners through the first rough months following the stock-market crash. Any reason to feel confidence in the future, Perkins had told F. Scott Fitzgerald, was largely due to Willard, "whose books seem not to be affected by the Depression—in fact, almost to have gained by it." There was little his publishers wouldn't do for Willard then, as Hollywood studios competed for screen rights to his novels and publicists stoked the fires of popular journalism. In his prime, Willard was one of the most interviewed writers in America, and one of the most affluent.

But times had changed, and with them the audience for detective fiction. Realism in crime-solving was the new order of the day, a shift in taste that had a damaging effect on the income and self-confidence of Philo Vance's creator. Willard had no flair for the "hard-boiled" school of detective writing that followed his own more delicate style. He loathed Dashiell Hammett's novels— "all booze and erections," he complained to a friend—but he could see that his rival's world was the one the public knew and wanted. Throughout the Thirties he watched his influence erode, in Hollywood and New York. One humiliating truth was especially clear: the time was fast approaching when he would be a liability at Scribners. But the more Willard anguished over his situation, the less he was able to do about it. Rex Stout had appeared on the scene in that time, Dorothy Sayers' novels had found their audience, and Agatha Christie was more prolific than ever. From all sides, he saw himself beaten. Nero Wolfe, Peter Wimsey, and Hercule Poirot didn't leave any room for the elegant cynicism of Philo Vance, who seemed more than ever a holdover from the day of the flapper and the speakeasy.

It was to Perkins that Willard regularly turned in his decline to vent his anger and frustration. Their sessions together could be nerve-racking, but Perkins was a patient, diplomatic man, especially good at bringing Willard round to a more philosophical calm. As an editor at Scribners for more than twenty years, he had coped in his time with Hemingway's anxieties, Fitzgerald's collapse, and the legendary indulgences of Thomas Wolfe. Max Perkins knew about unhappy writers. If he found himself sorely tried by Willard's grim monologues and ramblings, especially those stirred by a second or a third drink, he was too gracious to say so. On his part, Willard certainly understood how difficult he could be—he had alienated more than his share of friends over the years—and appreciated his editor's forbearance.

By the end of 1938, though, it was proving harder for Perkins, or anyone, to relieve Willard's desperate state of mind. He looked exhausted and, at fifty-one, was often taken for a man well into his sixties. The famous beard was almost white. He was obsessed by events in Europe and the drift toward war, by the fickleness of the public, and by his own failure. A well-read man with a passion for the arts, like the detective he wrote about, Willard had always been able to find what sustenance he needed in his library or among his pictures, but that wasn't true any longer. The part of him that had once been an adventurous editor and a controversial art critic was long dead. Only one pleasure remained intact. "I'm so glad for all the brandy I've had," Willard told Perkins that afternoon before they parted. "I've enjoyed the brandy. I only regret that I didn't drink more of it."

Back in his apartment on Central Park West, overlooking the park at 84th Street, Willard had ample cause to lose himself in brandy. He left Perkins to return home to work on a plot outline that disgusted and embarrassed him. *The Winter Murder Case*, which would eventually become the twelfth and last S. S. Van Dine novel, wasn't even being written as an original Scribners publication. It had been conceived as a plot idea by the story department at Twentieth Century–Fox. It was Willard's task, for the ample sum of $25,000, to prod it into shape as the basis for a B-movie. Only when the deal on the movie was set and an audience for the story guaranteed would *The Winter Murder Case* be reshaped into a full-length novel and published by Scribners.

This was the second time Willard had reversed the usual process of turning a novel into a screenplay. His most recent book, *The Gracie Allen Murder Case*, which Scribners was halfheartedly pushing in its Christmas ads, had been pieced together in the same way. It was a sorry pattern, and the meaning of it was obvious to everyone who knew Willard. To pay for a standard of living that far outdistanced his royalties, he had swallowed his pride and announced himself willing to write to order. For anyone, without any conditions, if the money was right. Under the circumstances, Willard could hardly be called a novelist anymore.

The first draft proceeded slowly. Philo Vance, once dapper and energetic, creaked across the pages of this dull murder mystery. Even the detective's traditional setting, the streets and apartments of Manhattan, had been abandoned. The studio wanted picturesque wintry shots and ice-skating scenes; the studio wanted the female lead written with Sonja Henie, a new starlet, in mind (a woman of some grave limitations, the producers hinted to Willard); the studio wanted a happy ending. Willard dutifully complied. Acutely aware that he was writing trash, he was determined to prostitute himself like a professional—to hold nothing back. Indeed, Willard became so obsequious in his correspondence with the Fox story department, so eager to know their wishes, that company executives were made uneasy by the novelist they had hired. After all, wasn't Willard Huntington Wright supposed to be the most temperamental of New York authors?

Friends saw less of Willard and his wife, Claire, that autumn than at any time previously. It wasn't unusual for the Wrights to hibernate in the penthouse when Willard was in the middle of a book or during a period of intense manuscript revision, but there were some people who wondered if Willard ever planned to emerge from this new seclusion. His social relationships had grown increasingly tense and awkward. Any conversation about his career, any hints of condescension or sympathy or disapproval, set him on edge. But it was hard for those who had known Willard for years to pretend that all was well. He talked about money incessantly and, despite his doctor's warnings, continued to drink too much.

When, in mid-November, Willard learned from a producer at

Twentieth Century–Fox that the story he was working on for them wouldn't be billed as a Philo Vance mystery, though the studio had no objection to Vance's appearance in the movie or any concern with what role he played, he had even more reason to be discouraged. At that moment it was clear to Willard, if he hadn't realized it before, that the principal feature of his writing since he had given up his art and literary criticism, the character with whom he was most identified, had become a negligible commodity even in Hollywood. There was nothing now to distinguish him from any other writer whose price the companies could meet. And eventually, he knew, that source of income would dry up as well. Within a few years there wouldn't be any reason for the studios to meet his price. No one would want or remember S. S. Van Dine.

As if he suspected that this project would be his last, Willard set about looking for an epigraph to his story, always a matter of fastidious concern to him, even before he completed the first draft. In Wordsworth he found the appropriate line: "Stern Winter loves a dirge-like sound." His secretary typed the quotation on a blank sheet of paper which he placed by the cover of the manuscript.

The atmosphere at the Wrights' penthouse became progressively more charged, almost eerie. Willard's doctor visited almost every day, monitoring his friend's condition. His butler continued to fill the brandy decanter by his desk each afternoon, as he had been directed to. Claire said nothing. Willard wrote and revised with feverish energy.

Shortly before Christmas Willard paid another visit to Max Perkins. On this occasion there wasn't any stepping out for "tea" or time for a walk down Fifth Avenue. He made his call to the fifth-floor offices at Scribners for a purpose, with a request that needed an immediate answer. Willard was preparing his will, he told Perkins, and he wanted him to be his executor. It was an uncomplicated document but he wanted to know that everything would be handled properly. The thought of such a task was agonizing to Perkins, who was himself preoccupied that year with his own aging and mortality. Thomas Wolfe had died only a few months earlier, and Perkins wasn't ready to contemplate the passing of any more of "his" writers. But he saw that he had no choice. It was important to Willard, who looked even more tired and restless than at the time of their previous meeting, and so Perkins reluctantly agreed. Satisfied to have the matter settled, Willard left the office, entered his car at the corner of 48th Street, and was chauffeured home to Central Park West to tend to the solving of Philo Vance's last case.

The end came soon, almost on schedule.

Several weeks after seeing Perkins, having coped with a number of long and gently critical letters from Fox on the subject of his handling of the narrative, Willard completed the last scene of the 20,000-word story. Two days later he suffered a mild heart attack at home. It appeared, at first, that he would recover, and he left the hospital after a brief stay to rest under his wife's care. He seemed to be getting stronger all the time. He could rouse himself to better humor than he had shown in months and was enjoying all the attention. He even worked a little more on the manuscript. But on the afternoon of Tuesday, April 11, as he relaxed in bed after lunch, with his wife still in the room, Willard slid back onto his pillow and closed his eyes. As Claire Wright told Max Perkins, it was an astonishingly quick and gentle end.

On his desk was a typed first draft of *The Winter Murder Case*—"complete to the last comma," Perkins noted.

Like most newspapers in the country, *The New York Times* on April 12, 1939, ran a long obituary for America's best-known detective novelist. The following day, in a still loftier tribute, a *Times* editorial praised Willard Huntington Wright as a master of his art who had known "a kind of subtler splendor in his way of life." Reviewing the popularity of the Van Dine murder mysteries and their author's famous style of living, the editorial concluded: "He who had killed so many harmlessly knew how to live with enjoyment." Of the fears and tensions that dominated Willard's last years, the public knew very little. The *Times* preserved the image of S. S. Van Dine, as aesthete and connoisseur, that Willard had long cultivated.

Reactions to Willard's death from among those who had been close to him at one time or another were more varied and complex. They hint at the many sides of Willard Huntington Wright and give some picture of the almost separate lives he had lived and the different identities he had tried to create.

Alfred Stieglitz, the great champion of modernism in New York, regretted the loss of an old ally from the cultural battles of an earlier day. He and Georgia O'Keeffe knew Willard as a man with a deep appreciation of modern art, with a passion for honest, original work and an eagerness to fight for it. The publisher Ben Heubsch remembered the feisty critic who, before the Great War, had done his part for American literature in the face of censorship and cultural ignorance. Others in the literary world recalled a generous and entertaining man whose life had always had something anguished and fabulous about it. Historians of detective fiction, like Howard Haycraft, honored him as the man who had created a vast new audience for detective novels in this country, opening doors for younger writers.

But there were plenty of people who remembered Willard in a different, less benevolent light. They were the friends who had seen him at his worst. When Theodore Dreiser mailed H. L. Mencken an obituary notice about their one-time protégé, the reply from Baltimore was unsentimental. Wright had been "a great liar," Mencken wrote back, "but nevertheless an amusing fellow." Having once taken Willard under his wing, Mencken had long since decided that he was too troublesome and untrustworthy a friend. Dreiser, with his own stories and suspicions about Willard, was inclined to agree. Willard might have been one of the staunchest defenders of *Sister Carrie*, but Dreiser knew a "lean and hungry look" when he saw one and kept his distance. More than a few people in New York were ready to dismiss Willard as a classic sellout, an intellectual turned popular novelist for the sake of the money, and quite possibly the nastiest man they had ever met. Drama critic George Jean Nathan never wanted to hear Willard's name mentioned again.

Appropriately enough, it was left to Max Perkins to describe Willard in the terms he would most have appreciated. In a preface to *The Winter Murder Case*, published later in 1939 just as it was found, he wrote about Willard as one, easily misjudged, who had suffered more than most people knew from his own sensitivity and the insensitivities of the age. The real man was well hidden from the world, the unsigned "Preface of an Editor" noted, and to understand such a person demanded a personal and a cultural context and a willingness to look beneath the surface.

For Willard Huntington Wright's story, Perkins implied, was an unusual drama that was also about the era and the country he lived in. Wright's life was explained by certain kinds of risks, desires, and conflicts that not every man chose to grapple with. Private needs, social turmoil, a nation's coming-of-age, poverty, and the difficult terms of success in America—Perkins hinted at complex pressures placed on "a gallant, gentle man" in a time that was "turbulent and crude."

In turning to his editor in his need for an executor, Willard had also, of course, been asking him to serve as caretaker of his name and reputation. Perkins undoubtedly knew this. But as Willard feared all along, it was a hopeless cause, and nothing Max Perkins could do or say had any effect. No American writer of comparable fame and wealth in his day suffered so abrupt an eclipse in the public mind as did Willard Huntington Wright. Ten years after his death most of his books were out-of-print, and by the 1960s he was a forgotten name in American literary history—though not, ironically, in the history of modern art and art criticism. His articles on behalf of Cézanne and the new abstract painting, the writing at which he could not make a living, in time earned him more regard than the books which made him known all over the world.

It was Willard Huntington Wright's fate to live a life more interesting than his work. That is not a thought that would have pleased him, but the truth of that statement applies to both his fiction and his critical writing. Not even the most extravagant exploits of Philo Vance can compare to the wealth of experience, the adventures and trials, of Willard's own life. Yet Willard did his best to hide this story, the one that matters, and destroyed much of his correspondence and left a monstrous trail of false information behind him.

As Perkins, Stieglitz, Mencken, and so many others knew, Willard was a remarkable man of great gifts and terrible flaws, eager to play a part in the modern world, to understand and belong. In the end, though, his was a story about failure on a grand scale, and about identity and its loss. Unable to resolve the contradictions of his life at the end, Willard Huntington Wright—the very image of American success in his day—died a tormented and angry man.

ALIAS

S. S. VAN DINE

WITH
THE SMART SET

"The public demand for a work being in inverse ratio to its quality, one exists by chance and a series of ignominies . . . the prudery of my country . . ."

—Ezra Pound to James Joyce, 1915

From the beginning, Willard Huntington Wright's objectives were lofty: the raising of American journalism and criticism to new heights and the emancipation of American literature. Timorous editors and complacent readers, provincial critics and Victorian values, the American fear of anything new and demanding in the arts—these had been Willard's themes throughout five rancorous years as a California journalist. Ezra Pound's complaint to James Joyce about "the prudery of my country" was a cry that frustrated American writers had been sounding for the better part of thirty years. As the newly appointed editor of a New York magazine with a six-figure circulation, Willard—at twenty-five and supremely self-confident—was sure that he could do something to change all that. In the process, he told his wife, he might even become rich and famous.

Given his age, character, and ambitions, Willard Huntington Wright was an odd choice for the editorship of a magazine like *The Smart Set,* and in January 1913 not many people outside Los Angeles actually knew much about him. But he came to his job in New York thanks to the glowing recommendation of H. L.

Mencken, the magazine's book reviewer, and he seemed to everyone to have won over John Adams Thayer, the publisher, in record time. He also had earned a name for himself as one of the most prolific columnists in American journalism, second only to Mencken himself. Still and all, a fair number of people in New York were uncertain of what to expect from a critic loud in his defense of controversial realists like Dreiser and Zola, shameless in his disdain for female novelists, and relentlessly cranky about most bestsellers.

Surely it was the right moment for a clever, driven young man to arrive on the scene. The world of American magazine journalism, so influential at molding public opinion and guiding public taste in the years before radio and television, was at a point of grotesque stagnation. With the exception of Mitchell Kennerley's enlightened and lively *Forum* or those journals like *McClure's* and *Collier's* that had given space to the muckrakers' exposés of corrupt politicians and greedy trusts, the monthlies had long since settled for the security of established contributors, "wholesome" fiction, well-mannered essays, and political commentary of a scrupulously unthreatening character. There seemed to be no place for satire, ribaldry, the realism the best new writers were exploring, or any hint of the European ferment in the arts. *The Dial, The New Republic, Seven Arts, The American Mercury, Vanity Fair, The New Yorker,* exciting periodicals both popular and more intellectual—all of those magazines were yet to come, while *Scribner's, Harper's, The Atlantic Monthly,* and so many more were notoriously cool to unknown authors and unusual proposals.

To Willard, to Mencken, to many of their friends, this was a situation that had to be changed, if ever America was to "come of age," and in *The Smart Set* they felt they had found the vehicle of that change. Although very little of it worked out quite as planned, the magazine nonetheless became (in the words of critic Alfred Kazin) "a token of vigorous experiment," part of a national movement that had "sounded a trumpet call" in a "joyous season of great beginnings."

It came as no surprise to Willard Huntington Wright that office politics at *The Smart Set* was stormy and conspiratorial when he arrived in Manhattan at the beginning of the new year. In order to bring in Mencken's "boy wonder" from the West, John

Adams Thayer had had to make some abrupt rearrangements in his personnel. The most significant change involved Norman Boyer, the magazine's competent but unimaginative senior editor. To the consternation of the staff, Boyer was now going to be "managing editor" under Willard. Throughout the next several months he nursed an understandable grudge, silently but obviously waiting for his young boss to fall on his face. Everyone else in the office, from assistant editors to the stenographers, seemed to think that Thayer's find was going to be an incompetent kid, easily manipulated and not to be taken too seriously. Willard calmly accepted this state of affairs. He was going to have to prove himself. He wrote to his wife, who had remained behind in California with their young daughter, that he expected that process to take about a month. When everyone understood that he couldn't be bullied, things would settle down.

One decision, wisely calculated, which Willard made before leaving Los Angeles was to change his appearance. His dark beard, grown three years before to make him look older, was gone now and in its place was a long, severe, upturned moustache. It was, flagrantly, a Kaiser Wilhelm look. He had himself photographed, and Thayer agreed to publish the startling picture of his editor in the March issue of *The Smart Set*. The photograph, retouched for the desired effect, appears to show a forty-year-old Prussian aristocrat, a prematurely balding but energetic, self-assured, slightly unsavory man. The new look made Willard seem even older than the "early thirties" he liked to claim as his age, just as it advertised to the world a carefully manufactured self-image.

Willard's hope was that the magazine he was taking over was ready to acquire its own new image. In spirit and circulation, it was floundering, and Thayer, Boyer, and everyone in the office knew it. The question was, exactly what were Willard's plans? No one seemed to know. And would those plans work? The skeptics assumed that Thayer, in buying *The Smart Set* two years before, had acquired, at no bargain price, a sinking ship.

The January issue of the magazine was technically the first during Willard's tenure. On the newsstands on the fifteenth of the month, as usual, it had of course nothing of Willard's imprint on it. With each issue ready to go to press six or seven weeks before it appeared, the March issue was the first he could hope to have even a limited influence on. Looking over the opening issue of 1913, which—with the exception of Mencken's book reviews and George Jean Nathan's theater chronicle—was filled with quaint, formulaic, or abominably written material, Willard could see that his work was cut out for him. That month's number showed as forcefully as any other the few strengths and the many weaknesses of *The Smart Set* tradition and the limitations of its publisher's taste. Willard's first impressions of John Adams Thayer were confirmed. The man was "just plain dopey," he concluded. Like most businessmen, Willard told his wife, Thayer was "a bone-head" who couldn't understand that money and good prose had very little to do with each other.

Yet if the package wasn't much to boast of, the new editor saw no reason to despair: more fertile ground for transformation could hardly be found. Thayer had looked at his balance sheets and nervously agreed to try anything, or almost anything, that would turn things around. Willard's dream, shared with Mencken and Nathan and never quite fathomed by Thayer, was of an American journal to rival the best avant-garde publications of Europe. He was certain that if anyone could steer and prod the magazine in that direction, he was the one to do it.

In the February *Smart Set,* in the end pages entitled "Something Personal" which Thayer reserved for his own monthly words of wisdom, Willard was "announced." A few people later suggested that Willard, rather than his employer, penned his own introduction to the magazine's readers, which might well be true. Reticence was not part of his nature. In any event, it is hard to imagine a newly installed editor-in-chief receiving a grander welcome: "We believe no literary critic in America is more sympathetically inclined to help mold the policies of this magazine or to give more intelligent critical service to its readers. . . . He is essentially modern and does not believe in the editorial policy which caters to the prejudices, superstitions, and sentimentalities of unintelligent readers." The column described Willard Huntington Wright as a man "barely in his thirties" (twenty-five years and six months was the truth), "educated at Harvard University" (Willard had once taken two courses there), who was at work on two books, one on the new movement in American letters from 1850 to 1912 and one on the writings of Friedrich Nietzsche. (Both books existed only in outline form, and only the Nietzsche volume ever appeared.) The spring issues of the magazine would illustrate, Thayer promised, a vigorous new approach.

The "Something Personal" column in March officially signaled the transfer of editorial power out of Thayer's hands, a move he was to regret loudly and bitterly by autumn. "This month I have surrendered my column to Mr. Wright," Thayer wrote, making use of the right verb. Willard's stern photograph appeared beneath the headline A NEW EDITOR COMES TO "THE SMART SET" and in "Something Personal" he issued a dramatic call for readers—more readers, better readers, more sophisticated readers. "I believe that this is the day of enlightenment on the part of magazine readers," Willard began. He was certain, he declared, that there was a vast untapped audience out there that wanted something more than what the safe, middle-of-the-road magazines like *Harper's, Scribner's, The Century,* or *The Atlantic Monthly* were providing. The problem was that most editors had been too timid to gamble on that audience's responsiveness.

> The intelligent reader of today is not seeking to have his point of view verified in the things he reads. . . . The average editor, fearful of offending the narrow-minded reader, has not only thwarted and stultified talent, but has also kept the best of the modern literary output from those capable of appreciating it.

The Smart Set was still "opposed to salacity or crudity," Willard reassured his audience, "as much [as it is to] inane or colorless fiction," but the bottom line was: "The hackneyed, the trivial, the false, and the bloodless in letters must go."

An example of what Willard had in mind was the most controversial piece—the only controversial piece—in that month's issue, his own satiric essay on his hometown. "Los Angeles: The Chemically Pure" was an article Willard and Thayer had discussed in the fall, when Willard was wrangling for a job in New York, and was part of the magazine's new series on American cities. Its impact was satisfyingly immediate.

This series was one of Thayer's few good ideas in all the time he owned the magazine, if indeed it was his idea and not Boyer's. "San Francisco the Joyous" had made a good impression five months earlier, and "Washington: Home of the Climber," with its pointed criticism of the status-conscious capital, had been printed in February. "Los Angeles: The Chemically Pure" was a different sort of travelogue, though. It was a loud lament for a romantic, libidinal past that was gone forever and a protest over a state of mind in which bustling business opportunities, "rustic intelligence," and "suburban respectability" were the norm. It was also vintage Willard Huntington Wright.

According to Willard, Los Angeles, whose population promised to grow faster than any other city's in the country and whose ambience and climate sounded so appealing to Easterners tired of the cold, had in reality the temperament and culture of a church bazaar. There the godhead was "a combination of Calvin and Anthony Comstock [the famous censor of books]—with Comstock predominating." Residents suffered from an excess of piety and complacency and a banal fear of sensual and artistic pleasure. But now, the more worldly influence of the Spanish having been expunged by "good Americans," Los Angeles suffered from a "virgin innocence of the joys of nightlife" and had no place for demimonde retreats, cafes, cabarets, or great gourmet restaurants where one could eat "gloriously and riotously."

Like "a West Coast Mencken," as some called him, Willard aimed his satirical reportage at the very readers most magazines sought to soothe and entertain. It was a misfortune, he maintained (sounding very much like Mencken), to be forced to live a proper Christian life amid Southern California's "sober and phlegmatic people, with [their] passion for marching in parades and wearing badges." The streets there were deserted by midnight, and the theater offerings were regulated with a strictness to rival Boston's. Instead of a Pacific "vie de bohème," Browning clubs met for monthly readings, and antivaccination movements offered endless forums.

What caused this stultification? As the author of "Los Angeles: The Chemically Pure" saw it, the problem was simple—the burgeoning Midwestern influence. The vast majority of those coming West to begin a new life or retire in the sun were from parts of the country ignorant of, and defiant toward, the urban values Willard was extolling. Willard had no trouble summarizing the characteristics of his old Santa Monica and Los Angeles neighbors.

> These good folks brought with them a complete stock of rural beliefs, pieties, superstitions, and habits—the Middle West bed hours, the Middle West love of corned beef, church bells, Munsey's Magazine, union suits and missionary societies. They

> brought a complacent and intransigent aversion to late dinners, malt liquor, grand opera, and hussies . . . they have a righteous horror of shapely legs . . . at concerts they applaud the high notes, and they vote their pastor's choice of candidate.

In contrast to the dour citizens from Wichita, Emmitsburg, and Sedalia were those from the East, still too few in number and power. Unfortunately, their influence on "the inflexible doctrine of Puritanism in Los Angeles," with its attendant gossip-mongering and prohibitive town ordinances, was small. "The pietist, the killjoy, the lawn sprinkler" was in control. "Genuine human beings and honest rascals" were hard to find in the "chemically pure," prohibition-minded City of the Angels.

Just as Willard had intended, his impressionistic article produced a brief but intense reaction. Mail poured into the *Smart Set* office applauding or condemning the new editor's sarcasm, depending on the correspondent's proximity to Los Angeles or Sedalia. Most significantly from Thayer's point of view, the magazine's circulation rose a little after that issue. His editor had all the right people hopping mad.

John Adams Thayer was essentially a prudish man, but a controversy of this kind, in which Westerners were patronized and Easterners flattered, wasn't anything to unsettle him. On the contrary, the small-scale uproar seemed to him a healthy thing. Younger readers, those *The Smart Set* needed to attract, appeared to appreciate it. It gave the magazine the "spice," as Thayer called it, that he had been asking for and which Mencken and Nathan had told him was crucial for success.

Unbeknownst to his boss, Willard had played a part in fueling the reaction. He advertised the article himself with a flurry of postcards to journalists and Chamber of Commerce officials back in Los Angeles and asked friends in California to write to Thayer, under their own names or otherwise, praising or attacking the essay. It didn't matter which. Yet somehow, for Willard, that wasn't enough. It was never enough. To his wife, Katharine, he complained, "If only some eminent divine would preach a sermon on me and the article calling me a degenerate and all the rest of it—that would be great. . . . Let me know if anyone comes through." To prod the lethargic clergy of Los Angeles along, Willard sent marked copies of the article to a few of the more prominent area ministers, but none did "come through" with the publicity-generating sermon he wanted. The clubwomen of the city were a little more obliging, and the clippings Katharine sent her husband cheered him: FORMAL ACTION CONDEMNING WRIGHT, PLAN OF WOMEN: *Los Angeles Club Leaders Urge Protest* was a front-page headline from one paper, while *The Los Angeles Examiner* asked, ARE GOOD MORALS A DEBIT OR A CREDIT? and suggested that California was well rid of Willard Huntington Wright.

As Willard looked over the pile of manuscript possibilities that winter, most of which had come into the office since his arrival, he experienced his first unpleasant surprise of the job. A willingness to publish controversial stories, one-act plays, poems, and essays about modern life "as it was really lived" was one thing. That policy he had openly committed himself to in the "Something Personal" column in March. The lack of such material was something Willard hadn't anticipated. He had always assumed that conservative editors were to blame for the confections encountered in most magazines. Now Willard grappled with the fear that the number of literary realists and innovators was not what he had imagined it to be. He wrote to his friend Jack London in Carmel, to see if he had any stories to sell; he spoke to publishers and agents out of town; he asked Mencken and Nathan to pass on any suggestions. But the response was meager. The same happy-ending stories and mawkish verse kept coming in. So the April issue of *The Smart Set* closed, like the issue before it, with a clarion call—this time not for readers, but for writers.

> It seems incredible, in a country where the authors are forever complaining of not receiving intelligent appreciation from editors, that it should be difficult for a magazine to get hold of first-class matter, when the one standard of that magazine's acceptance is merit. . . . But that is just the case with "The Smart Set." We find it difficult to get hold of stories, or poems, or essays . . . that we consider sufficiently meritorious to publish.

"Meritorious" meant different, troubling, rough, unsentimental, undidactic. At the *Smart Set* office it meant, as of now, just the opposite of what it signified at the offices of *The Century* or *Scribner's* or *Ainslee's*.

> We want [unconventional] stories. . . . We know that they exist in America, and that the majority of authors would rather write

stories which are a sincere expression of themselves than write down to the popular level at the behest of editors.

The Smart Set desired new writers as well as established names, and Willard's "A Word to Authors" encouraged unpublished writers to send in their manuscripts if the work was "fresh and vigorous and marked with a fidelity to life . . . and not executed according to the rubber-stamp literary formulas that should have been discarded with bustles and pantalettes."

Over the next few years *The Smart Set* was going to become not only the best magazine in America, its editor predicted, but the kind of journal, socially conscious and alert to new movements, that had never been attempted in this country before on such a scale. "The old maids of both sexes" were no longer in charge.

One writer who benefited from Boyer's ouster and Willard's arrival, even before the famous "A Word to Authors" appeared, was Floyd Dell. "Jessica Screams," in the April number, would have had a hard time finding its way into print at any time before the more liberal Twenties. Its author had tackled two themes in this story, both potentially offensive: female adolescent sexuality and rebellion, and male sexual hypocrisy.

In Dell's story an attractive teenage girl is much admired by Murray Swift, the young acting principal at her Indiana high school. Swift's interest in her is meant to seem suspicious from the start. Dell portrays him as an unconventional man, too sophisticated to adjust to the mores of the small town he temporarily finds himself in. He is also Jessica's potential seducer. But when Jessica escapes her stifling hometown to become a dancer in Chicago, unapologetically capitalizing on her erotic qualities, Swift is horrified. He happens to meet her in the city and sanctimoniously threatens to have the police send her home. Still underage, Jessica offers to go to bed with her ex-teacher to prevent any forced return to the town they both hate. Swift is disgusted by Jessica's boldness; she has claimed the role of the seducer for herself. He sees that the girl is brought back to her parents against her will, and the story ends on a sad but not a moralistic note. Dell's male protagonist can't accept that a young woman's needs, desires, and tactics might be similar to his own, and it is the girl who pays the price for his confusion and dishonesty.

"Jessica Screams" astonished Thayer's regular readers and

precipitated a real (if momentary) controversy, quite unlike "The Chemically Pure" episode. Willard, who loved the story, later told Dell that he received more complaints about this piece than anything else published by *The Smart Set* that year—a high compliment in the editor's eyes. Subscriptions were canceled, letters-to-the-editor covered his desk, newspaper columnists made mention of the outlandish Jessica, and Wall Street friends of the publisher asked just what was going on at the magazine. Thayer was made seriously uncomfortable by the whole matter, never having expected a row of this type. But this, Willard affirmed, was one of the ways one knew the quality of Dell's fiction. It made people tense. It struck a nerve. They knew it had truth in it, he told Thayer. Willard had once declared in an essay from his Los Angeles days that "all American literature seems to be written with the one purpose of proving there is no such thing as sex." He was relieved to have found a native example, post-Dreiser, to prove the contrary. He assured Dell that, when he wrote another story as hard-hitting, the door at *The Smart Set* was open to him.

If Floyd Dell was surprised by Willard's openness to his fiction, he also had cause to be surprised by the check he received after publication. Seventy-five dollars was far above the usual price for a short story by a less-than-established writer in 1913. Yet generosity to his authors, or at the very least the obliging manner due to serious writers, came naturally to Willard. Already, he felt, he had seen too many creative men and women affected by the inevitable problems of their profession: the financial grind, the lack of prestige and security, the sense of their marginal place in the public life of America. In this regard Willard's contract with Thayer had two desirable features to it. He himself enjoyed an ample starting salary of $80 a week with promises of large raises to come, and he was given unheard-of control over expenditures for the magazine. In effect, he could determine the prices for anything—play, poem, novella, essay, or one-line epigram—accepted by the magazine, with only a perfunctory obligation to consult the publisher. Only in this way, Willard explained to Thayer, was he going to be able to make the changes they wanted.

A strange new "system" followed, laced with a good dose of editorial subjectivity and whimsy. Poets used to receiving five or ten dollars per poem might find checks from Willard for five or ten times that amount, arriving by special delivery. Short stories previously bought for twenty-five or thirty dollars were now fetching $70 or $100 or more. A "name" author like Richard Le Gallienne always commanded in the $200 range, but a new-comer like Ludwig Lewisohn, expecting to receive ten dollars for a poem, was startled to receive $100 that spring. Yet other respected writers were sometimes asked to accept a little less than usual until Willard could square things with them later. There was much borrowing from Peter to pay Paul and reliance on goodwill. No one in New York could quite figure out the magazine's new method of payment. But if Willard liked something, if he thought the material artistically important, he acted as if the magazine owed it to the creator to pay full value; anything less would be immoral. It was a duty to do right by one's authors. Most importantly, it was the rigidity of the old formula at the magazine, so many cents per word or line, that Willard was eager to strike down. (Willard's largesse actually owed something to Theodore Dreiser. Dreiser had called Willard cheap after receiving his check for a story *The Smart Set* was to publish that summer, and Willard angrily vowed never again to be placed in that embarrassing position—the business manager be damned.)

The writers who gained exposure that year thanks to the new order at *The Smart Set* were a varied group. Proud as he was to publish work by Dreiser—his vignette, "Lily Edwards," in the July issue told of an encounter with a London waif attempting to become a prostitute—Willard was eager to give a helping hand to the next generation of realists, the younger crowd who were challenging the Genteel Tradition. When Barry Benefield, a Texas writer and friend of a young Scribners editor named Max Perkins, approached Willard with his short stories and the admission that every magazine he had sent his work to had rejected him, Willard was overjoyed. That the other monthlies had turned him away was the best possible recommendation, he told Benefield, and he bought "Daughters of Joy" for the May issue. It could be said that this story, if slightly less unsavory than Dell's, opened certain floodgates. It was the first in what seemed, to the horrified Thayer, an endless stream of stories about a subject his editor never tired of.

Benefield's account of the death and funeral of a young New

York prostitute and life in a "house" on the infamous West 28th Street block of brothels met with a predictable reaction. If Dell's heroine was a teenage girl unashamed of her body and ready to use her sexuality as a tool if she had to—and those notions were offensive enough—how much worse was it that the magazine that had begun life as a high-society entertainment sheet was now printing mournful tales about whores. The indignant letter-writers were at it again, this time with a vengeance. A few more subscribers signed on, a few more old subscribers dropped off. Thayer had to be handled very gently on the subject of Benefield and assured, by both Willard and Mencken, that the author of "Daughters of Joy" was an important young talent, not a por-nographer. A few of the other Benefield stories Willard bought were equally unusual: "Bachelor Embalmerus" in the June issue was a vintage piece of Southern black comedy (of the kind as-sociated today with Eudora Welty or Flannery O'Connor) about a slightly retarded man's determination to become his town's first embalmer, and "Jerry" in the August issue contained one of the most graphic descriptions of a white mob's brutality toward an unjustly accused black man published in the United States before the 1930s.

Albert Payson Terhune was another writer who quickly be-came a regular in *The Smart Set* fold, and Willard solicited ma-terial from him as often as he did from Benefield. Terhune's stories all made use of the same narrator, a jaunty Manhattan cabaret owner and ex-con man, one Aloysius Raegan. Slangy, wisecracking, and indiscreet, he was a far cry from the genteel narrators of Ethel Watts Mumford or Juliet Wilbur Tompkins, two writers Thayer enjoyed. Raegan, whose persona Willard helped Terhune to develop, was a believer in live-and-let-live, and nothing much that went on in the streets or in the under-world of the metropolis surprised him. His observations on women were the reverse of those of vice crusaders like Anthony Comstock, who were then monopolizing the press. The moralists had it backwards, as usual, Raegan maintained. It was hard for a woman "to go wrong." That was the sad truth of the matter, he had found. Everything conspired to keep the unmarried sweat-shop girls and overworked saleswomen poor and respectable rather than shameful and comfortable. In stories like "For Sale" and "The Girl Who Couldn't Go Wrong," Terhune's hero told about attractive young women subject to male harassment and the limited range of their choices. Mattie Mercer, the brothel owner in "The Merchant of Venus," was an American version of Shaw's Mrs. Warren, who came to a good end by being clever and realistic rather than a bad end for being indecent. This, to American readers before the Jazz Age, was scarcely tolerable. The wages of sin were not being suffered.

Though Willard privately thought of Terhune as "a conscientious hack" rather than a strong talent like Dell or Benefield, the fact that his stories bordered on the blasphemous appealed to him. When Thayer protested, Willard held firm, insisting that he knew what he was doing, and he appealed to Mencken to urge their employer to be more patient and trusting.

To those who knew Willard Huntington Wright at all well, his interest in affronting traditional values, and particularly his interest in women who lived by freer-than-ordinary sexual codes, wouldn't have been surprising. Katharine Wright had had to come to terms early in her marriage with her husband's inability to maintain a monogamous relationship; his bravado and good looks made him very attractive to plenty of women. Willard dressed well, now that he was a New York editor, looking—as Mencken's friend Ernest Boyd noted—"as if he had just left the Café de la Paix . . . a Right-Bank American, if ever there was one." Boyd also analyzed Willard perceptively as a man who "made no appeal to the affections, save those of certain members of the opposite sex." He struck many of the Baltimore crowd Mencken introduced him to as fascinating, elegant, intense, at times a little chilling and, always, too cocksure of himself. "He was the most interesting and attractive unlikable man I have ever known," Boyd later commented.

Pondering his problem of the lack of good manuscripts by American writers, poets, and especially dramatists, Willard devised a plan in his fifth month on the job that excited him and even sounded reasonable to Thayer. Willard's idea was to go to Europe himself to see as many writers, publishers, and literary agents as he could in a concentrated period, negotiating on the spot for more and better stories. Clearly the feelers he had sent out in New York weren't yielding as much as he had hoped, and if Thayer was serious about wanting to raise the quality and circulation of his magazine, some further financial risk had to be undertaken. Subject to the whirlwind effect of his editor's enthusiasm, Thayer agreed to finance a month abroad.

Willard had several objectives in hatching this idea, not all of which he discussed with Thayer. To start, he was sure Europe offered a better field for drama; the one-act plays that had been coming into the office were only getting worse, and Willard had been an early fan of the new British, French, and German playwrights. He was also interested in meeting Ezra Pound. Everyone seemed to think that Pound, a Yeats protégé living in London now, was the right man for an editor in search of original material to see. Willard was fairly confident that Pound hadn't seen the negative review of his poetry Willard had written for *The Los Angeles Times* in 1910—he had criticized the poet for the self-indulgent eccentricity of his style and labeled him "our ballyhoo bard"—and was hopeful that Pound would assist him.

Another reason for this venture was Willard's desire to join his magazine's drama critic, George Jean Nathan, for some fun in Paris, as Nathan was planning a private European tour for himself in June. Seeing the sights there, as well as in London and Vienna, all on a huge expense account, was a dream come true for Willard. Lastly, the more personal advantage such a trip would offer was connected to a growing need to see his brother. Stanton Wright, twenty-three and married at the age of seventeen, was a young man every bit as brilliant and dynamic as Willard. He had been living in France since 1907, studying to be a painter and absorbing the spirit and styles of Gauguin, Matisse, and Cézanne. Now on the verge of a turning point in his young career, Stanton was about to have his first exhibition, in Munich that June, and he wanted his brother to be there. It would be a momentous show, Stanton assured Willard, and an experience to remember.

Willard's well-financed month in Europe was fully as exciting as he imagined, though by no means as productive for the magazine as he had promised. In London he met with Ezra Pound, taking an approach that was a mixture of overbearing energy and fulsome flattery. He told his twenty-seven-year-old host that, as he understood it, there were only two classes of poets writing in English at the moment, Yeats and Pound himself on the one hand, and everyone else on the other. ("Such illumination cannot go without reward," Pound remarked to James Joyce.) Knowing that Pound knew everyone who mattered in avant-garde circles, Willard promised fair prices for whatever stories or poems he accepted by way of Pound's suggestion, and he painted a picture of *The Smart Set,* which Pound and his friends had none too high an opinion of, as a magazine in transition, on its way to becoming closer to Ford Madox Ford's highbrow *English Review.* Unfortunately, despite their common interest and shared antagonism toward "establishment periodicals," something didn't click between the two men. Willard almost made it seem as if he wanted Pound to be his exclusive London agent, funneling back the best work and all the undiscovered great names straight to *The Smart Set* offices. Eager as Pound was to see his peers find the audience they deserved, he wasn't entirely comfortable about being used in a fashion that relegated him to a businessman's role, scouting Bohemia for a fee. And, worse yet, something in Willard Wright's manner—perhaps a reflection of his own wariness, aggressiveness, and self-esteem—rubbed him the wrong way. To Joyce, Pound later confided his final, incredulous impression of the man: "Wright thinks me a bit cracked and regards himself as the sane and normal and practical male."

What Willard finally did get from Pound, or through Pound's auspices, was a small selection of his own poems (ten was the eventual total), one poem by Yeats, a story by Ford Madox Ford, and several poems and two excellent stories by D. H. Lawrence, then little known in the United States but ready to startle American readers with *Sons and Lovers* and his short fiction about Eastwood colliers and tormented lovers.

Before leaving London, where he treated himself to several costly nights on the town and met a few interesting women, Willard saw to the purchase of stories by Eden Phillpotts, George Moore, W. L. George, and May Sinclair and, most significantly, Joseph Conrad's only play, *One Day More.* Then it was on to Berlin and Vienna, "on the trail of a thousand girls" (his wife was, after all, six thousand miles away, waiting to join him in New York when she was called for) and in search of the beer gardens, the better brothels, the Kaiser's museums, the new painters (Klimt, Kokoschka, Kandinsky), and the new music—of Strauss, Korngold, Berg, Webern, and Schoenberg—that Stanton had told him to investigate. Vienna particularly appealed to Willard; it was, he wrote in a travel essay for *The Smart Set* that fall, a city "redolent with romance, bristling with intrigue."

John Adams Thayer, paying for this good time, might fairly have wondered why Berlin and Vienna had been included in Willard's itinerary at all. A Frank Wedekind play and an Arthur Schnitzler story had been secured for publication before Willard even left New York, and apparently not one poem, story, or play was bought by *The Smart Set* editor in either city, despite the long list of German and Austrian writers Willard had read and said he believed in.

There was a clearer reason to move on to Munich for a few days. There, on June 1, at Der Neue Kunst Salon Stanton's first major exhibition of paintings was held, and Willard saw for the first time the early, tentative—but striking—results of his brother's labors. The Munich exhibition was not a one-man show. Stanton, who called himself Stanton Macdonald-Wright now, had joined forces with another young expatriate American painter, Morgan Russell, and the twenty-nine paintings on view were the work of both men. But there was a unity of purpose to the Kunst Salon exhibition and something, vaguely, of a unity of style. Willard didn't have much time to learn about the intricacies of Stanton and Morgan Russell's antiacademic aesthetic experiment, which they were calling "Synchromism," but he did have the feeling during his eager reunion with his brother that Stanton was exploring authentically new ground in his dramatic use of color and the broken, blurry forms he was using. To Willard, the Munich show was a perplexing but an impressive spectacle. And, though no works were sold from the exhibition, there was an air of a cultural battle about the whole thing which captivated him.

After Munich, Paris. There Willard intended to call on the playwright Eugène Brieux and on Gabriele D'Annunzio's publishers and to lose himself on George Jean Nathan's grand tour. Willard was making his first visit to the City of Light in the right year and in the right season. The weather was perfect; the streets and cafés were packed. The artistic climate was even more provocative and enlivening than in Germany or Austria. Apollinaire had just brought out *Les Peintures Cubistes,* people were talking excitedly about the recent opening of *Le Sacre du printemps,* and everyone Willard met seemed to want to hear about the Armory Show in New York, which he could boast having seen. He was also able to pay his first visits to the Louvre, the Luxembourg, the Ballets Russes, and the Comédie-Française.

Business matters in Paris were easily settled. Willard called on Brieux and discussed the recent Broadway success of his play *Damaged Goods* (the first drama mentioning venereal disease to appear in New York, Willard proudly noted) and the possibilities for extending the French playwright's reputation among American readers still further. Brieux offered Willard a one-act play and a short story, both untranslated. Willard volunteered to do the translating himself, and that same week made a deal on a particularly good D'Annunzio story.

Still, it wasn't exactly a treasure trove Willard had gathered for *The Smart Set,* at least when compared to his London finds. Though Willard was remarkably well read in French literature, he made no attempt to solicit work from Gide, Proust, Cocteau, Mauriac, and any of the other major names he might have introduced to American audiences in a truly cosmopolitan journal in 1913. The likelihood is that he had forgotten his professional mission by this time, amid the many social and sensual attractions Paris offered.

Indeed, in the midst of a week of boisterous good times with Nathan, Willard was surprised by the arrival in town of Mr. and Mrs. Thayer. The publisher had decided on the spur of the moment, or so he said, to take a break himself and cross paths with his editor. He wanted company for a few days of healthful bathing at Carlsbad, an offer Nathan was free to decline, immediately and vehemently, but which Willard was not. A week of mudbaths and mineral water, "taking the vapors," strolls through the prim north Austrian town, and dull black-tie dinners, at a time when he could have been in the city with a bachelor friend who knew Paris intimately, put Willard in a black mood, which he struggled to hide from his hosts. He was relieved when the Thayers went their own way. He returned to London for a few days after they parted and, on June 22, almost five weeks after his arrival, left Europe in a first-class cabin on the *Mauritania.*

Proud of his work abroad, Willard let Mencken know when he returned of the contracts and stories he had gathered. Mencken was duly impressed. Everyone at the office could see that the autumn issues were going to be different from any they had printed before. Pound and Lawrence were relative unknowns, but Conrad, Moore, Brieux, D'Annunzio, May Sinclair, and Eden Phillpotts were prestigious names. But to novelist Harry Leon Wilson, Mencken confided his worries that, despite the plums of Willard's trip, there was grave trouble ahead. "If Thayer lets [Willard] alone, he will make the S.S. But I doubt that Thayer will stand pat long enough. Naturally, a good many kicks have been rolling in."

The "kicks" had thundered more than rolled in during Willard's unlucky absence and, without anyone on the scene to calm him on a daily basis, Thayer had grown nervous and angry. The unscheduled trip to Carlsbad had probably been designed to broach the subject of steering a more moderate course at the magazine. Thayer was finally grasping the nature of Willard's aspirations, and his conclusion, which he wasn't yet ready to articulate to Willard, was that he had made a mistake in giving a young man such a free hand. Their ever-erratic circulation, whose numbers Thayer watched like a poll-obsessed politician, was again dropping. The mail had turned fiercely antagonistic. As a result, Willard's euphoria after his month in Europe was short-lived. No sooner was he unpacked than it was back to battle with Thayer, the advertisers, and those thousands of readers who wanted a magazine to tell them that all was right in their world and always would be.

THAYER'S
REVENGE

" 'The Smart Set' for three or four years past has been appealing to the 'Ladies Home Journal' folks. They must be shaken out and more civilized readers found. Such a process tries a publisher's courage."
—H. L. Mencken, 1913

At lunch with the eminent critic James Gibbons Huneker a few days after his return to New York, Willard poured out his thoughts to a sympathetic listener. Huneker had been through it all himself. His own time as an editor and critic-spokesman for new artists, predating H. L. Mencken and Willard Wright by almost two decades, had left him war-weary and not fully convinced that he had effected any of the changes he thought important. Nor had Huneker grown rich in the process of writing several books, dozens of essays, and many thousands of reviews. America's foremost man of letters, at the age of fifty-six, was hard pressed for funds and couldn't afford to live in Manhattan any longer—not a heartening example for his colleague. Over an enormous quantity of beer, the two men compared notes on their experiences in Europe and Willard accepted two of Huneker's stories for publication that autumn. Neither story was designed to make matters go any easier with Thayer—one was about life in a high-class Manhattan brothel and the other about a Catholic priest dabbling in Satanism—but Willard assured Huneker that he was honored to have them.

The support of men like Huneker meant a great deal to Willard that summer, as he felt wounded to have to return to the office to cope with a barrage of questions, accusations, and dire predictions about the future of the magazine. "You don't know what it is to have to listen to this all day," he wrote Katharine. He had gone from being Thayer's "Great White Hope" in March, Willard told his wife, to an object of some suspicion. Looking over the summer selections—and, after all, Dreiser, Schnitzler, and Wedekind were international names—he felt that he had made a decent start toward dragging *The Smart Set* out of the rut it had been in. Who else in journalism was trying to do as much? He had also managed to buy, just before leaving for Europe, a Frank Harris novella (*An English Saint*) that proved to be very popular and a one-act Strindberg play (*Simmom*). Many of their readers didn't know Strindberg's work, most of which was slow in finding English translators and American distributors, but that was the whole point of a good magazine, Willard argued. People would first hear of these writers in their pages. Thayer took a different view. He was growing tired of "whores and horrors" or, more likely, tired of answering questions about what was happening to a once-respectable journal. *The Smart Set* carried a subtitle, "The Magazine of Cleverness," Thayer reminded Willard. So, naturally, their subscribers wanted to feel "clever," not swamped by life's misery. It wasn't even so much one story or one author that had set Thayer off. It was the pattern, the overall impression.

The June issue that was already on the stands, the July issue that was ready to go to press, and the August issue that was being discussed and laid out did suggest a pattern, a trend that was hard to overlook. First, there was "Owen Hatteras," the pseudonymous commentator whose column of reflections and epigrams was actually a collaborative effort by Mencken, Nathan, and Willard. The column was getting snider by the month, making innuendoes about women and marriage that were crossing the line of acceptable adult humor, as the publisher saw it, and there was no doubt about whose influence was steering "Hatteras" in that direction. Then there was Mencken's "The American" series. Meant to be collected for a book, which was never published, his essays on "The American" dissected month by month the language, the morals, the habits, the aesthetic and political ideas, of that mongrel "Homo Americanus." Mencken on his own, though, Thayer could have accepted. He wasn't opposed to literate, even mean satire. And Mencken was witty, and he rarely mentioned sex. Not so Benefield, Terhune, and Dreiser, who were relentless on the subject.

There were also stories that summer and fall like Edna Kenton's "Sisters," about two unmarried young women coming to terms with their sexual guilt after their illicit relationships, and Julius Furthman's "The Inn of Youth," a depiction of family violence that reminded too many people of Zola or Crane at their most unsparing. The playwright George Bronson Howard contributed his "Pages from the Book of Broadway," a rather formulaic series exploring "the subterranean world" of Broadway's hack writers, stage managers, actresses, chorus girls, boulevardiers, patrons, alcoholics, and hangers-on. Daniel Carson Goodman, fresh from an obscenity trial over his sensational novel *Hagar Revelly,* had been picked up by Willard as a kindred spirit in the battle against the whole lingering cult of the virginal and the maternal in America. Whether Goodman was writing about his novel's antiheroine in "Hagar Decides," or a more flagrant gold-digger in "Turkey Trot," or even a principled protagonist in "The Feminine Sense of Honor," his theme was the same: the sexual instinct in women was as potent and problematic as it was in men.

When seen as a whole, then, it was a vivid, promiscuous pageant from April to August: Benefield's scarlet women, Raegan "the cabaret philosopher," Kenton's unrepentant sisters, Bronson Howard's cynical exploiters, Hagar and her sisters like Jessica and Dreiser's Lily Edwards, and some ten or twelve others of the same mold. With advertisers to placate as stodgy as Monarch Typewriters, Steinway, Postum and Grape-Nuts, Tiffany's, and National Cars ("For Conservative People—who want the best, who will pay only a price commensurate with quality—a car of reliability, safety, and luxury"), Thayer was in an irreconcilable bind.

To all of this Mencken offered Willard stern and surprising advice: compromise. There was nothing to be gained by pushing too hard and too fast, he warned. The Thayers of the world had to be treated gently. Their power had to be understood. "Be careful with the sexual stuff, at least for the present," he warned, extending his caution even to the reprobate Owen Hatteras. Mencken and Nathan were willing to kill him off if he bothered Thayer all that much: the fun had been had. "Why have a row every month, all to no purpose?" Hatteras' column of acerbic jokes and observations was just "a dynamite bomb on the table," he wrote to Willard, an explosive that threatened to hurt the writers more than the publisher. "The one thing 'The Smart Set' needs above everything else is harmony," he added. "There must be a steady pull together, with no rowing over nonessentials."

But Willard wouldn't hear of it. The Hatteras column was too much fun, for one thing, and too close to his ideal of what the magazine should offer, to give up. Had he showed some flexibility in the matter of Owen Hatteras, Willard might have had more leverage later when he needed it. But the pleasure of flinging, from behind the safety of a pseudonym, some of his most biting thoughts about women, marriage, religion, and politics at a large audience had become a deeply satisfying need. That he was only replacing one kind of provincialism—American insularity—with another—an oppressive, knee-jerk cynicism—didn't seem to matter. Hatteras continued to bark and bait and insult.

Willard was also a little taken aback by Mencken's opinion that the European travel essays he was working on were too risqué and could benefit from some temperate editing. He had decided on the general title "The Night Romance of Europe," with his own survey of Vienna's night life to appear first, in October, Nathan's account of Paris the following month, his London essay in December, and Nathan's essay on Berlin in January. (The plan was that Mencken would prepare one in a similar jocular vein on Munich, and Willard would then undertake to see if all five could be put together in one book.) But Mencken found the title unnecessarily lurid, with its suggestion of sinful debauches and gatherings in dark places. When Willard sent the Vienna article to him for a critique, he offered some editorial revisions designed to make the series less sensational and more satirical of the stereotypical American tourist. Though Nathan was slowly coming round to the conclusion that Willard was "mussing up the magazine with pornography," he sided with Willard on this one. The Vienna, London, Paris, and Berlin sketches never actually detail any amorous adventures or sexual experiences, but they are heavy with innuendo. They each discuss a specific girl who served as the visiting writer's guide to the right places and hint at secrets the knowing male reader will understand.

When the travel sketches were gathered together in book form the following year, published by John Lane as *Europe After 8:15*, Mencken showed no interest in the book and rarely spoke of it afterwards. It was Willard's project, he implied, more than his or Nathan's.

Mencken took his commitments seriously. Having gotten Willard into this job far from California, he felt honor-bound to come to his aid, despite his annoyance at Willard's rigidity. When Thayer made a quick, heated visit to Baltimore—not the first— Mencken did his best to persuade him to be patient. He probably urged Thayer to withhold any final judgments about his editor for two more months to see if the new material from Europe made any difference. He was inclined to think it would. In any event, Willard's contract called for a review and renegotiation in October. Whatever the exact line of Mencken's argument, it worked. He was his usual cogent self. Thayer relented.

Even when he won a round, though, Willard lost, if only a little. He was one man against an office staff which had no reason to feel any loyalty to him, against a city of conservative big money, and against wider public opinion. The tension wore him out. He had always pretended to have more stamina than he really had, to enjoy a fight more than he did. By the end of the summer he was visibly run down and forced to spend a few days in bed.

When the two D. H. Lawrence stories which he had been eagerly waiting for arrived in the mail, via Pound, Willard wearily acknowledged the limits of his situation. He knew the stories were exceptional, and he knew that they would mean another horrendous scene with Thayer, possibly his dismissal. Lawrence's choices were recent works of which he was especially proud. "Once" was a story about a promiscuous young woman and her desperate search for the right man, the fulfilling lover. The second story was either "The Thorn in the Flesh," about the desertion and sexual involvements of a young soldier, or the now-famous "The Prussian Officer," Lawrence's classic story of power plays and latent homosexuality in the military. In their seriousness and craftsmanship, all three stories were of a caliber to make Terhune, Goodman, and Bronson Howard look silly, and Willard must have recognized this.

In returning them to Ezra Pound, Willard tried to be glib. "Glorious stuff," he wrote, "wish to God we could print it, but we shall find the magazine suppressed, and I should be languishing in a jail cell as I believe the phrase is." Pound was furious. Henceforth, Willard was "that brute in New York." To be fair, the two Lawrence stories Willard bought instead, "The Shadow in the Rose Garden" and "Christening," published in *The Smart Set* in early 1914, weren't much more delicate. But in being "prudent" and rejecting Lawrence's first offerings, having already printed so much highly controversial fiction, Willard found himself in the worst of all positions. Mencken thought him half-cocked, not as mature and well-balanced as he had expected, while Pound thought him a milquetoast and a philistine.

By the beginning of September Willard was feeling well enough to visit Mencken in Baltimore in company with Dreiser. He needed to talk all of this out in person. Willard must have appreciated Dreiser's companionship as well. He was publishing his one-act play, *A Girl in the Coffin,* in the October issue. No one had a kind word to say about Theodore Dreiser the dramatist, but Willard thought the play a strong one—only Dreiser could fit a labor strike, a married man's affair with a younger woman, and an abortion into one twenty-page drama—and he let the author know it.

On Saturday, September 12th, after a brief illness, Archibald Wright, Willard's sixty-three-year-old father, died. His mother wired the news to Willard, who left New York immediately. Thayer graciously lent Willard $500 before he left for Los Angeles. Not knowing how long he would have to be on the West Coast, or what personal or immediate funeral expenses he would have to contend with, Willard also approached several other friends for a few hundred dollars. If he could help it, his first appearance in California since his departure to become a New York editor wasn't going to be a penny-pinching display. That meant a new wardrobe. He also embellished the account of his trip West by telling reporters in Los Angeles that he had been en route from Europe, on board ship, when he received the wireless cable about his father's condition, and only had time to rush from the dock to catch the first westward-bound train.

Archie Wright's funeral was a dignified, well-attended ceremony. Everyone in the hotel and real-estate community in Southern California knew him to be an honest and conscientious businessman and a caring family man. The wonder to their neighbors had always been how Archie and Annie Wright had produced two such crazy sons, the one a "mad" painter who had traipsed off to Europe while still a teenager, and the other not much better, with all of his pretensions to be a great writer and no thought of his wife and five-year-old child. The one titillating piece of family business people couldn't stop talking about was the word on Archie's will. Willard assumed that he and Stanton would be inheriting a sizable portion of his father's estate, at least the son's traditional one-quarter each. The surprise, which even made it into the newspapers, was Archie's bequest of one dollar each to Willard and Stanton and the rest of the estate to Annie. Impressed as he might have been with all that his sons were trying to accomplish, and financially strapped as he was in his last year, Archie Wright knew that he couldn't rely on Willard and Stanton to be careful with anything he left behind or to look after their mother as she grew older. Stanton was as incredulous and disappointed as Willard when he heard about the terms of the will.

Willard returned to New York right after the funeral. He didn't see his wife or daughter, who were in Washington state for a prolonged stay with Katharine's relatives, and so he was spared the awkwardness of explaining, yet again, that he wasn't ready for them to join him.

The September issue of *The Smart Set* appeared while Willard was in California. The first fruit of his trip to Europe, it met—to its editor's delight—with a good reception, on the newsstands and in the office. The Brieux one-acters, D'Annunzio's lyrical story of an elderly aristocratic woman's efforts to locate the illegitimate son she gave up for adoption in her youth, and May Sinclair's "Pictures," about a British painter and his vindictive model, were less leaden, more cosmopolitan selections than the earnest realism of Benefield and Susan Glaspell in the same number, and readers responded to that change.

Incredibly, the October issue brought an even more positive

response, which seemed to solidify Willard's position. This development should have indicated to Thayer the pointlessness of running a magazine by attending solely to monthly figures and mail from subscribers—Mencken had been maintaining all along that dips in circulation were seasonal and across-the-board with New York periodicals and shouldn't be taken as definitive—because the October issue was no less strident than any other. Dreiser's somber play, Willard's Vienna sketch, Mencken on the American's ignorant notions of freedom, stories by Howard, Terhune, Goodman, and Benefield: it had even more potential to offend. However, bolstered by Mencken and Nathan and a slight circulation rise, Thayer was in a sufficiently reassured mood to renew Willard's contract and extend him a munificent raise, to $125 a week. Even harder to understand is Thayer's agreement to allow his editor the ultimate journalistic honor, his name on the cover of the magazine each month. Beginning with the December issue, "Willard Huntington Wright, Editor" appeared beneath the title, leaving no doubt, presumably, as to who was in charge.

Or at least that was the image, of control and editorial authority, Willard wished to convey. Far from feeling vindicated by the events of the fall, he was as uneasy as he had been in June. Working for John Adams Thayer was becoming a roller-coaster experience, and Willard was awakening to the possibility that it wasn't going to last much longer. There was no guessing from one month to the next how the man would react. Writing to Katharine to tell her of his troubles and to say something about the cause of his delay in sending for her, he vented his anger toward his boss. "Of course I have a contract with [him]," he wrote, "but I am not going to count much on my arrangement . . . he is a low, inherently dishonest fellow, with a vicious, nasty type of mind." Willard complained that Thayer's circulation hopes had been unrealistic all along. He had been pressured from the beginning by these impossible goals. He was also tired of dealing with an employer who criticized his work so freely and valued the opinions of less intelligent people. "Thayer puts a lot of stock in [his readers'] moral yelps. I'm getting sick and tired of their attitude, and I guess he is beginning to feel my resentment." By next summer, Willard predicted, he was sure to be in another job where he wouldn't have to associate "with a skunk like J.A.T."

Willard wanted to be able to feel some satisfaction in his accomplishments on their own terms, divorced from commercial considerations. He had written his own proclamation for the October cover, announcing his belief that this was "the best number of the 'The Smart Set' ever issued . . . a stimulating and generally different issue." Now, to his annoyance, Thayer was agreeing that it was good—because the complaints of "the nasty moralists" were momentarily fewer, for no apparent reason, not because he recognized the value of the magazine's contents.

That value did merit attention, obscured though it was by the magazine's reputation and the mixed quality of its roster. The real bounty of the autumn issues, the literary bounty, was probably its poetry. For the first time an unequivocal list of poets of real stature appeared in *The Smart Set*. The six short poems of Ezra Pound and the single poems by William Butler Yeats, Bliss Carman, Louis Untermeyer, and Witter Bynner in the September issue weren't anything to shock Thayer's subscribers, but Lawrence's "Violets," a raw, tender graveside dialogue in the vernacular, must have seemed forceful to those who followed the magazine's usually tepid poetry pages. Pound was irate that Willard declined to print Robert Frost's "The Death of the Hired Man"—his biggest literary mistake of the year—but in the following months other good D. H. Lawrence poems were included, and in each issue between September and December Willard used one from the folder Pound had given him. Strategically, he placed the Pound poems in ascending order of difficulty, beginning in September with simple lyrics like "An Immorality" ("Sing we for love and idleness / Naught else is worth the having") and culminating in December with the fragmented, imagistic "Zenia." The latter poem was radically unlike anything that had ever appeared in *The Smart Set* and elicited a fair number of letters condemning what everyone agreed must be a hoax. As Willard was known in the business to publish his own verse in the magazine under assumed names, some people who had never heard of Ezra Pound came to the conclusion that it was another of the editor's pseudonyms and the poem in question, too silly to worry over, just another of his jokes. Columnists remarked on still one more bit of modernist lunacy from Thayer's domain, but by that time it didn't matter. Thayer had turned on Willard again, for the last time.

The final unraveling of Willard's position on the magazine was as inevitable, and once it started as swift, as he had imagined it would be. By the end of November, Thayer was distressed about rising expenses. He and Willard quarreled more frequently and openly not only about the content of each issue, but even more about the cost. Thayer had never been happy with Willard's practice of (as he saw it) overpaying his authors and complained to Mencken that his protégé was putting *The Smart Set* on a course of financial ruin. With his new contract in hand, Willard tried to bluff his way through. He insisted to Mencken he had seen the books, and Thayer was still clearing a $3,000-a-month profit. But all around him he sensed his power eroding. When Willard was out sick for a few days with a case of ptomaine poisoning, Norman Boyer was left in charge. Boyer had resigned from the magazine for a short time in midyear, only to return at Thayer's urging. In Willard's absence, he gleefully rejected one of Terhune's stories, and the message wasn't lost on Terhune or anyone else who heard about it. Willard discreetly began to inquire, with no success, about other job prospects.

The crisis came in December. Circulation had slipped over a two-month period, the "Zenia" row was on, and Thayer caught Willard in a breach of professional conduct that jeopardized any slight security his contract gave him. Willard had ordered a short dummy issue of what was tentatively titled *The Blue Review,* a more iconoclastic journal he and Nathan and Mencken had been fantasizing about and discussing for over a year. It is unfortunate that there isn't a record of just what essays by the three men, or any other contributors, were included in this experimental piece of copy, but all that mattered to Thayer was the amazing discovery that Willard had charged the printer's bill to the *Smart Set* account. Thayer was stuck for a bill for a dummy copy of a radical intellectual journal he knew nothing about and which had nothing to do with his own periodical. Even Mencken was taken aback by Willard's maneuver and couldn't see how the two men were going to be reconciled, now that Thayer was so enraged. He advised Willard to get a lawyer.

With Thayer all but waiting to catch him in an error for which he would be legally responsible, Willard couldn't have chosen a less sensible moment in which to test the limits of his authority. But he had always refused to take financial facts seriously. For months he had been acting as if the magazine's coffers were bottomless, bragging to writers that he would soon be paying the best fees in the business. Then too he might have felt that he had nothing to lose, if his days on the magazine were numbered. There was a fierce and comical poetic justice in sticking a mogul of Thayer's literary tastes and prim temperament with the bill for something like *The Blue Review.* But there was just as likely another twist that entered into Willard's thinking that November, a personal development and a bit of timing too potent to be entirely coincidental. Stanton and his wife, Ida, had returned to America at the beginning of November. Their married life had evidently been no more fulfilling than Willard and Katharine's. Flat broke and worn out after a big Paris showing of his Synchromist work, Stanton packed Ida off to her relations not long after they arrived in New York. He moved in with Willard while he found his bearings, and the brothers had the chance to get reacquainted, a process they had started back in June, in Munich.

Good-looking and promiscuous, clever and arrogant, Stanton was a dangerous if invigorating influence. During these weeks Willard was exposed to Stanton's manner and attitudes in a more concentrated way than ever before. The image his younger brother conveyed to Willard was a blend of artistic challenge (Stanton was ready to present Synchromism to America, where he anticipated bountiful results), intense, almost threatening intellectual stimulation, and a real, not a lip-service, devotion to serious avant-garde goals. The editorship of *The Smart Set* was an impressive post to Willard's acquaintances in Los Angeles and New York. To Stanton, it wouldn't have signified all that much, unless it was going to lead to something else, something larger and more radical, as Willard kept implying it would. To be the editor of *The Blue Review*, however, meant to be more like Ezra Pound and Ford Madox Ford. It meant being more like Stanton Wright and Morgan Russell, who portrayed themselves as revolutionaries on the order of Delacroix and Cézanne. Willard's decision to see what a copy of his ideal journal would look like forced him to pass a point from which there was no return. With the kind of impolitic nerve Stanton was famous for, Willard was in effect announcing his priorities to Thayer and everyone else in their circle.

Recriminations were hurled in all directions—Thayer belligerently informed Willard that even Mencken agreed it was time for a parting of the ways—and lawyers were called in. A fair severance was arranged, the $500 debt to Thayer was canceled, and by New Year's Day Willard was out of work. Almost all of that severance money went to his lawyer, his landlady, his laundry service, tailor, and several other people who had been waiting patiently to be paid. After twelve months of good living and extended credit, Willard was almost broke.

This left Boyer and Thayer to put out the magazine themselves. One of their first acts, perfectly characteristic, was to decline three of James Joyce's "Dubliners" stories which Pound had sent on with Willard's approval. Ironically, some of Willard's best material appeared in the few issues following his departure, contributions like Joseph Conrad's play and D. H. Lawrence's stories. However, aware of his audience's discontent, Thayer quickly mailed postcards to all subscribers announcing the end of Wright's tenure and promising that their magazine would in the future "entertain, amuse, thrill, surprise . . . but never offend good taste." "Sex stories . . . and stories of gloom and hopelessness" were out. "CLEAN, CRISP, CLEVER" was the new motto, which in red letters emblazoned the cover of the April 1914 issue, almost as if to wash away the taint of Willard's name on past covers.

Once again Mencken did what he could to assist his friend. He helped Willard secure a lucrative position as a columnist for *The New York Mail,* taking over the "Always in Good Humor" page recently vacated by Franklin P. Adams. (Not the most aptly named title for Adams' successor.) In the three months he lasted at the *Mail,* Willard was deeply unhappy. From the duties and perquisites of an editor-in-chief's position to the hustle and pressure of the newsroom was a transition he found impossibly hard. There was also something demeaning about the role of "daily humorist," churning out gossip tidbits, limericks, snappy replies to those who wrote to the paper, wry commentary on current events, and sarcastic maxims for the man in the street. The result was a far cry from "the eruptions" of Owen Hatteras and the panache of the travel essays. To make matters worse, Willard complained to Mencken, the management was intellectually primitive, and to Katharine he wrote despairingly, "It's a Presbyterian paper and they are forever criticizing my vulgarities and irreverences. The mention of beer in the column sends them into a white heat. I can't stand it. They want me to write drool and I refuse." In March he quit and curtly informed his wife that any thoughts of moving East would have to be postponed indefinitely.

Proximity to Stanton and release from his ambiguous position at *The Smart Set* had made Willard less pliable, more uncompromising and risk-taking. He felt that he had been forced to capitulate too much already. He had an exciting time in February when he wasn't at the *Mail* office, helping Stanton hang his exhibition at the prestigious Carroll Gallery (the show turned out not to be the resounding success the Wrights had expected) and typing the manuscript of *Europe After 8:15,* which John Lane was considering for publication. Every minute that took him away from what was important to earn a salary at "hack work," as he bitterly termed it, was wasted time. Annie and Katharine, who had never wanted to see Willard prostitute his talents in the first place, became the unwitting focus of his anger when he left the *Mail.* The one woman had money and wouldn't give it to him, and the other woman wanted it from him. In a hectoring, fifteen-page typed letter to them, he suggested that a truly loving mother would understand her sons' ambitions enough to finance them, and a truly faithful wife would get a job to support their daughter so that her spouse could be freed from material and domestic pressures in his pursuit of higher goals. How right Nietzsche had been about women, he told Mencken.

Throughout March, Willard had been putting aside what he could from the *Mail,* knowing that his days there were numbered. He was also becoming aware of the difficulty of getting anything done in New York, where the cost of living and the distractions were such obstacles. Stanton, who loathed the city, agreed that they had to move. Even Mencken advised Willard that Manhattan was taking more from him now than he was getting back. He recommended Baltimore as the ideal place to do some serious writing. "There is no smell of Broadway here,"

he wrote to Willard, though he could promise him enough "for-
nicati" to keep him busy after working hours. Willard considered
moving to a suburb of New York for the solitude, but Stanton
eventually convinced his brother that Paris was the place for
both of them. Prices were cheaper, the annoyances fewer, and
the atmosphere more hospitable. The money for their passage
was obtained by less than honest means, Stanton mysteriously
implied to Morgan Russell, and Annie Wright was finally pre-
vailed upon to send them each a small allowance, fifty dollars a
month, during their first year abroad. Willard borrowed some
money from publisher Ben Huebsch, an especially generous
friend, and approached some of the writers he had recently
published in *The Smart Set*. He felt they owed it to him.

On March 28, 1914, one distinct era in Willard's life ended as
he and Stanton sailed for Europe. Oblivious to politics, as always,
they anticipated two or three years of uninterrupted study and
work under conditions more favorable than those New York
could offer.

BEGINNINGS

"Sons have always a rebellious wish to be disillusioned by that which charmed their fathers."

—*Aldous Huxley*

Willard Huntington Wright never held his Southern origins in high esteem. "I was born in Virginia by accident," he once told an interviewer. A more likely birthplace in his eyes would have been New York or San Francisco—or, better still, Vienna under the Hapsburgs or Paris in "la belle epoque." The fact that Wright senior had bought property in quiet, muddy Charlottesville two years before his elder son's birth could not, as that elder son saw it, be held against either of his children.

Willard's path from his Virginia childhood to the editorship of *The Smart Set,* and through all the accomplishments and defeats that followed that eventful year, was anything but a predictable one. His beginnings offer a kind of fabulous tale in itself, a roundabout story of egoism and ambition in the making, most of which Willard later did his best to falsify.

Charlottesville was home to Willard for barely seven years, and his memories of his childhood days there were shadowy. The move had been regarded by the family as only a temporary one, anyway. Archibald Davenport Wright and Annie Van Vranken, married in New York City in 1884, had left their native

35

Northeast right after their wedding to live for a year in Fay-etteville, North Carolina, before moving to "the Athens of the South," as Jefferson's university town is still known. The vigor-ous expansion of the Southern Railroad and a real-estate boom in Virginia in the 1880s meant opportunity to Archie Wright, a hotel proprietor and restaurateur. Hence, the couple's drift from Upstate New York to Manhattan, then to Fayetteville and Char-lottesville, and on to Lynchburg in 1894. The tides of commerce eventually led the family to Los Angeles, in 1901. Only in Cali-fornia were the Wrights and their two unusual sons to find the stability and sense of belonging they had given up on leaving their Oneonta, New York, relatives behind. In Virginia, they were outsiders, opportunists of a kind, latter-day carpetbaggers (though of a less grasping variety) profiting now not from the South's defeat but from its bustling recovery.

If there was never much question for the Wrights about set-tling permanently in Virginia, there wasn't any question about seeing their sons, Willard and Stanton, educated and raised to adulthood there. Charlottesville in 1888, the year of its incorpo-ration, was a far cry from the gracious brick town it is today. The amenities and cultural advantages were few. Revivals and evan-gelical campaigns were the popular fare. The mud and potholes that Woodrow Wilson (Virginia Law School, '80) had complained of a few years earlier were disappearing as more roads were being paved all the time, but even in the early 1890s a town reporter felt justified in labeling Main Street "a manure and dust bonanza in dry weather, a mud puddle in wet weather . . . a disgrace to a place calling itself a city."

That "manure and dust bonanza" was the street on which Willard Huntington Wright was born on October 15, 1887, and Stanton Macdonald-Wright on July 8, 1890.

To Annie Wright, in her twenties, raised in middle-class com-fort in Schenectady, related by marriage to the magnates Solon and Collis Huntington, this was an alien environment but not necessarily a threatening one. She was a quiet, hardworking, witty, determined woman and, like many of her Southern neigh-bors, deeply religious. Known for a wry sense of humor and an even more striking sense of duty and propriety, Annie was also patient and uncomplaining, ready to help her husband as he made his start in business, wherever that took them. Archie Wright, by all accounts, was just as even-tempered, if a little less tradition-bound and more broadminded than his wife. "A man of silent mien and devout habits," as Willard later described him, but a thinker and a reader all the same, he ran their small hotel and restaurant by the depot efficiently and economically. In most ways that counted, then, Archie and Annie were much like their Charlottesville friends and acquaintances: sober citizens and family-minded churchgoers.

There was one significant difference, though. In their attitude toward their children and what they saw in them and what they wanted for them, the Wrights were anything but typical of their time and place. They treated their sons as boys far removed from the common mold. Annie, especially, pampered and doted on them. Willard even more than Stanton enjoyed his mother's consuming love and attention. They were, to be sure, remarkably precocious children, reading and writing long before their peers, displaying an eagerness for music and drawing almost as soon as they could talk and hold a pencil. "Willard matured very young," his Aunt Julia approvingly recollected fifty years later, "and, shall I say, very skillfully." This intellectual progress was something Archie and Annie watched with proud amazement. They knew that Willard and Stanton were bright and capable, more than normally energetic and inquisitive, and decided that they required special attention. While the boys later attended public schools in Lynchburg, the Wrights often employed private tutors for them when they could be found and encouraged them in their study of art, music, and foreign languages.

Less prudently, perhaps, the Wrights didn't believe in discipline or anything approaching an authoritarian rule in the house. By the time they decided that they had been too lax in raising Willard and Stanton, it was late in the day to effect any change. There was a wild streak, as well as a creative impulse, in both boys. More playful than mean-spirited, at home they were apt to take their prerogatives for granted. They delighted in being irreverent and sarcastic. They recognized that they could get away with more than most children did, a realization that encouraged more rebelliousness. When a woman staying at the hotel commented to Annie about Willard's noisy antics, Annie quickly let her know whose presence in the hotel mattered more. When it involved her sons, Annie's traditional values, born of the conservative Protestant aura of her own childhood, paled.

The implications of so much parental indulgence, of their parents' faith in them, of Annie's favoritism toward Willard (a family truth that Stanton and Willard both acknowledged), and of the later, dramatic rivalries which necessarily develop between independent, talented brothers were played out on a wider field than Wright's Hotel and Junction Restaurant. Archie and Annie's children thought and dreamed large from the beginning. Willard in his teenage years anticipated a vocation as a great poet, a Byronic rebel, and Stanton in adolescence aspired to be a master painter. The brothers evolved in an atmosphere in which their specialness was never doubted. Their background was an exceptional one that offered unlimited potential for self-confidence and some equally treacherous obstacles to success and happiness.

As hotel children in Lynchburg, where Archie moved his family in 1894 and bought two much grander establishments than the one in Charlottesville, Willard and Stanton lived a privileged life. Every day, in the lobby and the dining room, there was the drama of change and movement going on all around them—a satisfying spectacle for imaginative boys—and a measure of luxury for them to assume as their right. Eventually Archie rented a house in town, giving the family more of a semblance of normal domestic life, but there is every indication that Willard and Stanton had become contentedly spoiled children long before adolescence, very used to being the center of attention. By the end of the 1890s, Archie Wright had established himself as one of the city's more prominent businessmen, and his children knew their position.

These early years were also the time in which Willard and Stanton enjoyed their greatest, most genuine closeness, a brotherly bond that would weather years of separation, jealousy, and contention. In appearance, Willard and Stanton were similar—handsome, robust, attractive to most of the girls they knew. The resemblance increased over the years until Willard began to lose weight. They shared many of the same enthusiasms and responses to the same situations. They were amused and angered by the same kinds of people and encouraged each other in subtle ways.

In the rowdy world of a small town or city, Willard was a good brother to emulate for a boy just three years younger. He was outgoing and athletic, always connected to a circle of friends. In fact, as Stanton remembered it, Willard was the very opposite of the portrait he drew of himself as a young boy and adolescent in his autobiographical novel, *The Man of Promise*. In that book, published when Willard was in his thirties, the artist-hero, named Stanford West, is a Stephen Daedalus, introspective and misunderstood. Stanton's recollections, confirmed by others later, was of a boy who was sociable and well liked, more fun-loving than brooding.

But Willard could also be a prankster and a loudmouth. Probably connected to this high-spiritedness, a great rupture took place in the Wright household the summer before Willard's thirteenth birthday. Archie decided that Willard should go away to school, to a more controlled environment. Whether he felt that Willard was becoming too rambunctious to be managed at home any longer, while both parents were busy at the hotel, or that Willard and Stanton needed to be separated for a time, or whether some other, entirely different reason or isolated incident was involved isn't clear today. However, hinting that there was a fair amount of trauma involved in his father's decision is the odd fact that in later life Willard never made mention of his year away. As a cadet in the Preparatory Department of the New York Military Academy at Cornwall-on-Hudson, he lived a life both more rigorous and more structured than it had been at home, and after ten months there he insisted on dropping out.

At the end of that school year, in the summer of 1901, Willard left the Academy and rejoined his mother, father, and brother. The family was to be together, all four of them, for only another five years before a series of separations permanently divided them. Yet the home Willard traveled to that year was not Virginia, but the far-distant town of Santa Monica.

Archie Wright moved his family west right at the turn of the century. Like tens of thousands of Easterners, he wanted to profit by the awesome real-estate and transportational developments his wife's relatives, the Huntingtons of the Southern Pacific Railroad, had effected in California. The Wrights settled in what seemed at first to be an unlikely location. Santa Monica had a population of 3,000 in 1900, making it considerably smaller than Lynchburg. Its beachfront was breathtaking, but the town was less accessible to travelers than some of the other resort areas along the California coast. But Archie knew the direction of Santa Monica's future. And when the Huntington trolley lines connected the little town on the water to downtown Los Angeles shortly after the Wrights' arrival, the commute from the city was reduced to a scant thirty minutes and the result, along with the completion in 1903 of the Southern Pacific's coastal line between San Francisco and Los Angeles, ensured the area's status as a great tourist center.

As Willard and Stanton entered their teenage years at the Arcadia Hotel, a steepled, five-story wood-frame building that was one of the showplaces of its day, their father was at the peak of his earning and his optimism about his future. Shortly after, he was able to buy a few apartment houses in town, and eventually he sold his interest in the Arcadia to buy a part ownership in a hotel, the Astoria, in downtown Los Angeles. Archie Wright wasn't avaricious, and he didn't suffer from delusions of matching the success of the much wealthier, more ruthless side of the family. The Huntingtons were tycoons, while he simply took his opportunities as he saw them and made the most of his circumstances. Willard and Stanton, though, were never able to see their father in any other light than the one in which he appeared to them when they were young: the man with the golden touch, a benevolent Midas and an ever-secure provider who could, if he wanted to, meet all their needs and demands. In later years, when Archie had overextended himself and owed people money or when conditions were against him, Willard and Stanton found it impossible to rethink their image of their father.

Santa Monica was a quiet place to live, and Willard never had cause to feel any greater nostalgia for his life there than in Virginia. With his warmer feeling for the landscape and the climate, Stanton was more at home in Southern California. (His earliest surviving painting is a small, lush view of Santa Monica.) Life at the Arcadia was comfortable—a sharp contrast to the rigors of a military academy—but the town itself was pious and conservative. For amusement, Willard and Stanton regularly frequented the town's bars when they were old enough, or looked old enough, to be admitted. Often, the conduct of Archie Wright's sons was enough in itself to convince the active local prohibitionists of the justice of their cause. An undated clipping from an area paper about this time refers to a bar brawl at William Reckitts' Cafe in which Willard was fined a staggering $120 in damages, which Archie had to pay.

But that was only one side of Willard in his youth. He was also testing his talents and wondering about his future. Despite his parents' desire to see him prepare in a practical way for a career that would support him, Willard was voluble in announcing that the life of the artist, not the businessman, was for him. But which art form was the question. At one point, it was to be music; Willard loved to pore over the scores of favorite composers like Brahms, Debussy, and Mahler and wrote a few of his own piano compositions. He was also interested in painting and drawing (he showed great facility at sketching), though in that area he experienced some nagging doubts about the extent of his ability and had to cope with the impressive steadiness of Stanton's artistic development.

To Willard's chagrin, Stanton seemed to proceed without any doubts. He was always sure of himself, annoyingly so. In both his capacity for mischief and for creative accomplishments, Stanton was a fair match for his older brother by the time he reached his teens, when they began, slowly and inevitably, to drift apart. He cost his parents as much worry and almost as much money. About his childhood in Santa Monica, Stanton as an older man liked to do his own mythmaking. He told his friends of running away from home when he was fourteen on a steamer bound for the Orient and being brought back from a stopover in Hawaii by detectives hired by his father. There is an apocryphal air to this particular tale of rebelliousness, but the motivation behind it is understandable. Stanton was unpredictable and determined, and he quickly outdid Willard in his show of nerve and stamina. The year he turned fourteen he was taking classes at the Art Students League in Los Angeles, and it was apparent to everyone in the family that Stanton was meant to be a painter. As a Sunday painter himself, Archie heartily approved.

Willard's decision to concentrate exclusively on literature and writing was only gradually arrived at. A few years passed before he finally put aside his dreams of composing and conducting. It came to seem to him, though, that writing was more satisfying, easier to work on and win a response to, and a more natural means of expression for him. (It was also his brother's weak spot. Despite a facility with languages, Stanton never showed any flair for writing.) Once begun in earnest, he found that the writing of poems and plays and the keeping of a journal became a compulsive, pleasurable activity. Hours of solitude, spent in struggling to master rhyme forms and to create fresh dialogue and interesting characters, followed. "He wanted to escape, to pay no heed save to his own thoughts, to follow out the dreams with which his mind overflowed, to spend his whole time in the only affair which gratified him—his writing." So Willard described Stanford West at the moment of his realization of his vocation.

Willard's extensive reading in his adolescence, which became a compulsion in itself the more he wrote, was sometimes a cause for concern to his parents. Not only did he spend a small fortune on the volumes he bought from area booksellers, but he refused to be monitored or guided in his choices. Robert Louis Stevenson, Poe, and Conan Doyle were his passions for a time, and that was pleasing to everyone. But his interest in Shaw and Maupassant, Baudelaire and Rimbaud, Conrad and Hardy were troubling to a woman of Annie's background. These were potentially immoral influences. Admonishing Willard did no good: if Archie would have been more at ease watching his son absorbed with Dickens or Fenimore Cooper, Willard had to read *Nana* or *Bel-Ami*. If Annie turned to the Bible for inspiration, hoping her example would encourage her son, he was apt to flaunt his copies of *Les Fleurs du Mal* or *Tess of the D'Urbervilles*. Even more distressingly, Willard—and Stanton—seemed positively obsessed for a time with Balzac and Oscar Wilde.

An enthusiasm for Wilde, in two adolescent boys no less, was guaranteed to shock anyone in their parents' circle who took notice. The scandal of the libel trials was still an awkward topic, the plays went unperformed, and books like *Dorian Gray* were considered the very model of the sort of literature that had to be kept from impressionable minds. This edge of notoriety, like the aesthetic amorality of Wilde's Henry Wooton ("self denial mars our lives . . . be always searching for new sensations, be afraid of nothing"), was just what Willard and Stanton were looking for. Masculine and aggressively heterosexual themselves, they weren't especially sympathetic to homosexuals. But Wilde's homosexuality was somehow acceptable: it was a dandy's pose and an affront to the middle class as much as it was a reality to them. Likewise, Balzac's fantastic, meticulous, plot-heavy stories of young men rising in the world, facing temptations and losing their small-town innocence, having what women they wanted and accepting the world as it was, struck Willard's imagination in these years and remained with him long after Stevenson and Poe, or even Shaw and Maupassant, were set aside.

For Stanton, there was always something of an ill-fated Balzac hero about his brother, enough to wonder if Willard wasn't acting at times with this prototype in mind. "If you want a real portrait of Willard," Stanton wrote to a friend in the 1970s, "read the series of books [by Balzac] that start with the Poet in the Provinces—and in Paris—the life story of Lucien de Rubempré [*Illusions Perdues* and *Splendeurs et misères des courtisanes*; usually translated as *Lost Illusions* and *A Harlot High and Low*]." That character's "vanity, ambition, greed, weakness, accomplishments and final suicide—as well as his attitudes toward his mistresses—his looks and psychology" were remarkably, strangely, similar to Willard's, Stanton told his correspondent. But then too, Stanton noted, there was more than a little of Vautrin in his brother. He could be both the young man on the make and the jaded, manipulative corrupter.

At sixteen Willard was, as he described his fictional self Stanford West at the same age, "hale, clear-eyed, and conspicuously able." There was every reason for Archie and Annie Wright to feel confidence in their elder son, to assume that in spite of his adolescent troubles he was going to justify their high hopes in him. Not surprisingly, though, Willard's experiences with college life, which began for him in the fall of 1903, were anything but orthodox and encouraging. He lasted one year at nearby St. Vincent's College (a forerunner of today's Loyola-Marymount University), one term at the University of Southern California, several weeks at Syracuse University, and one year at Pomona. As Edwin Schallert, a fellow student at St. Vincent's and later a writer for *The Los Angeles Times* remembered it, Willard was "a rare exhibit" in such conventional surroundings. He came to class in peg-top trousers, the latest in high fashion, talked

43

about European poets no one had heard of, cross-examined his teachers, spent more time on the football field or in the library than in class, and seemed loaded with "amazing opinions."

At Harvard, where he applied for admission as "a special student" who would only take instruction in English and wouldn't matriculate, Willard fared no better. (Willard's application to Harvard in the summer of 1906 marks the beginning of a pattern of serious public deceptions. He listed W. C. Morrow as a tutor and reference. Morrow was a short-story and travel writer in San Francisco enjoying a brief vogue at the time—Willard hadn't even met him, but was never caught in the lie. Though his entrance exam scores were high, he wasn't going to trust to the truth alone to get him in.) Willard approached Harvard with unnaturally high expectations. His new school wasn't going to duplicate the world of St. Vincent's and Pomona, religiously strict and morally provincial, but would be the meeting ground of original scholars and uninhibited thinkers. He saw himself as a poet among poets, learning in the shadow of great philosophers and living with other young men who had left behind them the values of their parents. The fact that the teachers and student body did not measure up to these lofty ideals—and, by Harvard's standards, that Willard did not measure up—was just the last in a series of disappointments that Willard's wandering "educational experiment" represented.

Harvard in 1906 was a place of striking contrasts. A part of what Willard was looking for was to be found there in the first decade of the century. The list of famous teachers was awesome (William James, George Santayana, Josiah Royce, George Pierce Baker), the student body contained some able young men—one of the first classmates Willard met that fall was Lee Simonson, an aspiring poet and painter himself—and the *Harvard Monthly* was a prestigious forum for the short stories and poems Willard published there. Yet Harvard had some flagrant drawbacks, too, and Willard wasn't the only one to feel that way. There was an air of "a well-kept orchard" about the college, in Simonson's words, a rarefied staleness, the product of affluence and complacency. The administration wasn't known for its flexibility and, in Willard's view, the students were often no less entrenched in their prejudices, no more critical of conservative traditions, than their teachers or parents. He was amazed to discover that the

44

fraternities and snobbish dining clubs were high priorities among the student body, and that few of his peers took literature as seriously as he did. Too many young men seemed to be at Harvard for the sake of the useful social contacts they would make. Simonson observed Willard when he "drifted in" to Cambridge, writing his "consciously fleshy Swinburnian verse." He was "the picture of a romantic poet," Simonson wrote in his memoirs, with his long hair "brushed back off a high forehead and his alabaster neck in a Byronic collar." It wasn't likely that he would fit in. What Willard later called the "tepidity, the inertia, the listlessness of life at [Harvard]" was a sore disappointment to him, though no doubt he was an alienating, arrogant presence himself.

As a "special," non-matriculated student, Willard was not obligated to take a full load of courses. The two he selected were "The History and Development of English Literature," a broad survey course for freshmen taught by Professor Barrett Wendell, and Charles Townsend Copeland's "English Composition," an intensive writing class with weekly criticism sessions. Wendell was a fanatic Anglophile—"all Boston Brahmin"—with scant regard for American literature or those who sang its praises. He preached "clearness, force, and elegance" in writing, regardless of subject matter, and had a legitimate following at Harvard. Willard wasn't part of that group. A doctrinaire lecturer whose aesthetic ideal didn't embrace Wilde or Shaw (let alone Willard's native favorites, Poe and Twain) wasn't a man Willard could respect. In various ways he let him know it. Willard found his teacher's pomposity and narrow literary judgments unbearable, and by midyear he was cutting more classes than he was attending.

Copeland's classes were another matter. They weren't really "classes," to begin with, and Copey, as he was affectionately known, wasn't at all in the establishment-figure Barrett Wendell mode. Copey had been an actor and a journalist before coming to Harvard and, once he abandoned his own career as a writer, the encouragement of serious young writers became his mission in life. He was a searingly honest critic of his students' work, and there was a sort of purifying integrity attached to the rituals of "English 12," the weekly reading-aloud and criticism sessions in Hollis Hall conducted before a small group of fellow sufferers.

Like T. S. Eliot, Walter Lippmann, Robert Benchley, John Dos Passos, Brooks Atkinson, Robert Sherwood, and S. N. Behrman, all of whom studied with Copeland at about that time, Willard recognized the special value of what he was learning from his teacher; he earned the "A" from Copey that he wanted. The time spent in "English 12," and in auditing the brilliant Hugo Münsterberg's "Psychology"—where the psychology of crime was a topic, connected to Münsterberg's belief that those who investigated crimes needed to be more aware of hidden motives and psychological patterns—were the high points of an otherwise trying period.

A predictable complication of Willard's life in Boston was that relationships with women were very pressingly on his mind in his eighteenth year. Living off campus, he had one tempestuous affair which quickly took on a frightening intensity. Neglecting his schoolwork and his friends to be with this beautiful older woman—"Irene," in his autobiographical novel—Willard was quite happy to lose himself in feverish lovemaking. "The desire for sensation overcame the desire for achievement," Willard wrote of his protagonist in *The Man of Promise,* describing his alter-ego character as a victim of a sexual obsession that obliterated all sense of time and dailiness and obligation. Only slowly and awkwardly, after his standing at school had been seriously undermined, was Willard able—like Stanford West—to extricate himself from the relationship. Also not surprisingly, the city itself became as much an enticement for Willard that year, luring him away from the library, as any individual, male or female. Restaurants, cafés, concert halls, and theaters existed in greater numbers, and provided better fare, than in Los Angeles. And the women of the night, who added their own element to "the crowded glamour" of the city, as Willard wrote of it, were a new and addicting discovery that year.

In March Willard was "excluded" from English 28, his survey course with Barrett Wendell. The cause of this invitation not to return to class could have been any number of things. Willard hadn't been doing the work, and he wasn't the most tractable of pupils. He later told friends of appearing in class one day with a glass of absinthe which he proceeded to sip in the back row while Wendell droned on. This anecdote might well be in the vein of Stanton's story of running away to Hawaii at fourteen (as most tales of which Willard was the only source usually are), but the spirit behind it is authentic. Willard was becoming defiantly rude. "Our undisciplinables are our proudest product," William James had boasted in a famous commencement address in 1903. However, James' generous definition of the independent Harvard man wasn't meant to include anyone who went quite as far as Willard Wright, or so Dean Hurlburt felt. He asked Willard to come to his office for a private talk.

In a terse letter dated March 21, 1907, following their conference, Dean Hurlburt notified his recalcitrant charge that his dismissal from class was final, as Wendell was adamant, and that, no, he could not advance Willard the money that he had—incredibly—asked to borrow from him. Furthermore, he suggested that, since Willard intended to make writing his career, he devote himself wholly to that endeavor. It was time "to get out into the world," the dean wrote, and give up the game at Cambridge.

Graciously nudged rather than kicked out the door, Willard left Harvard at the end of the month. He had no plans and only limited funds. Surprised, hurt, and discouraged by this turn of events, Archie let Willard know that his ample allowance was finally coming to an end. He suggested that his son give some thought to finding work. If he wasn't going to get a degree or continue his studies in a regular fashion, it was high time he began to support himself.

Willard took his time heading back to California. He stopped in Oneonta and visited his maiden aunts and the cousin who lived with them, Margaret Beatrice Child, a favorite playmate from his summer visits to his father's side of the family. Then he moved on to Washington state where he decided to spend a few weeks in the company of a family friend his own age. The two young men enjoyed several weeks in Olympia of impoverished but, as the friend, Jay Dinsmore, remembered it, "supremely happy days." For Willard, it was a time of anxious release, of freedom from deadlines and people to please and some nervousness about what to do next. Relocating to Seattle, where Dinsmore had some affluent acquaintances known for their good parties, he made the social rounds and came to relish the part of the visiting poet. Given his good looks, it was a role that always had an effect on literary young women. At a gathering at the end of June, just before he was to leave for Los Angeles, Willard met a woman his own age whom he liked and who was obviously taken with him. In fact, he decided it might be worth lingering in Washington a while longer to get to know her better. Coming from an educated family of very limited means, Katharine Belle Boynton was exactly the sort of girl to interest Willard and, at first glance, she even appeared unconventional enough to hold his respect. The daughter of a newspaper publisher in the small town of Elma and a temperamental, neurotic musician mother, Katharine had been on her own longer than Willard, since she was seventeen. She was an avid reader and writer of poetry, and had supported herself, precariously, as a stenographer while she traveled throughout the Northwest. There was an odd mixture in Katharine Boynton of diffident and adventurous qualities, of an idealistic and a practical nature.

After a few days' acquaintance, Katharine struck Willard as sufficiently independent to think for herself, sufficiently respectable and inexperienced to be shocked (when Willard wanted that reaction), and pretty enough to court. Intelligent, curious, and reserved, she was eager to be taught about the writers and composers Willard appeared familiar with, and she loved to hear his stories about Harvard and California. Best of all, she took for granted that Willard was all that he seemed to be. He was the first man she had met in the Northwest with ambitions she approved of. Not normally given to impulsiveness, Katharine found herself irresistibly attracted to this tall poet with the long, curly hair and athletic build, who was alternately funny and eccentric and gravely, pompously serious. Willard was by no means uninterested in her and asked to see her each day that he was in Seattle.

Willard's amorous attentions to Katharine might have remained a pleasant memory for both of them after Willard's departure for the South but for one development. In early July Willard heard from his parents the surprising news that Stanton, already a star pupil at the Art Students League, was going to be married. He would be leaving home before the end of the summer. Stanton's bride-to-be was a girl he had been seeing for some months, Ida Wyman, and in company with the well-to-do Mrs. Wyman the couple was setting off for Paris in August where

Stanton would enroll at the Sorbonne. A short time after, without any further communication with his parents or brother, Willard proposed to Katharine, who immediately accepted.

On Saturday evening, July 13th, having known each other for only two weeks, Katharine Boynton and Willard Huntington Wright were married by a Unitarian minister in Seattle. In acknowledging the quiet ceremony, the local society page described Willard as "a clever and rising young poet" and printed one of his poems, while Katharine was lauded as "also a writer of no mean ability." The page in the bride's wedding book marked "Congratulations of Guests" was left blank. Like the Wrights, Katharine's parents, sisters, and one brother weren't notified until after the wedding. It didn't seem to matter. The Boyntons weren't in a position to give them any money, to pay for a reception, or even to offer the newly married couple a honeymoon.

As Willard was down to his last few dollars and Katharine's savings weren't much, their honeymoon took them no farther than the beaches of Oregon. But they were happy with that. Willard told his daughter almost thirty years later that a wedding-night scene had marred their first few hours together as husband and wife when Katharine discovered that her husband wasn't as romantically inexperienced as she was and had assumed him to be. The idea seemed almost funny to Willard—that a man more than eighteen years old would still be a virgin wasn't plausible—but he and Katharine soon made up. She had her own naive ideas about the world, Willard decided, and that was probably to be expected. What mattered was that he had found a mate, a friend and a support with which to face whatever lay ahead. Stanton wasn't the only member of the family with a wife, a goal, and the promise of an interesting future.

THE SCHOOL OF
MENCKEN

"The critic who is modest is lost."

—*George Bernard Shaw*

By the end of summer Willard was back in Los Angeles with his young wife but with no degree, no money, no literary accomplishments to boast of, no place to live—and, most importantly, no means of support. He had missed Stanton's departure by several weeks, thus averting an awkward comparison of new brides and future prospects. For Stanton, whatever the circumstances involved in the marriage of two seventeen-year-olds, at least had a plan the Wrights could understand, and he had already proven his talent and dedication to his art. He also had his mother-in-law, Mrs. Wyman, in tow. And he had known his bride for more than two weeks. Willard was lacking more than a plan, as the Wrights saw it. He was lacking common sense, even rationality.

As they couldn't afford to support him any longer, Archie and Annie had counseled Willard to stay in the Northwest and look for work there, a piece of advice all too quickly rejected. And with Willard and Katharine on their doorstep—two nineteen-year-olds with a few bags, a few books, and no place to stay—the Wrights had small choice in the matter. The couple moved in with them, Katharine found a secretarial job, and Archie set about trying to find something suitable for his son. Willard's two attempts at making a living out of the real-estate market, almost a sure thing for an ambitious young man in California in 1907, ended in failure—Willard preferred to spend the day reading novels and writing love letters to Katharine at her office. A third and final try at commercial success was his lamentable experience as cofounder of the Cheer-ee Beverage Company. Organized in January 1908 "for the purpose of selling the non-alcoholic drink, cheeree," three partners put up $2,500 each (Willard's share was borrowed from his father). The company operated, or floundered, out of a small office and factory on South San Pedro Street. In April, though, Willard had decided—wisely in this case—to bail out by summer, losing all of his father's investment but managing to escape incurring his partners' debts as bankruptcy loomed.

The spring and summer that followed was a difficult time at the Astoria Hotel. In the ninth month of her marriage, Katharine discovered that she was pregnant, a situation that meant loss of the household's only stable income other than Archie's, while Willard continued to spend his days writing poetry and avoiding the job-hunting everyone expected of him. His attitude toward his new responsibilities couldn't have been a surprise to his parents, but Katharine was stunned by her husband's odd manner. Making matters worse, as the weeks went by, it was hard for Willard to conceal the panic he felt at the thought of an unplanned child. Proud as he was of his sexual expertise, he hadn't known enough to prevent his wife's pregnancy, and he experienced a disturbing fear of the future and the trap into which he was falling. Fatherhood, at twenty-one, promised to limit his freedom and endanger the goals of his life even more than marriage had, and this, for Willard, was intolerable.

While contemplating his predicament, Willard met an older woman in Los Angeles to whom he confided his worries. Nothing more passed between them than a few earnest, sympathetic conversations. There was, apparently, no affair. Yet Willard was attracted to this elegant, educated woman and relished their private meetings and long, intimate talks. When the lady, who signed her letters only with the initials MVM, left the city to live in New York, Willard found that the need for feminine understanding and romantic escape had been stirred by this first "infidelity." A short time before his daughter's birth, and married for not quite two years, he recognized that his ties to his wife were already weakening.

When Willard abandoned the Cheer-ee enterprise, Archie's worst fears were realized. In due course he turned to the one man on his wife's side of the family who could help. Henry Huntington, having taken over the reins of his father's business, was able to provide work for his cousin's son without a moment's hesitation. The job "Cousin Henry" offered Willard was one he thought commensurate with his young relative's age and experience: ticket-taking on the Huntington-initiated commuter railway line of the greater Los Angeles area. As Harry Carr of *The Los Angeles Times,* later a friend of Willard's, summarized the matter, "Huntington did not recognize the light of genius" in his kin but, always ready to help, "gave him a cap with a gilt band" and a gate on the Pasadena Line. For a would-be writer who had walked Harvard Square and studied with Copey, who had relished Balzac and Oscar Wilde while his peers were reading Booth Tarkington and Zane Grey, and whose younger brother was an artist in Paris, his days serving the short-tempered commuters at the Pacific Electric Depot were excruciating. Ironically, though, the job secured Willard his first break as a writer. A chance meeting at the depot with John Daggett, a reporter for the *Times,* the principal newspaper in Los Angeles, led to an interview with Harry Andrews, the paper's managing editor, and a trial spot as a reviewer and reporter. All of this took place in October, the very week Beverley Wright was born.

In later life Willard never referred to his hapless days as a businessman or a ticket-taker. He preferred the common notion that he had moved from his random college studies straight to the pages of *The Los Angeles Times,* with no false starts in between.

For a young man of Willard Wright's views and ambitions, *The Los Angeles Times* was an ideal place at which to begin a literary career. The newspaper that had originated in a two-story brick building with a water-powered press back in 1881 (when the population of Los Angeles was 12,000) had grown in twenty-seven years into a vast, powerful, controversial forum. Dominated by the reactionary Harrison Gray Otis, the paper was conservative in its politics but flexible with its new writers (assuming they showed no hint of left-wing sympathies), new enough to need still more and younger journalists, and widespread—almost absolute—in its influence in Southern California. To work for the *Times,* whose circulation then was 52,000 for the daily paper and 76,000 for the weekend edition, was to work for the most commanding, and the most prejudiced, source of information in the state south of San Francisco. That was a bigger audience than most fledgling writers could hope to reach, as Willard realized. Furthermore, the *Times* appreciated strong opinions and strong language. Willard could honestly promise his editor plenty of that.

It wasn't long before Harry Andrews' newest writer was being assigned more books to review than anyone else and more exciting features to prepare than he had a right to expect, tasks that involved reporting on everything from bullfights in Tijuana to the gambling dens of Los Angeles. Liberated from mindless labor, Willard took to his duties with a ferocious enthusiasm and, for a newcomer to the business, an almost eerie self-confidence, a strength of opinion that seemed to bypass the usual hesitant apprentice-work period. Otis and Andrews were impressed, and within a few months Willard succeeded to the title he wanted: literary editor.

Faced with piles of books with titles like *Home Occupation for Boys and Girls, That Pup* ("a short novel about a lovable and vitally human dog"), and *The Mascot of Sweet Briar Gulch*—some of the touted Christmas offerings in 1908—Willard did his best to secure for himself more sophisticated fare. He was the man, he told Harry Andrews, to review the more serious criticism and fiction. The obvious junk could be farmed out to somebody else. His "Harvard education" helped, as few other reviewers could boast those credentials, as did the lie he told about spending a year studying art and literature in Europe. So the latest books by Conrad, Kipling, Wells, Maugham, George Moore, Anatole France, Edith Wharton, Ellen Glasgow, and Mark Twain went to Willard, along with almost all of the poetry and literary and music criticism. He quickly hit his stride and acquired in local literary circles just the reputation he wanted, that of a feisty, well-read reviewer who could separate the imitation from the genuine work of art.

The models he had in mind, critics whose work he had been reading since his college days, were an impressive lot. James Gibbons Huneker, Percival Pollard, and William Marion Reedy were among the most prolific of the new breed of writers who were unconnected to university life, free from the narrowness of academic criticism and specialization, and eager to analyze modern literature and theater rather than established classics or the ordinary publishing fare. Huneker, Pollard, and Reedy were also unashamed of their calling as journalists; they lived contentedly in the rough-and-tumble world of contemporary letters.

When Willard couldn't escape his share of the weaker books, of which there were plenty, he used the opportunity to vent his ire and hone an increasingly terse, acerbic reviewer's style. It was appalling to him to discover how much inane and trivial literature was published each month. "The tedious and gentlemanly art of reviewing books," as he described his new profession, gave way to breezy judgments and unapologetic sarcasm.

If it took the *Times* readers a while to discover what kind of literature Willard Huntington Wright approved of, it took no time to learn the specific nature of his complaints. Even the briefest survey of the several hundred reviews Willard wrote offers a clear picture of an opinionated young man who had seized the literary page as his personal platform. High on Willard's list of literary horrors were books that aimed to teach an explicit lesson, moral or political, or those that tried to turn the pleasure of reading into a dry, scholarly exercise. This meant that Socialists, feminists, and academics were never to be encouraged to move from the lecture hall to the writing table. Willard regularly lambasted Upton Sinclair and Charlotte Perkins Gilman for their efforts to use the novel as a propaganda vehicle for their causes, while he savored the chance to comment on Professor Barrett Wendell's academic studies as empty books expressed in "an overworked, sedentary style."

Willard also let it be known that an author's international reputation meant nothing to him either. He had slight regard for Mrs. Humphrey Ward, guilty of the ultimate sin of sentimentalizing reality, Charles Dickens (a writer of "cartoon characters" and "bourgeois humor"), or "that superficial poseur" Horace Walpole, and it made no difference to the *Times* literary editor how popular Ward, Dickens, or Walpole were with American readers. The prolific novelist Anne Warner, a national favorite, was another personage who never received a kind notice during Willard's years on the paper. In Willard's mind, Anne Warner, "the ne plus ultra of 'The Ladies Home Journal,' " was the epitome of everything effete and insipid that was embodied in the dread term "popular female novelist."

Nor were regional writers, who were sometimes treated more gently in the pages of California journals, given any special treatment by Willard merely because of their local followings. "The raucous and tautological atrocities of Gertrude Atherton's English . . . the awkwardness and cacophonies of her style" could not be excused by her fame or her good intentions. Most of her novels, Willard argued, ended in melodrama or maudlin sentiment. (To the many women who loudly complained that Willard was opposed to any female author simply because she was a female, Willard could counter, though he seldom cared to dispel that idea, with the names of Edith Wharton and Ellen Glasgow, both of whom he rated highly.)

After Atherton, Ambrose Bierce was the other sacred name in California literary circles. A few people even thought that Willard might have had Bierce in mind as a prototype for his own brand of commentary. From his misogyny to the crusty impatience with bad writing, there are obvious similarities. As "a professional cynic" and a libelously sarcastic columnist for Hearst's *San Francisco Examiner,* Bierce lived to shock and tease his audience. He became a cult figure for many young writers. But when a Bierce collection of essays appeared in 1909, Willard took the occasion to distance himself from any comparisons. Bierce was too purely a derider and a misanthrope. "He has nothing to supply in place of his devastation," Willard wrote. Bierce's problem, Willard believed, was that he lacked the desire to help create a better artistic climate. He was satisfied with the job of lashing out at complacent ideas and undeserved reputations, nothing more. Nonetheless, the comparisons between the two were often made in Willard's years on the *Times.* Bierce with the vinegar diluted, was the verdict of a few colleagues.

But whatever his complaints about serious writers like Ward, Walpole, Atherton, and Bierce, Willard reserved for another kind of literary animal his deepest scorn. That was the commercial novelist, the man or woman who published with the primary intention of making money by working a formula or appealing to the lowest tastes of the burgeoning mass audience. The group might include writers of romances, historical novels, or pulp adventures. It certainly included mystery and detective writers. "Mystery yarns are at best sad affairs," he decided. "They make their strongest appeal to children, divinity students, savages, stenographers, and other people of inferior intelligence and faulty education." By 1912, nearing the end of his reviewing days, he was moved to press the point even further. "The woods are full of detective stories—most of them bad. In fact, any serious detective story is of necessity bad. It appeals to the most primitive cravings within us."

The reactions to Willard's testy columns, almost from the beginning, were just what the *Times* management had hoped they would be. The book-review page had a bite to it now that was rare for newspapers of that time, and while most commentary and reportage was still unsigned in the early 1900s, the name of Harrison Gray Otis' new critic got around. Willard had taken fellow reporter Harry Carr's doctrine to heart, to good effect. "No one reads uncontroversial journalism" was Carr's motto. Rile enough readers, he told Willard, and you'll have a steadfast following. It even became desirable to give Willard a byline as he settled into the role of baiter and iconoclast.

Those writers Willard did commend to his readers were apt to be European or at least more cosmopolitan than bestsellers like Harold Bell Wright or Booth Tarkington. That some of Willard's literary heroes were new names to the California public didn't matter. He wrote as if any educated person should know who they were and what they stood for, or would take the time to find out. The new dramatists like Wedekind, Schnitzler, Sudermann, Brieux, Granville-Barker, Synge, and Andreyev, and of course the not-so-new playwrights like Ibsen, Shaw, Chekhov, and Strindberg, the "disreputable" poets Swinburne, Rossetti, and Baudelaire, and the great contemporary realists like Bennett, Galsworthy, Moore, Gorky, Zola, Norris, Crane, and especially Dreiser were the kind of artists Willard believed Americans had not paid sufficient attention to in their clamor for a more uplifting or moralizing literature.

Some of Willard's judgments were woefully wrong; he wrote, frequently, about Henry Milner Rideout as if he were an equal to

Thomas Hardy and proclaimed Stephen French Whitman the great American novelist. But more often than not he was on the mark. And unlike Bierce, Willard came to see himself as a man with a dual task. The vicious or amusing part of his job was to mock insipid or timorous authors. But the equally important part of the job, ultimately, was to promote the cause of those writers who were more honest, original, and challenging than the majority.

"The most uncompromising and zealous literary critic the West ever saw," Harry Carr described his friend thirty years later. He further reminisced that "[Willard] had all the authors scared to come out from under the bed . . . he had a rapier point for his pen whenever he wrote of those who had commercialized their gifts." By 1910 the college dropout and embarrassed ticket-taker had skillfully refashioned himself into a developing voice for the avant-garde and a taskmaster for all those writers who failed to meet the highest standards.

One *Times* reporter who was of even more immediate help to Willard than Carr was the affable John McGroarty, a regional poet and playwright and something of an inspired crazy himself. He helped Willard by giving him another, less restricted avenue into print. Eager to do his part in making a cultural capital out of a backwater, McGroarty had started his own small-circulation magazine in 1906, *The West Coast Magazine,* using his *Times* salary to help finance the project and his *Times* contacts to locate the freelance writers. He met Willard in 1909 and knew he had the sort of contributor he was in the market for—one who would come cheap, write frequently, and keep the reader awake. For Willard, the arrangement was agreeable. The more exposure, the better, and any extra money, however little, was welcome.

The West Coast Magazine was John McGroarty's noble attempt to broadcast and further California's intellectual coming-of-age, and beyond a doubt the most eccentric pages of this unusual brainchild were given over to the essays of Willard Huntington Wright. In the ample space allotted him, Willard let loose on the subjects of aesthetic struggle and moral restraints, the rights of the modern artist, the dangers of domesticity, and the joys of sex and wine. He wrote with a freedom of expression the *Times*, conscious of its advertisers and middle-class audience, would never permit. What the readers of *The West Coast Magazine* thought of Willard's rambling, impressionistic pieces can only be imagined. By 1910, though, McGroarty hinted that too much of a good thing was going to kill his magazine, and Willard's duties were changed to theater and book reviewing.

Essays like "The Uselessness of Art," "Respectability vs. Art," "The Artistic Temperament," and "Estheticism and Unmorality" are pure Oscar Wilde. In these pages with their thick, leafy Art Nouveau borders, Willard was paying his debt to the great British writer he and Stanton revered while preaching a doctrine, straight out of *Dorian Gray* and *The Decay of Lying*, that wouldn't have found space in *The Century* or *The Atlantic Monthly*. His thesis in the *West Coast* essays is very much the doctrine of a turn-of-the-century dandy or a young man bored by pious pictures, sermons masquerading as stories, and insensitive audiences. "Art is never understood or appreciated except by the artist," he proclaimed in the first essay, "The Uselessness of Art," which appeared in April 1909. As Willard saw him, the artist was a being whose perceptions necessarily set him apart from his fellows: therefore, "for the artist to cry for appreciation is to cry for the impossible." Neglect by the majority was to be expected. Nor should it trouble any serious creator, Willard maintained, because "art is solely a means of intoxication for the artist," no different from religious ecstasy for the believer or alcohol for the drinker. What follows is a Decadent's litany: Art does not serve any ethical or practical purposes. It does not aim to improve the world. It exists for its own sake. Furthermore, great art was likely to be stunted in a democratic environment with its emphasis on mass appeal, popular interests, and common bonds. For the *West Coast Magazine* critic, the truth was sobering and could be concisely, belligerently phrased: democracy was "the antithesis of all art . . . the apotheosis of the mean average, the glorification of the mediocre" and a democratic state like America was necessarily the trivial man's homeland, "the paradise of the insignificant."

In his other pieces for McGroarty, like "The Sex Impulse in Art" (an attack on the "passionless" novels of William Dean Howells, among others), or "Should Artists Marry?" (the answer was an emphatic "no"), or in book review columns like "The Suffragette in Fiction" (Willard's point was that the less attention paid to these vocal neurotic women the better), Willard continued straining to be as audacious as he could, or as much as a well-read but poorly educated writer in his early twenties could be. The odd value to Willard's writing of this period, even at its most rhetorical and repetitive, is that he was willing to articulate opinions other people might have shared but were too proper to express in print or ideas others might have read elsewhere (he was surely not the only resident of Los Angeles to have read Wilde, Pater, Gautier, or Huysmans) but didn't venture to discuss in the insular world of Southern California.

Willard's thinking in the years 1908 to 1912, before he moved to New York and joined *The Smart Set,* was that the less he respected liberal sentiment or the boundaries of "common sense" and "good taste," the more notice he would attract, and for a time John McGroarty played along. With each issue of *The West Coast Magazine,* until readers decided that he had gone too far in the "sex impulse" essay, Willard did in fact become a name that sold magazines, and McGroarty flamboyantly advertised him as "The Literary Vivisectionist," a local Bernard Shaw.

In time, Willard's California writings also became a means to another end and a reflection of another influence, a new journalistic voice, that Willard had discovered. He wasn't alone, he found out, in his swagger and bluntness and in his delight in issuing vast cultural pronouncements (at the age of twenty-two) and scathing commentaries.

Henry L. Mencken was in his third year with *The Baltimore Sun* in 1909 when Willard started to follow his columns and his advancing literary career. He had only recently become the lead book reviewer for *The Smart Set.* From the start, everything Willard heard or read about Mencken appealed to him. Mencken was ambitious, clever, opinionated, and strategically irreverent. He was anathema to prissy academic critics and excited about the new realists. Here was another of the kindred spirits Willard had always been searching for, and this was one who was younger, brisker, and more famous and less local than his newest friends, the *Times* art critic Antony Anderson and theater critic Julian Johnson. He might also be a useful contact in the East, Willard concluded, a man with access to the right publishers and editors.

Mencken was a man to learn from, too. He seemed even more

certain of himself than Willard, was better read in some areas, and exhibited a remarkable openness for male friendship, the exchange of ideas, mischief and controversy. He represented the best in the new style of cultural criticism and was refining a style that Willard was only too happy to mimic. He eventually played a far greater role in Willard's life than did Carr, Anderson, Johnson, or any other journalist. If Willard was uncomfortable in admitting in later years how much he owed to Mencken, on many levels, that is not surprising but it is no coincidence that Willard's career and reputation began to soar at the same time Mencken became a figure on the national scene. It was a profitable relationship.

Willard began to correspond with H. L. Mencken in the spring of 1909, praising his work and later suggesting that he might find freelance space for him in the pages of the *Times*. The *Times* reviews of Mencken's book about Shaw, in April, and his Nietzsche study, in May, were decidedly friendly overtures. Neither book was new (the Shaw book was published in 1905, the Nietzsche in 1908) and so the point of Willard's articles—a desire to make contact with Mencken—was clear enough. After such an auspicious beginning, it took no time at all for the two men to discover how much they had in common.

The crucial intellectual link between Mencken and Wright was the cause of those writers they wished to champion. The right allegiances were prerequisites for friendship for both men, and in this they were perfectly matched. Conrad, among European novelists, and Dreiser, among Americans, were their mutual passions. A third common interest—the tie that secured a friendship even before they met—was Friedrich Nietzsche. Nietzsche was experiencing a vogue in America just after the turn of the century, a tide of intelligent appreciation that came to an abrupt halt in 1914–1918 with the war in Europe when American "Nietzscheans" became a highly suspect group. Mencken's *The Philosophy of Friedrich Nietzsche,* his second book, was only one of many commentaries to appear between 1905 and 1915, but it was Willard's favorable review of the book in *The Los Angeles Times* of May 9, 1909, that prompted Mencken to take serious note of his fellow journalist. In fact, Willard's own interest in Nietzsche probably began in the wake of

Mencken's venture. He purchased a complete set of a new translation over the course of the next year and set himself to the task of reading all the volumes. Impressed with the eagerness of the *Times* critic, Mencken expressed the hope that they might meet someday. At his first opportunity to come East, Willard promised to look Mencken up.

That opportunity presented itself sooner than Willard expected. Katharine decided that she and Beverley would spend part of the summer in Washington, visiting her family, escaping the heat, and easing the financial strain in Los Angeles. She also feared that her husband was seeing another woman at the time (he was, briefly) and hoped that a separation from his daughter, whom he was beginning to warm to, would help her cause. At the same time the management of the paper let it be known that it was looking for someone to travel to New York in September to meet with the company's advertising and circulation men in Manhattan and then in Philadelphia and Boston. Willard volunteered. No one questioned his fitness for the job, if pushiness was the only qualification, and he wrote to Katharine asking her to stay in the north through October. As Willard explained, this was a career opportunity too good to be overlooked. It was dawning on him that Southern California might not be the beginning and the end of his career.

Willard's expedition that autumn, the first of three such trips he made for the paper over the next four years, was both exhausting and exciting. "I find here in the East I am pretty well known, adversely and otherwise," he noted to Katharine. Manhattan was the revelatory experience he expected and, with its competitive atmosphere and more glamorous nightlife, its libraries and concert halls, confirmed him in the feeling that one day he had to escape the quiet and narrowness of Los Angeles. The people he secured introductions to on these trips led Willard to believe that there was, or could be, a place for him in their circle. There was Mitchell Kennerley, the publisher who brought out the prestigious *Forum* magazine and bought a few of Willard's poems for future issues; there was the publisher Ben Huebsch, who took an immediate interest in his new friend's prospects; there were the poets Bliss Carman and George Sylvester Viereck, the critics Pollard and Huneker, and the dozens of editors and reporters Willard added to his list of promising contacts. To all of them, Willard dropped hints about his willingness to leave the *Times* for greener pastures.

The highlight of the trip East, naturally, was the long-awaited visit to Baltimore for the last weekend of October. "I got into Baltimore about 4 p.m. and went straight to H. L. Mencken's," Willard wrote Katharine. "We had a corking good time. He is just like his book reviews—a kind of Human Ham." Their areas of agreement were "very numerous" and, over a superb oyster dinner and many bottles, the two "got on wonderfully well." Part of Willard's description was calculated for its shock effect on Katharine: "His hair grows straight out in all directions and he talks like a sewer."

Some of the topics of conversation, which might have called for profane language, were the hopeless limitations of American editors and publishers, the dismal state of American fiction, the shoddy treatment Dreiser had to put up with, the prissiness of most contemporary magazines, and the desperate need for a journal that could offer something other than morality tales, Horatio Alger imitations, and light verse. The last topic was especially important to both men. Mencken was given considerably leeway in his book reviews for *The Smart Set* but wasn't entirely happy with that publication, either. He had the itch to start his own review, or to gather a group of like-minded men to form one, that could provide more daring short fiction and hard-hitting essays for sophisticated readers. In this fantasy about what would eventually become the *American Mercury,* Mencken was sufficiently taken with Willard on their first meeting to decide that he would be one of their contributors; he was, Mencken said, "elected and inaugurated" on the spot. "When the time comes, you must come in," Mencken urged. This was the offer Willard had traveled East to hear. No real urging was called for.

And if Mencken needed more proof than the *Times* articles he had already seen that Willard was his man, Willard was able to provide it in the form of some essays he had written for *The West Coast Magazine.* Toward these further evidences of Willard's iconoclasm, Mencken was particularly gracious.

> Believe me, your two essays knocked me over—not because their doctrine startled me, for I knew your position, in part, and suspected the rest, but because of their electric style. You have

here got into English the thing Nietzsche got into German—a loud heart beat, an assertive clang. There is the resounding wallop of heavy strokes, the clash of hammer on anvil.

He also issued his young colleague the warning that "if anyone talks to you of style, bidding you read Addison and Walter Pater—my curses on him! . . . your style is already there: guard it, by all means, from feminization." When Willard arrived home, having piled up bills far in excess of the expense account the paper had given him, it was with the happy sense that he had an ally near to New York with his best interests at heart. Nor could it have been displeasing to Mencken that the style he praised was so similar to, even at times borrowed from, his own.

H. L. Mencken and Willard Huntington Wright were more than intellectual allies, though, in their closest years. And Willard was more than a disciple, although he was that too. There was also a temperamental affinity, a mutual playing-off of the best and the worst in each other. Mencken's understanding of literary criticism, which he later described as "prejudices made plausible," was appealing to Willard. They shared an innate suspicion of academics, liberals, reformers, and teetotalers. Both men looked upon democracy, or so they said, as a dubious improvement on old-world aristocracy; humility and sympathy for the downtrodden were never their strong suits. Particularly in his attitude toward women, not one of the most enlightened areas of Mencken's thinking, the Maryland bachelor (who, like Willard, enjoyed a strong tie to his mother) was just the kind of model Willard was seeking. Mencken knew that Willard was a married man and a father but didn't take those facts any more seriously than was called for and introduced his friend to more than a few young ladies in the several years they were friends. Nor were they strangers in their time to the classier brothels of Baltimore or "the working girls" of New York.

Over the course of the next three years Willard did his best to make a more visible name for himself. He poured out reviews for the *Times*, essays and theater chronicles for McGroarty, and poems and short stories for any periodical he could place them with. He became a widely sought-after lecturer, with two bizarre specialties: explicating Nietzsche and presenting the case against suffrage for women, both topics dear to Mencken's heart. These antisuffrage lectures were often tempestuous affairs. He also broadened his base by traveling from one end of the state to the other, in search of good feature articles on California life. ("Hotbed of Soulful Culture," his full-page *Times* article of May 22, 1910, was especially popular. This satirical piece on the Bohemianism of the Carmel artists' colony spared none of the writers who congregated there—including his friend the poet George Sterling and the novelists Mary Austin and Upton Sinclair, two authors Willard never ceased teasing.) In these days Willard hatched more projects than any single man could ever have brought to completion, and at one time he was meeting with Antony Anderson of the *Times* to coauthor a drawing-room comedy in the style of Maugham (the working title was "Sex") and with a local composer to produce a libretto, all the while interviewing people and taking notes for a biography of the American poet Richard Hovey, recently deceased and much admired in 1910. None of these undertakings was ever finished—but that didn't seem to discourage Willard, who could afford to revel in the sheer energy and optimism of the moment.

The one serious interruption to Willard's pace at the *Times,* which might have had calamitous consequences for him, took place in the fall of 1910. The anarchist bombing of the *Los Angeles Times* building during the night of October 1 was among the most divisive and traumatic events in the history of Southern California. When the McNamara brothers' sixteen carefully planted sticks of dynamite went off at 1 A.M., near the peak of the evening shift, twenty *Times* men were killed, most of them instantly. Almost the entire block-long building was destroyed. Had the bombing occurred four hours earlier, or had Willard worked late that night, he would probably have been among the seriously or fatally injured.

The bombing of Harrison Gray Otis' building, a plainly symbolic act in the face of the paper's political conservatism and antiunion campaigns, had been planned for maximum effect by two radicals, John and James McNamara. The sticks of dynamite and the timing device were placed in Ink Alley, a passageway separating the stereotyping and the press rooms. The initial blast demolished the first-floor wall, precipitating the explosion of tons of ink stored in the alley. Within minutes the three-story structure was ablaze. The one hundred writers, typists, and press men on duty made desperate efforts to escape, but many of those in the basement or on the upper floors were trapped. Churchill Harvey-Elder, the acting night editor, was forced to jump from his top-floor office window and died at the hospital a few hours later. It was a gruesome episode in California and American labor history.

Within a few years, when he was no longer living amid people who might contradict him, Willard altered the story of his own involvement in the bombing until it bore no more relation to the truth than most of his anecdotes about his early life. The whole event was after all a made-to-order drama, too good to leave to the mercy of the facts. As Willard told it, he had worked late on the night of September 30th, straining over a review of a godawful concert Julian Johnson had talked him into covering. At a few minutes to one, he turned to Harvey-Elder at the next desk and told him that he would have to leave with the review undone as his migraine headache was making it impossible for him to continue. In a cab a few blocks away, Willard heard the deafening explosion and returned to see the building, and the office he shared with Harvey-Elder, in flames. In the years of his greatest fame as S. S. Van Dine, when he was interviewed and quoted on a regular basis, Willard liked to tie this anecdote in to what he saw as an emerging theme of his life: illness as a benefit in disguise. His "brush with death" in the McNamara bombing—having been saved only by the pain of his headache—was the first, he claimed, in a line of similar ironic happenings.

The truth was considerably less grand. Willard left the office before ten o'clock that night and returned home for a long, much-needed sleep. He was nowhere near sight or sound of the trouble. When he was awakened at nine on the morning of the 1st by the delivery of a frantic telegram from Katharine, who was out of town and had already heard the news (and assumed the worst about her husband), Willard hadn't the slightest idea of the cause of Katharine's hysteria. As he didn't believe in subscribing to the morning papers himself, he only learned of the explosion from a neighbor an hour later. He then had breakfast, which nothing ever interfered with, dressed, and headed for the scene to find out what was expected of him. After all, he had the upcoming Christmas "Special Book Section" to work on.

Indeed, the most authentic achievement of Willard's early

years, which earned him the regard of East Coast publishers, was this special literary supplement section he prepared every six months for the *Times*. Brought out each July and December, these twenty or more pages of reviews and essays, book advertisements and "Recommended Reading" lists, were an excruciating labor to organize but well worth the trouble. The supplement was a classy product with a heavy emphasis on the better realistic writers, and those who said that Otis' *Times* offered California as much first-rate reportage as Adolph Ochs' *Times* gave New York had a strong argument in their favor whenever Willard's creation, the "Special Book Section," appeared. Given the state of literary journalism in the West in the early 1900s, this aspect of the newspaper seems astoundingly cosmopolitan today. It surprised no one then, after the death of the respected critic Percival Pollard in 1911, when Willard was offered Pollard's freelance position with *Town Topics*. An eccentric New York gazette—part gossip sheet, part cultural review—*Town Topics* was, as Willard calculated, his foothold in the door. From Los Angeles each month, he mailed out a column on the arts that shared the same un-stodgy, un-parochial qualities that had endeared Pollard to his small but faithful readership in the East.

Throughout 1912 John Adams Thayer had been impressing upon H. L. Mencken his need for a new editor-in-chief for *The Smart Set*, someone with fresh ideas and talent as a manager. Thayer's feeling was that Mencken himself was the man to make something great of his magazine. But no matter how agreeable the terms, and Thayer wasn't known, really, for his generosity, Mencken never had any intention of leaving Baltimore for the killing pace of New York, a city he intensely disliked. When Thayer pressed him yet again in the fall of that year, he had a strong suggestion to make instead: a young writer in Southern California he knew, a twenty-five-year-old critic and editor of similar views, who would do just as well. Thayer knew very little about Willard Huntington Wright, but he had enjoyed his *Town Topics* columns and was willing to meet with him, and so Mencken pushed the suggestion all he could.

Given Thayer's lack of acumen and Willard's sense of a critical opportunity at hand, it was small wonder that Willard, a glib conversationalist, awed the *Smart Set* publisher at their first meeting. He must have been as erudite, talkative, charming, and even fulsome as he had ever been because Thayer decided on the spot that Mencken was correct. (Obviously Thayer had never seen Willard's book review of his memoirs the year before, in which the *Times* critic made fun of the businessman as a colossal bore puffed up by his own self-importance.) He offered Willard the position as editor of the magazine beginning with the new year. In joy and disbelief, Willard sent word to Katharine and his parents that, at last, he was going to have the chance that he had always hoped would come his way. Once back in Los Angeles to make his arrangements with the *Times* and to talk his father into a loan, he deftly got out of bringing Katharine and Beverley with him by pleading that he needed a while to establish himself in his new position, save some money, and find decent housing for them all. By this time Katharine knew better than to protest. Willard would do what he wanted to, anyway. She already knew of at least three affairs he had had in the first four years of their marriage.

A fitting note to signal Willard's departure from the West was the appearance before Christmas of a short story he had written, which several adventurous newspapers around the country asked to reprint. "The Second Child," autobiographical in spirit rather than in fact, was a story of a young man whose wife has become pregnant for the second time. This is a desperate development for the poverty-stricken couple, as they can barely feed their first child, and the husband appeals to various doctors for "help." Rebuffed by the respectable medical men he approaches, he finally finds a back-alley abortionist who performs the operation and spares them the unwanted baby. The Maupassant twist to the story, though, is the death of the wife, a victim of the ineptness of the abortionist. As he was packing to leave, Willard happily clipped and saved some of the better, angrier letter-to-the-editor responses that his abortion story elicited.

By the end of the month he was in New York, in time to join Mencken and his drinking friends for New Year's in Baltimore. The events that were to follow that celebration Willard couldn't have foreseen: a year of high hopes and grating trials at *The Smart Set*, embarrassing defeat, and an unexpected reunion with Stanton. Still less could Willard have imagined his imminent involvement with the tangled theory and bitter politics of modern art.

THE BIRTH OF SYNCHROMISM

"Were realism the object of art, painting would always be infinitely inferior to life—a mere simulacrum of our daily life, ever inadequate in its illusion. . . . Our minds call for a more forceful emotion than the simple imitation of life can give. We require problems, inspirations, incentives to thought."

—*Willard Huntington Wright, 1915*

The infamous Armory Show, that great carnival display of the latest painting and sculpture from Europe and America, was a litmus test—the first of many—for art lovers, patrons, and critics in the early years of the century. Many visitors reacted with hostility to the mammoth exhibition of Post-Impressionist, Fauve, and Cubist art. A fair number struggled to grasp the intentions behind the new trends, while some (a minority) rejoiced in the attack on academic, representational styles. Willard had taken time off from his duties at *The Smart Set* office to see the show at the Lexington Avenue and 26th Street armory in March of 1913, but his responses to the new art had not been particularly enlightened.

In fact, the four jocular postcards he mailed to Katharine are straight out of *Babbitt*. On the back of a card reproducing Sousa-Cardoza's "Parade" Willard scrawled, "This is not a plate of tripe, but a street parade as seen by a Futurist. There are a hundred like it at the exhibit." Duchamp's "Nude Descending a Staircase" elicited the comment: "The most talked of picture in New York. It's too deep for me." The card showing Picabia's "Danse à la

Source" contained the message, "I translate this so you will believe it. The cubist's idea of art. Picabia is one of the leaders. Can you see the dance or the spring? This has sold for an enormous price." And in reference to Lehmbruck's elongated "The Kneeling One": "Doesn't she make you jealous?" It was characteristic of Willard Huntington Wright that he might be woefully ignorant of the principles of modern art in 1913 but ready to declare himself an advocate and an expert two years later. In this transformation, he was aided by Stanton and some wonderfully advantageous circumstances.

Willard owed his first serious art education, such as it was, to his friend Antony Anderson, the *Los Angeles Times* art critic. Together they would go to exhibitions and studio gatherings during Willard's years on the paper, where Anderson shared his knowledge and opinions with his much younger but very receptive colleague. Unfortunately, the opportunities to see the paintings of the best new artists, or the Old Masters for that matter, were few and far between in Southern California. Inness, Hassam, La Farge, Henri, Homer, Whistler: those whose work Willard had occasion to see (and sparingly at that) were remarkable but by-then conservative artists, inspired but certainly not provocative painters to a 1910 audience. Moreover, Anderson's own background as a painter was in portraiture and representational art, and he had only a small idea of the radical direction Willard's brother was pursuing abroad. There was only so far Willard could go with such a mentor. Indeed, for Willard in the pre-1913 period, a great artist was someone like Edwin Austin Abbey, Cézanne was just a name, and Cubism an amusing French joke.

The change came when Willard moved to New York and slowly realized that in his understanding of the visual arts he was as provincial as the people out West he loved to satirize. He failed to perceive the meaning of everything, or much of anything, he saw at the Armory Show, but he understood soon enough that something unusual and significant was happening. New galleries were opening, the newspapers and magazines were full of conflicting reports on the current "isms," and some of the most intelligent people he knew, like Mitchell Kennerley and the lawyer John Quinn, had taken a serious interest. His curiosity was roused. When Willard met Alfred Stieglitz later that year, he encountered an especially potent influence in that area. Stieglitz was the sort of pragmatic visionary Willard was most in awe of, and at Stieglitz's gallery at 291 Fifth Avenue he was able to see over the next four years some of the best examples of modernist painting and sculpture and to meet the artists the gallery was promoting. The two men never formed the kind of mentor-disciple relationship, though, that might have been expected. Despite the fact that Stieglitz was twenty-four years Willard's senior and very interested in gathering disciples into the fold at "291," that arrangement would never have worked in this case. Stieglitz and Willard were too much alike: colossal egos, passionate workers, and rancorous personalities. Once Willard had mastered "the lesson," they settled into the position of respectful allies.

The real turning point in Willard's awareness of modern art is probably, and ironically, owed to John Adams Thayer. The June 1913 trip to Europe which Thayer promoted for his troublesome editor enabled Willard for the first time to taste some of the excitement the more advanced European art circles were experiencing on the eve of the War and to confront the reality of his brother's experiments in the six years since he had seen him. It was an excellent piece of timing that allowed Willard to be in Munich to see the paintings at the Neue Kunst Salon Synchromism exhibition, to meet Morgan Russell, to hear the theories and the hopes directly from Stanton, and to savor the controversy.

Full of self-confidence and plans for a great future, Stanton had left Santa Monica in the summer of 1907 without any clear or specific sense of where he was headed as a painter. He simply knew that California wasn't going to provide him with the opportunities, exposure, or influences he craved. He also left home with a wife (and her mother, for a time) who was made to order for a struggling artist. Ida Wyman Wright was meek, doting, and reasonably affluent. In the fall they arrived in Paris, where Stanton enrolled at the Sorbonne and later at three of the best art schools. For the better part of the next six years, in a blissful situation very unlike his brother's, Stanton had little to do but worry about the development of his art. (He contemplated writing a biography of Oscar Wilde, but nothing came of this project.) Wyman money, and occasional checks squeezed out of Archie, supported the couple in a comfortable (but not luxurious) fashion as they set up house in town, periodically visited London, Amsterdam, Munich, and other art centers, and spent months at a time in the village of Cassis on the Mediterranean. From the ages of seventeen to twenty-three, Stanton read, sketched, painted, and studied the works of other artists, aware of his technical inexperience and free from the pressure to sell pictures in order to live. Of that vast contingent of American painters who traveled to Europe before war broke out, he was the most fortunate in his circumstances.

It was of course a privileged moment in which to be young, curious, artistically inclined—and in Paris. With great robustness, Stanton made the most of it. He availed himself of every chance to see the new Cubist still-lifes of Picasso, Braque, and Gris, the Fauvist landscapes of Matisse, Vlaminck, and Derain, and the by-then hallowed paintings of Post-Impressionists like Van Gogh, Gauguin, and Cézanne. He met Leo Stein, but didn't particularly care for Gertrude (he once referred to the "Steinitis" of Gertrude's circle as "the Disease of Paris"). In any event, almost everything about the life Stanton encountered in France seemed reassuringly distant from Southern California, the mores of Annie Wright, Los Angeles art school teachers who preached "proper" craftsmanship, and a cultural climate that saw "Ash Can" realism as daring new art.

It was probably inevitable, as he became more intense, sophisticated, and preoccupied with his work in the studio, that Stanton would drift away from Ida, and that happened, by degrees. The little that can be inferred from the family letters presents a startling picture in one respect: Ida might have been Katharine Boynton's sister. Both brothers had managed to find women who bore their husband's gradual estrangement and compulsive promiscuity stoically and assumed, or hoped, that they would eventually find time for them again. Meeting men of stature like Rodin, Signac, and Delaunay confirmed Stanton in his belief that he had been right to leave home to develop an identity as more than an American artist and that questions of husbandly duty were of limited importance. A step in that identity-forming process involved an alteration of his name. Tired of being asked if he were related to Frank Lloyd Wright, Stanton Wright decided to make use of his middle name and to sign his work "Stanton Macdonald-Wright."

None of Stanton's early paintings are known to be extant, but the photographs of his pre-Synchromist work that have come to light offer a tantalizing hint of the direction he was moving in. A self-portrait of 1909 indicates a young painter who has been studying Impressionism and Post-Impressionism, not academic portraiture, with a special interest in Cézanne's patchy applications of paint and Gauguin's and Matisse's colors. "Self-Portrait with Simonson" of 1912 is a more accomplished and ambitious venture in the same vein. (Stanton had met Lee Simonson, Willard's old Harvard acquaintance, in 1910, and they quickly became fast friends and painting partners, sharing models and ideas about painting.) In his usual fashion, a method both rigorous and haphazard, Stanton pursued his aesthetic education as he pleased through the Louvre and the galleries, studios, and private collections of Paris. He exercised a sensible, indefatigable openness. Michelangelo, Rubens, Constable, Turner, Géricault, Delacroix, Renoir, Gauguin, Matisse, Cézanne: the artists Stanton appreciated, analyzed, sketched from, or repeatedly, even obsessively, returned to were a diverse, seemingly random group. The common tie, if there was one, was their interest in the dynamic or rhythmic qualities of their media, a concern with solidity or movement or intensity of experience that raised them out of traditional or academic molds. Elegance, refinement, or stasis were less important in the men Stanton chose as his artistic heroes than spectacular color, rugged forms, vigorous modeling, and animating energy. In these general influences the groundwork was being laid for the more systematic evolution of what came to be called Synchromism.

Two developments in 1911 provided some crucial and unanticipated focus to Stanton's explorations. That year he began to attend the classes of Ernest Percyval Tudor-Hart and, through Simonson, he met a fellow expatriate of a similarly independent bent, Morgan Russell. Tudor-Hart was a Canadian painter and teacher whose unusual classes emphasized the importance of color as a primary functioning element in a modern painting. Well informed about the research and theorizing of the last century on the subject of color relationships and optical effects, he urged his students to read the texts of Chevreul, von Helmholtz,

Ogden Rood, and Charles Blanc, whose writings about "receding" and "advancing" colors, color contrasts and blends, were only vaguely understood. Tudor-Hart didn't agree with everything in Rood's *Modern Chromatics* or Chevreul's *Principles of Harmony and Contrasts of Color,* but he wanted his students to move beyond a superficial, subjective use of color. He was considered a hopeless crank by some, but for two of his students in particular, he was a serious and thought-provoking instructor.

As a former student in New York of the unconventional realist painter Robert Henri, and as a former student in Paris of the much more innovative Henri Matisse, Morgan Russell was ripe for conversion to Tudor-Hart's faith in the power of color. He also saw himself as the man to turn that faith into tangible, original accomplishment, which his teacher had failed to do. Russell knew the modern movements in art and had found them all wanting: none seemed to go quite far enough, to satisfy him as the best ancient sculpture or classical music did. Ambitious for his art form as much as for himself, Russell wrote that he wanted to make painting "capable of moving people to the degree that music does." To this end, he ultimately concluded, painting had to move away from its preoccupation with illustration, verisimilitude, storytelling, or even image-making itself, devising means for color to convey aesthetic sensations in the way that notes alone, divorced from words and stories, provided satisfaction in music. As early as September 1912, in a notebook annotation, Russell speculated on an idea for a kinetic light machine that could render color relationships more effectively than oil on canvas, an invention of the future in which waves of light of different colors could be projected past the viewer, immersing him in pure color. In this desire to make painting less bound to literary or sentimental associations or biographical and social concerns, Russell was hardly alone in the years after 1910. That goal was shared by many turn-of-the-century painters of different or even competing schools. In assuming that draftsmanship and recognizable subject matter might have to be abandoned altogether (a decision he was later to alter), Russell was in a much smaller minority. But at the time he and Stanton met, all of these thoughts were still in a formative stage, and Morgan Russell's work from this period was still either sculptural or representational in a style that suggested Matisse or Derain.

73

Stanton Macdonald-Wright and Morgan Russell never became warm or intimate friends. (It is unlikely that Stanton ever knew about Russell's penchant for cross-dressing in private.) They were allied more by their shared professional interests and their conclusions that everybody else in Europe was on the wrong track. As Russell eloquently phrased it in his journal, they wanted to keep "the palpitation or undulation" in their paintings and "sacrifice the fact." In those terms, Cubism and Fauvism—styles based in still-life and landscape traditions, however revolutionary they seemed to the uninitiated—weren't breaking such new ground after all. The two Americans, in their early twenties, felt that they were groping their way toward a much more radical definition of modern painting.

The historical morass concerning just how much the paintings of Macdonald-Wright and Russell owe to the Cubists, to Cézanne, Kupka, Kandinsky, and particularly to the "Orphist" color abstractions of Robert and Sonia Delaunay is still being sorted out by scholars of twentieth-century art (well into the 1970s Sonia Delaunay insisted that she and her husband were the first to use the terms "synchrome" and "synchromique"), but the claims for originality on the part of the Synchromists are more highly regarded today. Similarly, the differences, visual and theoretical, between the work of Russell and Wright and the Delaunays' "Orphism"—a brighter, flatter, more tightly geometric, and more decorative mode of abstraction—have been studied with greater care in recent years.

So what was Synchromism, after all? Inspired by the Post-Impressionists or not, born of the Delaunays' earlier example or not, does it have characteristics of its own? It does, but they are annoyingly elusive in that the two individuals who developed the term were anything but identical in their style, evolved in slightly different ways, and sometimes responded to different artistic traditions. Unlike many of the Cubist works of Picasso and Braque, which even for connoisseurs can be difficult to tell apart, the paintings of Stanton Macdonald-Wright and Morgan Russell are not interchangeable. When one refers to "a Synchromist painting," then, one might be referring to any one of several kinds. Further complicating the matter is the fact that some Synchromies are abstractions, while others are not.

The artists' mutual premise was clear at any rate. They took

Cézanne's celebrated dictum "when color is at its richest, form is at its fullest" as a springboard. Hence, objects or figures, or the faint suggestions of them, in a Synchromist oil are not drawn onto the canvas; they are molded and positioned without outlines, by the color arrangements themselves. The physical properties of color, painted in broad patches or subtle gradations, in pairs or triads of complementary colors, in modulations of warm or cold colors, are used to convey a sense of volume and depth. The Synchromists set out to devalue anecdotal, psychological, or decorative content in a painting, just as they were going to herald, by their example, the end of precise draftsmanship, that tool of an earlier age. Like the student of music and abstract dance, the viewer of a Synchromy had to respond in a nonliterary, nonreferential way. Meaning was found in form alone (as Morgan Russell said about the first work he labeled a Synchromy, exhibited in early 1913, "[its] subject is deep blue") or in its transcendent potential. A Synchromist still-life and an abstract Synchromy could be said, then, to evoke identical responses: immersion in the experience of color rather than "content." The difficulty of achieving these aesthetic goals is suggested by the uneven quality of the Synchromist body of work, but the aspirations can still strike us as impressive—and prescient in terms of the Color-Field art of the 1950s and '60s that Synchromism anticipated.

Throughout the years he worked in this style, Morgan Russell, who began his career as an architect and a sculptor, often looked to sculptural forms as the source for his compositions and the rhythmic power of his paintings. A sort of modern-day Emersonian, he was apt to think in Transcendentalist terms about art, as the title of one of his most famous works ("Cosmic Synchromy") implies. He was also more open than Stanton to the possibility of devising nonrepresentational compositions (after Arthur Dove, Morgan Russell was probably the first American abstract painter), and the term "Synchromism" itself—meaning "with color"—was chosen by Russell in late 1912.

A more assured colorist than his friend, Stanton was less ready to come to terms with pure abstraction, and for a while he hovered between the two poles. It was not until a few years after the Munich show that he acknowledged the limitation he had imposed on his early Synchromies by grounding them so emphatically in suggestions of external realities. But for Stanton, child of California light and water, color and openness, it wasn't desirable for the modern artist, even for the painter who was forsaking naturalism and Impressionism, to stray too far from nature and the human body. Yet it wasn't the depiction of limbs or bodies that interested Macdonald-Wright and Russell, as one art historian has written, but something closer to "a rippling surface movement," a pattern calling to mind "the flexing of limbs held under tension." The Synchromists made use of the broken planes of the Cubists, but their lavishly colored, swirling hues sometimes looked, as the historian Abraham Davidson has fairly described them, like "eddies of mist, the droplets of which collect to form parts of a straining torso." The hard-edged geometric style of abstraction then emerging elsewhere in Europe, and which later played such a large part in the development of modernism, was antithetical to the Synchromists' spirit. Theirs was an abstraction of reverberations, textures, and sinuous or colossal movement.

The most important point to be made about Synchromism now, probably, is that it was less an authentic "system," "school," or "movement"—though those labels are almost unavoidable—than an attitude toward painting, or a set of general, highly principled beliefs with a theoretical underpinning. This was a point Willard himself made on several occasions. That lack of a cogent, easily digested program with disciples, imitators, avid collectors, and respected spokesmen accounts in part for its obscurity today, as does the brevity of the period in which the Synchromist painters remained in the limelight. Stanton Macdonald-Wright and Morgan Russell were enormously talented but not, in the long run, particularly lucky or wise in their strategies. The other piece of the puzzle which explains Synchromism's odd position in art history was the nature of the campaign itself waged first by the artists and later, in New York, by Willard.

When Willard Huntington Wright met Morgan Russell in June of 1913 and saw the Synchromist exhibition in Munich in his brother's company, he experienced a shock equal to anything he felt at the Armory Show three months earlier. Four paintings were reproduced in the catalogue that accompanied the show:

Russell's "Synchromy in Green," a studio interior with two figures and a statue, Stanton's portrait of Jean Dracopoli, a collector who had befriended him, and two back views of Michelangelo's "Dying Slave" in the Louvre, one by each artist. All were representational works, as were the twenty-five other paintings in the exhibition; the first completely abstract Synchromist canvas wasn't completed until later that year. But they were hardly conventional scenes or still-lifes. The two painters' diminishing interest in line and growing desire to allow color to express shape and depth were evident, and though we can only know the paintings from the Munich show by photographs and later descriptions in print (they are all lost works now), the bluntness of the broken planes of color is easy to imagine. This was a step beyond the controversial Fauve exhibitions of the decade before. If Synchromism wasn't a clear-cut style as of the spring of 1913, it was more than an embryonic development. The opening of the show was loud and hectic, and the whole adventure excited a fair amount of attention, leading to the promise of a major Paris show the following autumn. The reviews were not heartening, but Willard was impressed with his brother's achievements.

"In Explanation of Synchromism," the catalogue essay written by Stanton and Russell, was a somewhat pretentious document—though nothing compared to their catalogue statements that followed. They discussed their work as an outgrowth of Impressionism's concern with light and artistic freedom, though they had no wish to be further associated with the crowd-pleasers who came under that heading. From the Synchromist point of view, Monet, Pissarro, and Sisley were essentially illustrators of pretty scenes rather than visionaries or artists of "genuine inner strength." As the legitimate heirs of Renoir and Cézanne, the Synchromists were going to surpass their fathers in examining the properties of light and color and forging an art of enduring value. The Cubist rejection of strong color for a muted palette came in for a full measure of condescension, as did the Italian Futurists' mania for movement and technology. The catalogue undoubtedly failed to win any adherents—it could have been a *Smart Set* editorial—but it did imply, if a bit obscurely, the emerging tenets of the new movement and its lofty purposes.

Willard could be the most willing of pupils when intellectually challenged by something new and strange. In Munich he didn't have much time to absorb everything Stanton wanted to tell him, as he had to get on with his search for good manuscripts for the magazine, but he did his best. Though no letters survive to prove it, it seems likely that the brothers corresponded at length during the summer and fall when Willard was back in New York. Certainly by the end of the year he was much more knowledgeable, and biased in new ways, about the different trends of modern art than he had been at the start of the year.

The autumn exhibition at the Bernheim-Jeune Gallery, which ran from October 27 through November 8, saw the display of the first abstract Synchromy. Morgan Russell's "Synchromy in Deep-Blue Violet" was dedicated to Gertrude Vanderbilt Whitney, who had for some time been helping to finance the painter's study abroad. He considered it "the heart of [his] development," a "rhythmic ensemble" that conveyed "the bursting of the central spectrum . . . on one's consciousness." Though the painting apparently bore no resemblance to the human form, it took its compositional premise, Willard later wrote, from the twists and spirals of "Dying Slave," that monumental Renaissance sculpture which so fascinated both Morgan Russell and Stanton. The rest of the paintings in the Paris show, like those in the earlier Munich exhibition, were more clearly based on recognizable forms. The vision of the Synchromists, as one scholar has accurately noted, was in advance of their accomplishment.

Showing these works in the art capital of Paris, though, rather than in a foreign city, was bound to provoke a heated reaction, and in that sense Stanton wasn't disappointed. In fact, he did all he could to fan the flames. The new catalogue, all 5,000 copies of which were gone by the second day of the show, was more aggressive than its predecessor as well as more helpful in detailing the Synchromist intentions. Again, though, the Cubists and the Futurists were dismissed as "superficial and of secondary interest" in that they failed to see color relationships as the significant aesthetic exploration of the new century. Picasso was remarked on simply as a vulgarizer of the lessons of Cézanne. And the Delaunays, those annoying Orphists, implicitly acknowledged now as the rivals bent on misleading the critics and the public, were disposed of as latter-day Impressionists. To mistake the Synchromists for the Orphists, Stanton and Russell wrote, was to confuse a tiger and zebra on the pretext that both are striped. The one style was profound and searching, the other shallow and ingratiating. More modestly, the Synchromist painters suggested that perhaps they were only precursors of a yet-unknown approach to picture-making "that would surpass contemporary painting in emotional power as the modern orchestra outdoes the harpsichord's old solo."

Sharp battle lines were drawn after the Bernheim-Jeune show, with many more sympathizers on the side of the Delaunays than on the side of the impolitic Synchromists, who seemed incapable of advancing their own cause without denigrating everyone else in sight. Critic Andre Salmon rejected the Americans' work as "a vulgar art, without nobility, unlikely to live, as it carries the principles of death in itself." A reviewer for *Les Arts et Les Artistes* was harsher—"the house painter at the corner can, when he wished, claim that he belongs to this school"—while even a sympathetic critic like Gustave Kahn thought the whole thing "un peu audacieuse."

The row reached a peak the following winter when Morgan Russell exhibited his huge, colorful "Synchromy in Orange: To Form" at the Salon des Indépendents. Charges of willful obscurity and plagiarizing from the Orphists were heard in the press. President Poincaré, a visitor to the Salon, was visibly displeased. But Stanton wasn't there to enjoy any of this. He had returned to America in November. Preoccupied with the plans for his Paris show, he hadn't been able to go home at the time of Archie's death in September. He left Paris not long after the Bernheim-Jeune exhibition closed to be with Willard and to see to his family affairs. He also wanted to arrange a separation from Ida, and he was clearly curious to see what the chances were for a Synchromist exhibition in New York. It must have seemed a plausible idea: if the Delaunays couldn't be surpassed and put to rest on his own territory, they might be in New York, where few people had heard of Orphism, Kupka, or the art battles of Montmartre.

With the disintegration of the Macdonald-Wright marriage, a union as foolish as Willard and Katharine's, the Wyman family funds tapered off. Stanton arrived in Manhattan financially strapped and with no immediate prospects of getting more money. Ida went to live with relatives, apparently ready to rejoin her husband whenever he called. But Stanton, taking up residence with Willard on a part-time basis, wanted to be on his own. What followed were five months of frenetic, misdirected activity and hand-to-mouth living, culminating in some major changes in the lives of both brothers.

Stanton was as surprised and angry as Willard when he heard about Archie's will and learned that only Annie was inheriting any money. He had even more cause than Willard to be saddened by his father's death; he had been closer to Archie, just as Willard had been closer to Annie. But, with perhaps more equanimity than Willard, who could see the handwriting on the wall at *The Smart Set* and was nervous about the future, Stanton came to terms with the fact that he was going to have to support himself. He talked about writing a musical comedy to earn some quick cash, futilely appealed to Morgan Russell's patron, Gertrude Whitney, for an artist's allowance, and finally ended by landing a job as a French-English translator. All the while the possibility of a New York exhibition was on his mind. For the rest of the time, it was meals at Willard's and nights out on the editor's credit, a diligent search for female companionship, attempts at studio work, and carousing with friends.

The two men Stanton spent the most time with that winter, and cordially introduced to Willard, were American friends he had known in Paris, the painter Thomas Hart Benton and the poet Thomas Craven. Benton especially was fond of Stanton, whom he thought of as the most well-rounded and gifted man he knew. He also became, after the painter Andrew Dasburg, Synchromism's most ardent if confused disciple. Twenty years before he achieved fame as the nation's great Regionalist, folksy portrayer of the American Scene, Benton was doing his best to follow the lead of Morgan Russell and Stanton Macdonald-Wright. He was always grateful to Stanton for taking him under his wing in Paris during his times of self-doubt and for believing in his talent. Stanton could be very giving in his relationships with men he liked and respected. He made his Missouri friend feel that he had chosen the correct path and would ultimately succeed.

Thomas Hart Benton also knew the other side of the Wrights. He remembered Stanton as "full of picturesque blasphemy" on

his return to New York, and he honored him as "the most devoted skirt-chaser among us and our most continuous philosopher on the perplexities of sex." Various letters describe some
aggressive womanizing in these weeks, and swapping of sexual
partners with Willard. Benton was in tight straits himself in 1913
and enjoyed as much of Willard's largesse as he could help himself to. They indulged in several contentedly boisterous evenings
in Willard's midtown apartment and, when Craven and the two
painters were present, Willard had to take some chaffing for
being the "establishment" figure of the group. In this Bohemian
context, though, that simply meant he had a desk job and a
weekly paycheck.

Stanton's only immediate means of repaying his brother's hospitality, which he might have stretched to the limit, was through
his art. It was at this time that Stanton painted, or at least began,
his portrait of Willard, a picture now owned by the National
Portrait Gallery in Washington. With his high forehead, thick
but receding reddish-brown hair, a full beard now as well as a
moustache, and protruding ears, seated at his desk surrounded
by books and papers, Willard looks the bona fide New York
intellectual. In Stanton's version of him, the *Smart Set* editor is a
prosperous and productive man, gazing right at the viewer with
an intense, serious expression. The hands are barely suggested,
while the face is painted in the manner imitative of Cézanne
which Stanton had been working on since 1908. Just what kind
of homage Stanton intended this portrait to be, and what role he
was casting his sibling in, is clear to anyone familiar with
Cézanne's work in the Louvre. "Portrait of the Artist's Brother,"
or "Portrait of S. S. Van Dine" as it later became known, is a copy
in almost all points of Cézanne's 1895 portrait of Gustave Geffroy. Stanton's choice is telling. Geffroy was one of the first journalists to write in support of the Provence master, predicting
that the artist, then outrageously neglected, would one day grace
the Louvre. Willard, it seems, was to be the Geffroy to Stanton's
Cézanne. He was being groomed for a lofty part.

The opening salvo in the campaign for the newest art cause in
America, and the ostensible beginning of Willard's career as an
art critic, was an essay that appeared in the December *Forum*. It
was entitled "Impressionism to Synchromism." Its author was
listed as Willard Huntington Wright. Given the tenor of most art

criticism of the day, in which great names were treated respectfully and euphemistic wording was the norm, "Impressionism to Synchromism" was an unusual polemic. Mitchell Kennerley's magazine was one of the few that would even have considered its publication. Many readers weren't sure what to make of it at all.

In an archly learned, almost patrician tone, the *Forum* essay briskly surveyed the history of modern painting beginning with the years when the supremacy of David and Ingres as artistic models was challenged by the new, freer objectives of Constable, Géricault, Delacroix, Daumier, and Courbet. The legacy of Impressionism as a breakthrough style was given its due, though the lack of a scientific basis in Monet and Pissarro, a failure to conduct a real study of chromatic laws, was cited as their crippling weakness. Brilliant "illustrators" like Degas and Lautrec, or hopelessly misguided color-experimenters like Seurat and Signac, or delicate academics like Bonnard and Vuillard ("fat with the argot of their craft"), were kindly or abruptly put in their place. The disparagement of Cubism, Futurism, and Orphism, initiated in the catalogue statements in Munich and Paris, was reiterated and emphasized even more strongly. According to the *Forum* essayist, these seemingly novel schools directed their energies toward goals that were essentially superfluous or old-hat. Picasso was "an amateur metaphysician on the loose," ensnared by Cubism's "craze for the static . . . the immovable and the geometric." Only Renoir, Matisse, and Cézanne, as innovators in their merging of form and color, were spared the writer's scorn, and the real value of those three giants was in pointing the way toward that phase of painting "which seems destined to have the most far-reaching effects," offering "signs of an inner and radical transformation in art." That next phase in this evolutionary view of art was Synchromism, "sired by S. Macdonald-Wright and Morgan Russell." An apotheosis awaited art lovers in the next few years, the article suggested, as the implications of pure color were examined. A brief but not overly technical summary of the Synchromist style followed.

Despite the name beneath the title, there is good reason to regard "Impressionism to Synchromism" as Stanton's creation as much as Willard's, or at the very least to assume that it expresses Stanton's investigations and ideas in Willard's prose. The author of this piece was well acquainted with the European paintings, art theories, schools, collectors, and galleries then in vogue, more so than a harried literary man could have been after a rushed month in Europe spent in five different cities. Leo Stein's collection, for example, is alluded to in discussing Cézanne's achievements in watercolor. But it was Stanton, not Willard, who had visited the Stein collection. The 1913 show of late Renoirs at Bernheim-Jeune is offered as further proof of that artist's advances over traditional Impressionism. Yet the exhibition closed several weeks before Willard arrived in Paris. And Stanton had sent Willard a packet of "art notes" in October. Willard was pleased to take credit for the essay, which Mencken among others found interesting and informative. He was a believer in his brother's work, and it showed him to be more aware of developments in the visual arts abroad than anyone else in New York. Stanton's purposes were well served, too. An appreciation by the editor of a major magazine, published in a respected national journal, was a splendid way to introduce Synchromism to an American audience. Nowhere in the essay, of course, is mention made of the fact that the critic extending the praise and the artist being praised are brothers.

The *Forum* essay and Willard's position must have had some influence in New York in January 1914, because the hoped-for chance to exhibit came through for Stanton not long after. The Carroll Gallery, a new art gallery off Fifth Avenue on East 44th Street, extended the invitation to Stanton to show his and Morgan Russell's paintings from March 2nd to the 16th. The short notice between the time of the offer and the date of the opening didn't allow for preparation of an illustrated catalogue, but Stanton and Willard threw themselves into the work of preparing catalogue essays, advertising the exhibition, and selecting and hanging paintings in a mood of sheer exhilaration. For Willard, it was also a chance to forget the atmosphere of the *Mail,* now that he was finally done with Thayer, and his otherwise dwindling prospects.

Trouble was brewing from the start, though, even before the exhibition opened, which ensured its failure. Andrew Dasburg and Arthur Lee, artist-friends of Russell, were in New York at that time and wrote indignant letters to him in Paris, announcing that Stanton was claiming all the credit for the development of Synchromism and was liable to hurt Russell's reputation. This led to a temporary but deeply felt rift between the two men. Stanton had to write back to Russell, in his most diplomatic style, to assure him that his paintings were being hung with care and in the best places and that he was always going to be given his fair share of attention. Then, in the wake of the *Forum* essay's jibes at everyone from Manet to Van Gogh, from Picasso to Duchamp, many New York artists with some experience of French art reacted with understandable hostility when they heard that the Synchromists were to have a show. According to Benton, the feeling that winter was: who did these two impudent unknown Americans think they were to establish a school in Paris in competition with their Parisian superiors? The Carroll Gallery exhibition opened to an undercurrent of ill-will, an inauspicious circumstance for such a tentative venture.

Rather disingenuously, considering his role in the strident propagandizing of "Impressionism to Synchromism," Stanton complained in later years to museum director Lloyd Goodrich and others that Willard had been to blame for the mess that resulted. He had undermined their chances for acceptance, Stanton said, by his abrasiveness toward other artists and art movements. Stanton also claimed, with perhaps more justice, that Willard's flair for the melodramatic led him to persuade Benton to dress as a French apache to skulk about the gallery, while he planted crazy stories with his friends in the press about dark Parisian plots against the American painters.

The reviews for the first New York showing of Synchromism were neither overly encouraging nor as severe as they might have been. The Armory Show had changed all that. Only the most obtuse reviewers on a big-city paper could automatically dismiss every new painting style as a joke. Art from abroad now had to be dealt with as a critical problem for those who disapproved, and many people were beginning to feel the stirrings of that uneasiness about missing the point and appearing behind the times.

J. E. Chamberlain, Willard's colleague on the *Mail,* offered a typical example of the new ambivalence. In his review, he welcomed the arrival of a struggling new talent in New York, printed the exaggerated biographical facts about Stanton which Willard fed to him, praised several pictures for their startling color and massive forms, and finally admitted that he had been "left floundering in the midst of a sense of utter strangeness." The *Times* report was equally gracious. *Town Topics,* however, despite Willard's affiliation, had fewer qualms and made fun of the "artistic Barnums and [their] gullible audience," these foreign "sacred pink elephants . . . and their cryptic theories." More to the point, and more depressingly for Stanton and Willard, was the lack of the commercial success they had anticipated and boasted of to their friends. This exhibition was supposed to have made them the money Archie had robbed them of. But sales from the two-week show were sparse, and most collectors, dealers, and painters shrugged the whole thing off as a joke.

Synchromism was one of the most short-lived "movements" of modern art. By the 1920s the creative work of Stanton Macdonald-Wright and Morgan Russell had taken a different turn, and it was not until the 1960s and '70s that the importance of their early paintings in the history of abstract art was studied in a serious way by critics and art historians. Only in 1990 was the first Morgan Russell retrospective held, providing a belated overview of his productive career. Still, despite these first setbacks, the Wrights were convinced that they were involved in something original and momentous, a cultural development that would simply have to be fought for.

BATTLING FOR
MODERN ART

"I only regret that the artists did not get more substantial results, but they must remember that they are fighting a long, hard fight and that their enemies have power. . . ."

—*Willard Wright to Alfred Stieglitz, a letter about the Forum Exhibition, 1916*

When the *Olympia* left port on March 28, 1914, Willard could think of only one consolation to calm him in his present plight. "I'm glad to be near Stanton," he wrote to Katharine. After struggling and maneuvering for years to get to New York, he felt it amazing that he should be abandoning that great city only fourteen months later. But there seemed no other way. For a writer without a steady independent income, the one American city he would consider living in was out of the question. In Europe, as Stanton told it, another way of life was possible for the man who was too busy educating himself to make a living.

Traveling second class was Willard's first unpleasant adjustment. His *Smart Set* excursion the previous spring, financed by a man worth millions, had been a luxurious experience. The people, food, and accommodations were of a different order this trip across the Atlantic, "but I suppose paupers shouldn't kick," Willard decided.

Upon arrival in Paris, Stanton and Willard moved in with Morgan Russell on the rue Vercingetorix in the Quartier de

Maine. When they finally found their own small apartment, one room with a "sleeping balcony" at 14 rue de Moulin de Buerre, they considered themselves lucky enough, given their combined savings, to get what they could. It was a far cry from childhood days at their father's hotels. There was neither gas nor electricity. They cooked with alcohol on a hot plate and took one meal a day at a cheap neighborhood restaurant. The skylight wasn't waterproof, and the concierge was less than honest. Yet, at least at first, Willard accepted the terms of his new life calmly and uncomplainingly. Freed from his old responsibilities, he had time to reflect, read, write, and look carefully at paintings in a way that he had never known before.

At a distance from New York, Willard also had the opportunity to reconsider his year at *The Smart Set*. Bitter at the memory of time wasted and compromises submitted to, he resolved never to get himself into a similar situation again, never to relinquish control. Suspicions of betrayal that had been simmering before he departed New York made their way to the surface. Mencken was now "that fat Dutchman from Baltimore" when Willard referred to him in a letter to Ben Huebsch. Of all his old Manhattan comrades, Huebsch was the only one whom Willard cared to remember fondly and the only one with whom he regularly kept in contact during his time away. However, when Mencken and George Jean Nathan made a trip to Paris two months later, in May, Willard was feeling more favorably disposed toward both of them. They treated him to an evening at the ballet, stood him drinks, and brought fresh gossip from home. They also inquired about the progress of his writing. *Europe After 8:15* was due out that summer; that was a bond in itself that couldn't be dismissed.

The writing Willard had in mind to do while in Europe covered a range of topics and genres. The biography of Richard Hovey, for which he had accepted a $500 advance from Mitchell Kennerley, was one possibility, though it appears that Willard had pretty much given up on that project—without ever intending to return the advance. He was more interested in mailing to Huebsch an anthology of Nietzsche's writings which he had promised to complete by the end of the summer, in starting a book-length study of modern art that would expand on the themes of "Impressionism to Synchromism," and in outlining a novel he had been pondering for some time.

With enviable energy and ambition, Willard wasted no time in getting to work. These vast plans, though—three large endeavors in the making at once—paradoxically illustrate something of Willard's shortcomings. No man was likely to see all this through to a successful completion, certainly not without paying a heavy price. It was too much. The grandiosity of Willard's plans hints at their origin in a fierce competitiveness, a drive that didn't preclude a genuine, deep interest in the subjects he was studying. But Willard was going to turn twenty-seven in 1914. The time still to be seen as a prodigy was fast drawing to a close. Unlike Stanton, Mencken, Dreiser, and so many other brilliant men he knew, Willard was in danger of turning thirty, of growing old, without making his mark. Now was the time to show others, like Stanton, and to prove to himself, what he was actually capable of.

During the five months they stayed in Paris, Stanton undertook to educate his brother, a willing student, to see and think about art as he and Morgan Russell did. Willard learned from them, went with them again and again to the Louvre, the Luxembourg, and all the galleries, and eventually followed his own bent down even more theoretical and philosophical paths. His reading in these months, predictably catholic and intense, included the criticism of Baudelaire, the journals of Delacroix, the writings of all the color-theorists Tudor-Hart had recommended to his classes, the texts of men like Hugo Münsterberg, William James, Vernon Lee, Julpe, Groos, Hildebrand, and everything he could find by the French aesthetician Hippolyte Taine.

Taine's articulation of the principles of art was particularly important to Willard as he gradually altered his own aesthetic philosophy. At the time of his *West Coast Magazine* essays five years before, Willard had been concerned with art as a source of sensation, as an emotional and sensual rather than an intellectual experience. When a woman wrote to the magazine asking if Wright could possibly be serious in ranking Keats, Swinburne, Rossetti, and Wilde above the more "cerebral" Milton and Tennyson, Willard had replied that the greatest artistic achievements were necessarily as removed from "mathematics and mental processes" as from ethics and social reform. "When I want to satisfy the 'lasting appetite of the intellect,' " he had written as an aesthete of twenty-two, "I am not simple-minded enough to go to art for it, for it is beyond the domain of art. I go to Euclid."

But many of the painting styles Willard was trying to understand in Europe, like Cubism, and the new musical compositions he was interested in, like Webern's and Schoenberg's, were obviously appealing to more than the senses alone. Intellectual appreciation mattered, at least as much as any automatic visual or aural pleasures. Even his brother and Morgan Russell were basing their art on highly "mental processes," allegedly scientific, in which certain colors were used because they seemed to move toward the viewer or to "warm" an area of composition, while others were employed for their receding or cooling qualities.

Taine had prophesied that someday a rationale for criticism and art appreciation would be devised, a system that would free both artists and art lovers from the randomness of personal taste, subjective likes and dislikes, and put art on the surer footing of science and philosophy. To Willard, these ideas, coupled with the invigorating reality of his brother's paintings, had the impact of revelation. He began to see himself as the individual who might write a definitive, clarifying aesthetic analysis at this watershed moment in the history of painting, music, and literature. Taine also wrote of the need for art to evolve in form and speak to its time, and these sentiments also had an influence on Willard. Rather than looking to the classical past for the answers, the useful critic would establish first principles and underlying truths that would apply to Rubens and Michelangelo as well as Cézanne and Stanton Macdonald-Wright.

Stanton's development as an artist also seems to have reached a crucial stage in these months. This was the year of his "Abstraction on Spectrum (Organization No. 5)" and his first version of "Conception Synchromy," two of his most famous abstract paintings. Both Willard and Stanton, led by Russell's example, were in a frame of mind to rethink their original reservations about abstraction, which (they had always assumed) ran the risk of being nothing more significant than pretty but shallow design. Some of Stanton's experiments have a tentative air about them, but if both Synchromists believed in the analogy equating painting with music, a comparison often repeated, then an attempt to divorce their paintings from traditional references like apples, vases, heads, and torsos seemed necessary, even vital.

By the summer of 1914 it was clear that the years of civilized calm conducive to painting, writing, and meditation, which Willard and Stanton had come to France in search of, were coming to an abrupt end. Most people in their circle had long since anticipated the war and made their plans accordingly, but they chose to remain in Paris until the hostilities had actually started and panic seized the city. By mid-August it was impossible to arrange an orderly leave-taking from the capital, so the Wrights were forced to depart with many of their belongings, most importantly books and paintings, left behind in their apartment. Forcing their way onto a packed train leaving for Boulogne, Willard and Stanton headed toward London for what they assumed would be the duration of the war.

"Don't worry over me. I'll come through O.K.," Willard wrote to Katharine, who was now deeply worried about the fate of her husband and brother-in-law. "The old world was an anachronism to me," he announced to his wife. "I and my beliefs were out of place." Fresh from reading more Nietzsche, he concluded, "I belong to the new era and was born to be one of the pagan leaders of it—some more of [my] prophecies!" In Willard's estimation, the only effect the war would have "will be to delay our work a little, and there is plenty of compensating romance to it all."

Any unpleasantness which their forced uprooting from Paris caused Willard was mitigated by what was for him an even larger development that summer. In June the prestigious publishing firm of John Lane brought out *Europe After 8:15*, and Willard was at last able to see his name on a book jacket. Sharing the honor with two of America's most famous men of letters only increased the pleasure, and Willard sent complimentary copies off in every direction. It was a handsome volume with an odd yellow cover. Mencken had flippantly suggested that Willard ask his brother to do the illustrations "in a futurist style," but Willard got Benton, an artist with a flair for drawing the figure, to do the job instead. Mencken wrote a Sinclair Lewis–style preface, mocking the blinders with which American tourists protected themselves when abroad. The irony of the book's publication date, though, wasn't lost on any of its authors. In the entire history of travel writing before and since, there has never been a less auspicious, almost comical piece of timing. Appearing only a few weeks after the calamitous events at Sarajevo, *Europe After 8:15* sold very few copies and went quickly out of print.

■ ■ ■

In London Willard and Stanton decided to proceed with their work while doing their best to ignore the cataclysm taking shape around them. That wasn't always easy. Detectives from Scotland Yard paid their Fitzroy Square apartment a brusque visit to snoop among their papers and take the names of their British references. A man without a steady job, voluble in discussing the book he was preparing about one of Germany's great philosophers, wasn't necessarily considered a safe alien. Both Wrights, for that matter, were apt to be too vocal in their feelings about flag-waving patriotism.

Willard had dinner with the scholarly writers Oscar Levy and A. R. Orage to talk about Nietzsche and the war soon after arriving in England but otherwise seems not to have made many friends in his seven-month stay. He found the Londoners he did meet snobbish in their attitudes toward Americans and unbearable in their sudden and blanket condemnation of all things German. That Wedekind, Schnitzler, Rilke, and Mann could no longer be sold in London's bookstores, or Wagner played at Covent Garden, or Schopenhauer or Goethe taught in the schools of this otherwise civilized capital seemed incredible to him. The anti-German feeling that was soon to find its way to America, after "the rape of Belgium" and the British propaganda blitz, was a cultural reality Willard was to have serious problems with in the future.

Willard's notes for his art book grew to a first draft while he was in England, and he made progress on his plot outline for the autobiographical novel he was calling *The Man of Promise*. The Nietzsche book was finished that autumn and scheduled by Huebsch for a January publication. But money became more of a worry, threatening to slow his progress and Stanton's, as the mails held up their mother's checks and rationing began. Willard was forced for a while to take a job playing the piano in a movie theater for seven dollars a week, while Stanton found work as a waiter. By winter they had pawned everything worth pawning and borrowed from anyone who would lend. When their landlord badgered them about the overdue rent, Willard was incredulous. "They take debt much more seriously in Europe than we do in America," he wrote to Katharine.

Willard's need for release from the tensions he had placed

upon himself and which grim circumstances were forcing on him had been fulfilled innocently enough in Paris. Stanton had taken him around to some of the brothels he knew from his student days. He also enjoyed an affair with an American woman visiting in France that spring. But in London, anxious and over-worked and always on the hunt for experiences he considered romantic and dangerous, Willard began to take his pleasures from another source. Letters Stanton had written to Morgan Russell from New York the year before imply that Stanton in 1913 was no stranger to drug-taking, at least to the use of marijuana and opium. It's possible that he introduced his brother to the ways of the drug culture. But Stanton claimed in later years, and it is a plausible claim, that Willard took to this indulgence with a frightening voraciousness, and he blamed Willard for involving both of them in the then-shady world of drugs to a degree that Stanton himself never intended.

Willard's was a personality prone to binges. He would labor for weeks on a regimen of writing several hours a day, examining the collections of the National Gallery and the other museums of the city with Stanton, and reading at night. Then he would feel the urge to let loose. An excess of pleasure followed an excess of work. Afterward, everyone had a different idea of what drug Willard became most involved with. Mencken wrote sadly a few years later of heroin "having Willard by the neck." Randolph Bartlett, a freelance writer Willard had known since his *Smart Set* days, had reason to know firsthand about his friend's extensive use of marijuana and hashish. Stanton implied that opium was the trouble. (The composition of his 1918 painting owned by the Whitney Museum, "Oriental Synchromy," is supposedly derived from a gathering of men in a circle taking opium.) Willard himself rarely alluded to this aspect of his life. Whatever the drug or drugs, and it might have been all or any that he tried, some of Willard's letters from 1915 suggest the beginnings of a serious problem. Wild flights of ego, flashes of anger, and moments of fantasy intermingled in his correspondence to Katharine, who had moved in with Annie Wright in Santa Monica. Even his handwriting began to change. Still, Willard managed to push ahead. Not an addict, yet, he was determined to finish the two books he had started.

■ ■ ■

In February of 1915 Willard and Stanton returned to the United States on board the *Lusitania,* as it made one of its last westward voyages. They left England in a bitter mood, displaced and infuriated by a war neither of them supported. "I had hoped never to see [America] again," Willard wrote shortly after landing, but it was too hard to get anything done in the hysterical climate of wartime Europe. Nor had the Wrights been living among people whose side they believed in. "The only intelligent people left today are the Germans," Willard decided, "and the lice against them are so numerous that [Germany] may be set back fifty years by this war."

With no surplus cash, Willard couldn't even afford to live in Manhattan. He parted with Stanton and found his own quarters in a rooming house in the Bronx that allowed him to do his own cooking on a hot plate. He loathed his neighbors and kept his distance. The anthology *What Nietzsche Taught* had been generously reviewed in January when it came out, but sales were limited and, after subtracting the sum Willard had borrowed from Ben Huebsch to leave New York the year before, there wasn't a dime left from the royalties. All he could try to do was to reestablish as many of his old contacts as possible among those he could face.

Willard looked up Kennerley and Stieglitz with special interest and took to stopping in at "291," Stieglitz's gallery, whenever he could afford an afternoon off from his writing. There were always unusual new oils, drawings, and watercolors to see there, in what was something of an oasis from the commercial and political fervor occupying the crowds outside on Fifth Avenue. On one of these visits he met Leo Stein, Gertrude's avidly conversational brother, with whom he enjoyed discussing aesthetics, Cubism, Matisse, and Cézanne.

When Mencken made his periodic trips north, Willard often asked him to join him at the Metropolitan Museum or any of the newer, more progressive galleries that had opened in the wake of the Armory Show. Mencken was agreeable, and these sessions sometimes became events of hard-core proselytizing.

> Wright used to try to convince me that a man could stand before a great painting and get the same tremendous emotional effect

that a great symphony would produce [Mencken remembered].
I tried it over and over again, often with Wright whooping it up
on the spot, but there was never any thrill.

Mencken could agree that "Cézanne was no dub" and that Stanton was a comer, but the magic of the form was never there for him. For Willard the magic of painting only grew with exposure, and in even the crankiest articles he wrote that year and the next, it was clear that he was someone who cared passionately, even fanatically, about pictures and sculptures.

The publication of *Modern Painting: Its Tendency and Meaning* in October was the crucial event for Willard in his first year back in America. Mencken publicized the book's author as "one of the heralds of the new era," while most of the men whose opinions mattered to Willard—James Gibbons Huneker, Antony Anderson, Kennerley, Stieglitz—were just as lavish in their praise. Even Katharine and Annie, preoccupied with raising Beverley and still amazed at Willard's readiness to abandon his family for his career, were delighted. It lent some meaning to their sacrifices as well as Willard's. He was immensely pleased with himself.

Modern Painting, imperfect and eccentric as it is, was Willard's most valuable achievement in art criticism. It might have meant even more to those artists who read it and were battling the Academicians on their own terms, people like Georgia O'Keeffe and Marsden Hartley, than to those critics and students who were sympathetic. Beneath, or beyond, its propagandizing for Stanton and Morgan Russell, the book was a call for a new aesthetic, a way of understanding art that would help clear the way for Stieglitz's circle as well as for the Synchromists.

Willard stated his themes bluntly in his foreword and reiterated them at some point in almost every chapter. Art, he wrote, had consistently been judged by the wrong criteria, with too much concern for literary content and moral values; modern art was not so much a revolutionary as a natural evolutionary process; a great work of art need not, and perhaps should not, contain any recognizable objects; and, finally, "the development of form by means of color" would be the rightful wave of the future. *Modern Painting* argued for a break from rhapsodic criticism and excessively subjective responses ("the chaos of our

94

moods" as a guide to judgment). "A rationale of valuation," a sharper understanding of what was being commended in a good picture, was needed, Willard observed, but this couldn't be effectively formulated if educated people continued to think of art as a purely sensual or emotional experience. "An intellectual rapture" over the elements of composition and color, regardless of subject matter, would take the viewer beyond "prejudice, personal taste, metaphysics, and the predilections of sentiment."

Now, a stringently analytical enjoyment obviously makes greater demands upon the artist's audience, and it was on this point that Willard could be most insistently didactic: "A true appreciation of art cannot grow up without a complete understanding of the aesthetic laws governing it." A knowledge of color theories, for instance, would put one's pleasure and understanding on firmer ground. True art lovers, then, were advised to study Rood, Chevreul, and Helmholtz. Unfortunately and predictably, even when he was correct, Willard's tone was annoying and alienating. Only the most earnest students of modern art were ready to be lectured on their technical and scientific ignorance.

To prove the inevitability of his concept of modernism, which implied a movement in the direction of color-abstraction, Willard charted a historical line reminiscent of the earlier essay "Impressionism to Synchromism." *Modern Painting* honored Delacroix, Turner, Bonington, Courbet, and Daumier as the most inspiring leaders of the assault on classicism and the important precursors of the modern. (The book's strong emphasis on "the dramatic qualities of color" should have made Delacroix and Turner much the greater figures, but this is only one of a few inconsistencies never fully clarified. Like Leo Stein, his newest acquaintance, Willard was capable of adjusting an aesthetic system to include those painters he liked, and after his time in Paris he was devoted to the works of Courbet and Daumier.) The survey that followed, a consideration of the new ideas and explorations in painting from Manet and the Impressionists through the Cubists and Futurists, was really an elaboration on the *Forum* essay of 1914. The most original and penetrating art of the last hundred years, Willard argued, was that which turned its back on fine drawing and storytelling, exploited the resources of color and light, and made its appeal solely to aesthetic emotions—to an interest in what the British critic Clive Bell was calling "significant form."

To later readers, the real peculiarity of *Modern Painting* continues to be found in its last chapters. Kandinsky, the Italian Futurists, Braque, Gris, Bonnard, and Vuillard are among the many painters condescendingly dismissed as "the lesser Moderns," artists whose representational concerns were not sufficiently in line with the course of "aesthetic purity" Willard was plotting for his readers. And, naturally, it is Stanton Macdonald-Wright and Morgan Russell who are lauded as the superior artists of the age and the culmination of a century's struggle and experimentation. "Synchromism embraces every aesthetic aspiration from Delacroix to Cézanne and the Cubists" was the author's conclusion. Furthermore, no innovations on this triumph were possible. The end point had been reached: the Synchromist movement was the apex of the art form. At no time did Willard acknowledge he was writing about his own brother. And however accurate he was proved to be about the importance of pure color and color relationships in the painting of the twentieth century, he could not accept that even color-abstraction might have its variations and uncharted directions. *Modern Painting* was a feisty, impassioned book in a period of impossibly dull criticism. It was also a remarkably lopsided treatise with an outlook that was both astute and narrow.

Certain writers were only too ready to poke holes in the ideas Willard's book articulated. Frank Jewett Mather in *The Nation* likened Willard to "a young Lochinvar come out of the West . . . to set crooked matters straight once and for all," who argued a thesis that was "brilliant and perverse." But, his review finally warned, the book "emanates from the caves where phantoms acquire a monstrous consistency. A ray of sunlight, a single impulse of humor, would shatter the entire dream fabric." Many newspaper reviewers found the theorizing top-heavy and pretentious and voiced their doubts that abstract art would ever come to play a large part in the culture of America or Europe. The London *Times* confirmed Willard's view of the British as patronizing to Americans by suggesting that the author had "all the credulous eagerness of his countrymen for the latest thing."

Leo Stein, wary of a purely abstract art, was more charitable—his *New Republic* review was simply entitled "An Inadequate

Theory"—but he saw merit in any writer, especially an American, willing to see Cézanne in his proper light. The critic Christian Brinton recommended the book to his Yale audience when he gave the Trowbridge Lectures in New Haven that winter, and Andre Tridon in the January *Forum* pronounced Willard "America's first aesthetician." Little by little over the months, Willard's file grew to include more favorable than skeptical or negative reviews.

Willard didn't become a rich man with the release of *Modern Painting*. That was a naive hope, as friends were prompt to tell him. But he did become, almost overnight, one of the new forces to be reckoned with in the New York art world. The essays and reviews he was publishing regularly in *Forum* became a source of fierce debate and annoyance.

In his *Forum* essays Willard let loose with the kind of fire he had shown in his days on the *Times*. But now his focus was more refined, his tone less sarcastic, and his goals more specific. He wanted Americans to understand just what was important about the new influence in painting and what artists and attitudes had to be discarded if they were to appreciate the best art of their century. Willard's essay on Cézanne, really an excerpt from *Modern Painting,* was his first and appeared in the July 1915 issue of Kennerley's magazine. With all its affectations of style, his account of "that astounding and grotesque colossos" of modern art was by far the most informative, well considered, and persuasive (as well as the longest) analysis of the painter whose influence animated both Cubism and Synchromism that had yet appeared in America.

It was a good time to be starting out as an art reviewer, and Willard loved making the rounds. He wrote about exhibitions over the next several months, in both *Forum* and *International Studio,* that enabled him to single out adventurous contemporary talents as diverse as Man Ray and John Marin, Elie Nadelman and Charles Demuth, Marsden Hartley and Abraham Walkowitz. As he reminded his readers about these new men and their European teachers in "Art, Promise and Failure" in the January *Forum:*

> The average spectator, believing modern painting to be chaotic, imagines it easy to do. The reverse, however, is true. No old

painting is more tightly drawn together than are some Picassos; no subject of the masters fits its frame better than a Matisse; and the relations of forms and lines in a Cézanne are as intricate as in a Rubens.

When he turned his attention to the American art scene and its established artists, critics, and institutions, Willard found more to criticize than to advocate. Painters like J. Alden Weir and Childe Hassam, belated Impressionists and popular men in the New York art world, were among those Willard had in mind when he wrote against men and women who were "clinging to a musty and unvital past, serenely unconscious of the great march of events." His review of the annual show at the National Academy of Design, an academic stronghold, was entitled "Morituri Salutamus," and even Winslow Homer was attacked in a full-length essay. Willard saw the revered Homer as a "healthy but slight talent," lively but too bound to illustration and realistic subject matter. "Since we are rapidly shedding our provincialism and developing a more universal art instinct," he wrote, "we can well afford to stifle our untutored eulogy of him." But, of course, he noted, "in a country of blind men, the one-eyed man is king."

There were plenty of "blind men" among his colleagues in the press, Willard felt, who helped to confuse the issues and retard the progress of deserving painters. "The Aesthetic Struggle in America" was a brutal sideswipe at fellow art critics, like Royal Cortissoz of the *Tribune* and author-painter Kenyon Cox, whom he labeled "aesthetically illiterate" and hopelessly reactionary. Even sometime-allies like Frank Jewett Mather of Princeton, or Charles Caffin in Stieglitz's circle, or James Huneker himself, didn't measure up to the standards Willard and Stanton expected. Mather was too academic in his approach to art and equivocal in his praise of the new men; Caffin, an Englishman, was too dry, too much the chronicler of biographical facts (Willard speculated that Stieglitz must have hypnotized the bloodless Caffin to win him over to the cause); and the well-meaning Huneker was too flighty and impressionistic. Huneker's essays took his audience ever further from the precise, systematic art criticism that Willard longed to see established. In this essay only Christian Brinton was spared Willard's scorn.

None of the *Forum* articles, rude or polemical as they were, provoked quite the reaction that Willard's "exposé" of the Metropolitan Museum did. This November 1915 essay in *Forum* was exactly the kind of examination that most excited Willard: a slow skewering of a sacred cow, a belligerent study that allowed room for large, startling pronouncements and step-by-step elaboration. It brought his name back into nationwide circulation for a while as *Reedy's Mirror* in St. Louis and various Eastern and California papers quoted from or reprinted the piece.

In "Paintings of the Metropolitan Museum" Willard looked at New York City's only museum in 1915 and found it disastrous in every respect. His essay challenged the crowded hanging and poor lighting of the museum's rooms, the smugness of the trustees, the stunted taste of the curators and director, and the institution's conservative buying practices. It would make more sense, he suggested, to purchase copies of first-rate pictures than to crowd the museum with so many second-rate or anachronistic works. Gallery by gallery, he named the collection's shortcomings and ripped away at its excesses. Remarkable for its thoroughness and justice, Willard's exposé elicited the comment from Reedy that "Mr. Wright goes through that venerable and venerated institution with something of the effect of the Huns and Vandals on their first invasion of Rome."

It was wonderful, Willard told Stanton, to be back in the saddle in New York. In effect, his brother had provided him with a new career, a chance to find himself again after the *Smart Set* debacle, which Willard was grateful for. It wasn't much of a career yet in terms of income. The royalties from *Modern Painting* saw him through a few months, but not much more, and those from *What Nietzsche Taught* and *The Man of Promise* proved even less helpful. *Forum* and *International Studio* paid a meager rate for reviews. Yet Willard was able to feel a hopefulness about his future that had left him in the days of his trouble with Thayer. By the following spring he was important enough to be asked to share a lecture bill at the Astor Hotel with William Merritt Chase, as famous a painter as any at the time, and Edward Robinson, the director of the Metropolitan Museum.

Stanton's situation was very different, though. Without sales of his paintings, he didn't know how much longer he could hold out. Desperate for money and serious attention, he was "tired of chasing art up back alleys." To John Weichsel, the head of the People's Art Guild, an organization that arranged commission-free exhibitions for young artists, Stanton vented his frustration. "America the damnable," he wrote, "is no place for a man to go to hell among masterworks of beauty. I could stand my own sorrows in a Florence, a Paris, or a Munich, but I see no purpose served, no sense, in starving to death . . . in the midst of a colossal ugliness." Painters and whores were both pariahs in America, Stanton fumed, "but the obvious preference [here is] for the whores. At least they travel in automobiles and have charge accounts!" He considered giving up on New York altogether.

It was in pondering his brother's plight—and Morgan Russell's in Europe, which was no better—that Willard first conceived the idea for the Forum Exhibition. This thirteen-day show in 1916, which ran from March 13th to the 25th at the Anderson Galleries (a Kennerley building on Madison Avenue), has since become an almost landmark event in American art history. It has been interpreted, accurately so, as an effective, small-scale response to the "foreignness" of the Armory Show. A native plea for American modernism, it was one of the several most important "educational" exhibitions of modern art held in New York prior to the opening of the Museum of Modern Art more than a decade later. Ironically, had Stanton managed to sell a few paintings to support himself that year, the Forum show might never have taken place.

Willard was aware that if he tried to organize a large exhibition on his own, which he was sure he could manage, the chances of its receiving a decent reception were slim. Too many people were still waiting to watch him fall on his face, and enough people remembered the Carroll Gallery fiasco. So, after soliciting the necessary funds from Kennerley and deciding to name the show after Kennerley's magazine, Willard recruited five colleagues as co-organizers. His choices were strategically brilliant. Alfred Stieglitz and John Weichsel were respected even by conservative artists and critics and were quite willing to be involved. Robert Henri, spiritual father to the Ash Can painters, had for many years cultivated a reputation for openness to new styles, no matter how tame his own art had become. Christian Brinton, the critic who had praised *Modern Painting,* and W. H. de B. Nelson, a painter and editor at *International Studio,* completed the list, which seemed to touch every point of the pro-modern art spectrum. In reality, only three of the six men met during the winter of 1915–1916 to discuss which artists and which works to include. Henri, Brinton, and Nelson were the agreeable figureheads, lending their names and prestige.

The 166 paintings and twenty-seven drawings that eventually comprised the Forum Exhibition hardly presented a unified view of modern American art. The artists—Ben Benn, Thomas Hart Benton, Oscar Bluemner, Andrew Dasburg, Arthur Dove, Marsden Hartley, John Marin, Alfred Maurer, Henry McFee, George Of, Man Ray, Charles Sheeler, Abraham Walkowitz, William and Marguerite Zorach, Morgan Russell, and Stanton Macdonald-Wright—were too varied a group for that. (And had painters like Rockwell Kent, Maurice Sterne, and Max Weber, who were on the judges' preliminary list of fifty, been included, the show would have been even more varied—almost pointlessly so.) It was, though, precisely that heterogeneity that made the exhibition a good opportunity for studying what one writer has called "the divided character of early American modernism" and its differences from European modernism.

Of course none of this was exactly to Willard's purpose, however supportive he was of the work of these diverse artists, and when the time came to hang the pictures he made sure that the Synchromists were given the best or most conspicuous spaces on the wall. This irked certain painters, like Man Ray, who thought it odd that he should be invited to exhibit only to find his works hung in the corner. Others like Benton and the Zorachs were so pleased to be included at all that nothing could spoil their good humor. It was a plum for a young artist to be a participant in a major show like the Forum Exhibition and to be associated with the august names of Stieglitz and Henri. A fair amount of backbiting and envy had been apparent among the lesser-known New York artists when word of the show first got out.

Almost as fascinating as the art works themselves, and even more infuriating to some critics, was the show's catalogue. In its earnestness and its aspirations, it was in the inimitable spirit of the *Forum* essays and *Modern Painting*. A short essay by each of its organizers was included (Willard allowed himself two), along with a bibliography of helpful books and articles about modern art and sixteen brief "artists's statements." A few of the artists' commentaries on their work sounded as if they might have come

101

from Willard's notebook jottings, like Stanton's "I strive to divest my art of all anecdote and illustration, and to purify it to the point where the emotions of the spectator will be wholly aesthetic, as when listening to good music." We know now that two of these sixteen statements actually were "edited" by Willard to follow a party line on abstraction—one with the painter's permission (Benton's) and one without (Russell's). But in trying to straddle the fence that divided his roles—entrepreneur and objective critic—his own contributions to the catalogue were what raised the eyebrows of even friendly visitors to the show.

In a separate note to "The Buying Public," Willard played on "America-first" sympathies, shaking his head over those patrons who necessarily preferred European art when so much native talent was being overlooked all around them. He went even further by attempting to vouch for the enduring quality of the pictures in the exhibition. The men who had selected these particular works, Willard stated, were individuals of exceptional judgment and could guarantee the aesthetic and long-term investment worth of any purchases. It was an unusual assurance for an exhibition catalogue to make, and the responses were predictable.

One of the most persistent of the catalogue's detractors wasn't a reactionary at all, though, but a man with modernist credentials almost as good as Willard's. Robert J. Coady was the director of the Washington Square Gallery and an intelligent, if little appreciated, promoter of modern art. As an exhibitor of both new European and American paintings, he wasn't happy about the chauvinistic nationalism of the Forum show or the nature of the catalogue's claims, particularly the committee's "guarantee" of the art. In a letter to *The New York Sun,* Coady challenged the organizers to issue a legal assurance of the appreciating market value of the paintings on view. The *Sun* (whose art critic, Henry McBride, was an ally) showed Willard the letter and allowed him to provide a rejoinder which was printed below Coady's letter. Both letters appeared on the day before the exhibition opened.

But what could Willard say? He had never expected anyone to question his claim in a way that demanded an answer and so his reply was necessarily a weak one. He reiterated the qualifications of the committee members to testify to the worth of the paintings, restated the meritorious principles behind the show, and ignored the question of any binding legal guarantees of the art. He also referred to the paintings now as "among the very best examples" of new American work, rather than "the very best," as he had in the catalogue. Coady got in the last word with another letter to the *Sun* of a more goading nature, but the matter ended there. Coady was far more embarrassing to Willard than the curmudgeon Royal Cortissoz in the *Tribune,* or Mather or Caffin or Kenyon Cox, in part because he was of the modernist camp and in part because he was, everyone agreed, in the right.

The Forum Exhibition was well attended and furnished much to talk about for those New Yorkers interested in the emerging avant-garde in America. It was one of the most exciting cultural occasions of that winter. But the sales were painfully disappointing, and Stanton was again plunged into despair. The prices of the drawings on view had ranged from $10 to $150, the paintings from $35 (some of Maurer's) to $1,050 (Bluemner's two oils), but none of the artists could be said to have made a killing. (Stanton's oils were priced in the $300 range.) Still, everyone seemed pleased that the effort had been made, and in many respects this was Willard's shining hour. Obstacles and all, things would never again feel so right. "It was a magnificent show. Beautifully hung . . ." Stieglitz wrote to a friend, praising not so much the individual pictures as "the spirit underlying the whole affair and the presentation of the work." It was Willard who had provided that sustaining spirit.

Seeing so many beautiful paintings on the walls of the Anderson Galleries—Dove's "Nature Symbolized" series, Sheeler's landscapes, McFee's still-lifes, Marguerite Zorach's spectacular "The Garden"—had awakened in Willard the hunger of ownership. He wanted to buy two Marins and one Dove for himself and held on to them after the show's closing in the hopes of raising the money. He apparently knew better than to ask Stieglitz for a reduced price based on their professional association— Stieglitz's answer to that sort of request was invariably cutting— and Willard eventually, reluctantly, returned the paintings to "291." Morgan Russell did give, or offer on a long-term loan that became permanent, two of his works to Willard. One of them, "Au Lait," is now lost, but Russell's "Cosmic Synchromy," which remained in Willard's possession until his death, is today in the collection of the Munson-Proctor-Williams Institute in Utica—a recognized classic of American abstract art.

After 1916 Willard's involvement with the advances and conflicts of American painting declined. Other projects and other problems engaged his time. By 1918 he was a pariah in the publishing circles of the East, a man consumed by serious physical and financial troubles. For a brief time, Willard did enjoy a career as a lecturer on modern art in California in 1919, but the zenith, and the beginning of the end, of his work as a major art critic could be dated with the year of the Forum Exhibition.

Willard's last word on the subject of painting was a short book, printed by Ben Huebsch in a very small edition in 1923, entitled *The Future of Painting*. This book suggests that Willard stopped writing about art for reasons beyond his subsequent breakdown and move from New York; oil on canvas was for him a form with a diminishing role to play in our future art experiences. Probing and resistant to nostalgia as always, Willard didn't see this possibility in the Twenties as a grim or unfortunate prospect. He accepted that art forms changed, declined, or evolved. In *The Future of Painting* he wrote simply and prophetically, stripping his prose of the bombast and stridency he was prone to. He suggested that the art of color, not necessarily bound to pigment on canvas or crayon on paper, using methods not yet conceived at the time, was one day going to supersede the art of painting. Then those viewers still interested in the art of painting, linked as it was in their minds to representation and drawing, would no longer need to rail at the misunderstood work of the color-abstractionists. The art of painting and the art of color would be separate.

Incredibly, in *The Future of Painting*, Willard Huntington Wright was looking ahead, beyond the tentative experiments of his brother and Morgan Russell, beyond even the days of Mark Rothko and Morris Louis, to the light sculptures of the 1960s, experimental color films, laser shows, and much more that was taken for granted fifty years later. But with this intriguing little book, soundly ignored in 1923, Willard ceased writing about modern art.

A MAN OF
LETTERS

"The hope of fame—what hours of speculation, what pulses of enthusiasm, what fevers of effort. . . ."
— *Theodore Dreiser,* THE GENIUS

Willard and Stanton disembarked from the *Lusitania* in March 1915, all but collapsing from exhaustion and nervous strain. They had gone to Europe in search of a climate that would enable them to paint and write in peace. In retrospect, they could see that the timing of their trip had been, to put it mildly, a little naive. They were returning from a continent blighted by war, despair, and nationalist hysteria. They had been badly used by circumstances, and their most important work was far from done.

Willard was in a strange state that spring. He was at the height of his Germanophilia, which put him at odds with most of his countrymen and easily set him off into fiercely argumentative moods in which he lashed out at Woodrow Wilson ("of all the smug moralists, the lousiest"), the British, and even the French. He was anxious about finding work, yet determined not to look down-and-out in front of his old New York acquaintances. Even more troubling, Willard seemed to be suffering the effects of a prolonged drug withdrawal. He described himself as weak and edgy, still "full of hallucinations and phobias," and would have checked himself into a hospital for a few days had someone come through with the money. "If I could get a free mind and a little rest," he told Katharine, "I'd be all right."

Living in a boardinghouse in the Bronx, the only rent he could afford, didn't put Willard in a better humor. It was possible to romanticize a Parisian garret or a London flat, but not one room on Kelly Street in the Bronx. The only advantage to these quarters for Willard was that no one he knew would see him until he looked healthier and less drawn. It was lonely, too. Stanton had gone on his own, on the assumption that bumming about the artists' studios of Manhattan would give him a better chance to find what he needed.

Back in California, Katharine and Annie waited to hear about Willard's plans. They had made a life for themselves as best they could, but Katharine still carried on in the hope that Willard would be returning soon, that their marriage might become a normal union now that Willard had given up on Europe. Following Archie Wright's death, Annie had grown much closer to her daughter-in-law, whom she had always liked and respected. Katharine leaned on Annie for emotional and sometimes financial support, but it often wasn't enough. And promises and evasions weren't enough anymore, either. "The physical austerities I can bear most of the time," Katharine wrote to Willard once she realized that he intended to stay in New York, but she complained bitterly of the isolation that "seem[ed] beyond bearing for another moment." How much longer was she expected to wait, she wanted to know, in letters that became increasingly bitter and mournful. Katharine's situation as a single parent, neither widowed nor divorced, was another awkward problem. Beverley was going to turn seven that fall and had only the vaguest, rapidly fading recollections of her father, who had left Los Angeles when she was only four.

Torn between shame at his failure to help Katharine and fury at her for making any demands on him at all, and angry at himself for giving in to what he saw as the weakness of guilt, Willard wouldn't make any more promises. He knew what he was doing to his wife, his daughter, and his mother. Once he had established himself in the literary world, he would be able to look to his other responsibilities, but not a minute sooner—and no one, he argued vehemently, should ask that of him. The odds of his being able to support himself as a writer, especially "a cultural critic," weren't encouraging. When the Nietzsche anthology went out of print that year, its author received an ominous royalty statement: after all the advances were tallied, he owed Ben Huebsch $8.50! But he had to have the summer to get on his feet and see what his prospects were, and nothing Katharine or Annie said could dissuade him.

The next time his family heard from Willard was in June. He was in Cleveland, of all unlikely places, where he had gone (so he said) to see some movie investors about a screenwriting job. When the deal fell through, Willard was stranded with a mounting hotel bill and no train fare. Abandoning all pride, he wrote to his mother and to Ben Huebsch begging for money to get back to New York. To Huebsch he was more honest: he was out there with a woman from New York, and things hadn't worked out. "I don't know how in hell I'm going to explain my presence in Cleveland to [my mother]," Willard admitted to his publisher. "She knows me well enough to suspect." Hence, the screenplay-movie deal charade, a tale which even Annie Wright found hard to believe. Under certain circumstances, Willard's deceptions were masterful, but at other times his lies were threadbare and almost silly.

By autumn Willard's situation had improved. His state of mind was more optimistic, even eager, and he was making a living of sorts. The essays for *Forum* and the art reviews for *International Studio*, the advances from John Lane on *Modern Painting* and the novel he had started in Europe, a few hackwork assignments—it didn't amount to much, and it allowed for only the smallest checks to Katharine ($10 or $15 at irregular intervals), but for the first time in a year and a half Willard was moderately self-sufficient. Desperate to leave the Bronx, he took a two-room apartment over a store at 787 Lexington Avenue in Manhattan. The building was in a dilapidated state, but at $35 a month, the rent was just affordable.

The hackwork Willard found for himself in those months was of the lowest order, the kind of degrading tasks he would never have touched a year or two earlier. Using the pseudonym "Albert Otis Pearsons" (the middle name a nod in the direction of his old *Times* employer, Harrison Gray Otis), Willard turned out made-to-order romance and adventure stories for pulp magazines and adapted a schlock play, *The Eternal Magdalene,* into a novella.

One reason, other than necessity, for Willard's willingness to humble himself with formula thrillers and hokey novels, as long as his name was not revealed, was connected to the publication of *What Nietzsche Taught. Europe After 8:15* was a literary curiosity, of no intellectual weight; the Nietzsche book was Willard's first serious book, his validation. No one was going to question his intellectual credentials now. The reviews had been good, with Mencken touting the book in *The Smart Set* and Huneker in *Seven Arts,* and even periodicals leery of the Nietzschean doctrines, like *The Nation,* had admitted that Willard's was one of the more useful and well presented of the recent publications on its controversial subject.

Dedicated to Mencken ("the critic who has given the greatest impetus to the study of Nietzsche in America") and handsomely printed by Huebsch's firm, *What Nietzsche Taught* came out while Willard was still in London. It had the earmarks of a timely project. If Nietzsche was a virtual unknown to the English-speaking world at the time of his mental collapse in 1889, that was no longer the case twenty-five years later. In the 1910s the German philosopher's ideas about tragedy, ethics, Christianity, and the "übermensch" were having a decided impact on the lives of American artists and intellectuals as varied as Jack London, Upton Sinclair, Max Eastman, Randolph Bourne, Walter Lippmann, Van Wyck Brooks, Emma Goldman, Clarence Darrow, Isadora Duncan, and Eugene O'Neill, not to mention Dreiser and Mencken. But Willard's book wasn't really meant for that audience. It was devised as a guide for the general reader, to inspire the uninitiated to read the new translations, or as a clarification to those students who had been misled by the wild notions that attached themselves to the name behind *Zarathustra.* After an introductory essay and a biographical sketch, Willard had included, with his own brief commentaries and summaries, excerpts from nine of Nietzsche's books, beginning with *Human, All-Too-Human* and culminating in *The Will to Power.* Far from sneering at popularizing texts in 1915, the literary world applauded such straightforward didactic efforts. The only one who seemed unhappy with Willard's choice of subject matter for his first major book was his mother. For Annie Wright, Nietzsche was nothing short of "a devil," in her words, who had tempted her impressionable son down the paths of atheism and egoism.

Fashionable as his anthology might have sounded when Willard began work on it in 1914, there was something brave and almost foolhardy in insisting a year later on a correct, broad-minded, un-nationalistic reading of Friedrich Nietzsche. The events of August 1914 had changed everything having to do with this writer. Tabloid dailies and staid literary journals suddenly made the same point: Nietzsche was to blame, in some measure, for the war. He was the prophet of the Iron Fist and Teutonic Superman, the enemy of all decent people. The very month Willard's book came out, *The North American Review* printed an incredible essay by William Archer entitled "Fighting a Philosopher." The "mad philosophy" behind *The Will to Power* was responsible for the militarism then convulsing the world, the eminent British critic warned. "In a very real sense," Archer wrote, "it is the philosophy of Nietzsche we are fighting." Plenty of American academics, led by Paul Elmer More, Irving Babbitt, and Stuart Sherman, prepared their own battery of essays and lectures to prove the same crude point. To all of this, Willard's opening essay in *What Nietzsche Taught* stood as a quiet counter, a reminder that Nietzsche's real interests weren't land for Germany or glory for the Kaiser, but "strength, confidence, exuberance, and affirmation . . . life intensified to its highest degree, life charged with a maximum of beauty, power, enthusiasm. . . ."

It is easy to believe, though, that Willard was thrilled by being part (almost by chance in this case) of a social and intellectual broil. How much duller it would have been if everyone had agreed to take Nietzsche spiritually and metaphorically and not out of context! Certainly the Nietzschean drama of these days provoked even more posturing from Willard. Thomas Hart Benton, who could be as irreverent as Willard, remembered his friend in this period as a dedicated übermensch, "taking haughty attitudes with doorkeepers, elevator men, hotel flunkies, and any of his acquaintances who would stand it." As Benton told it, "[Willard] patronized German delicatessen stores, going into them with the airs of a Junker aristocrat and combing his beard over the potato salads to the consternation of the Teutonic proprietors, who were afraid to say anything for fear that he might really be one of the great ones from the Fatherland on some secret mission."

When Willard wasn't busy imagining himself as one of the supermen his idol had written about, he could apply himself to the more mundane tasks of promoting the study of the books themselves. In 1916 he went to Connecticut to debate Paul Elmer More before a Hartford lecture society on the true meaning and implications of Nietzsche's teachings, and in a long interview that year in *The New York Tribune* he tried to separate the myths from the facts for a skeptical audience. In New York, at art gallery openings and literary receptions, the message was the same: "Nietzscheanism" was the tide of the future.

There were problems with Willard in the role of preacher and explicator. As a man known to be pro-German in his views on the war, he was naturally suspect as a critic-advocate of a German author. When Willard published "The Conscience of Germany," a book review-essay in the May 1916 *Forum*, which urged Americans to see Germany less as a British-concocted caricature and more as a diverse and culturally progressive modern state, many New Yorkers were convinced that Willard Huntington Wright was someone whose patriotism and intellectual allegiances were questionable, at best. These grumblings were later to catch up with him and cause considerable trouble.

In the fall of 1915 Annie Wright made a trip East. It had been eight years since she had seen Stanton, now twenty-five, and two years since she had seen Willard. None of the family letters survive to offer a picture of the reunion between these two young men and the woman who had always found it impossible to control or understand them and, in her heart, impossible to let go of them. It was surely an emotional if disorienting occasion. Yet by the time Annie had a chance to write to Katharine she was not in an uncritical mood. All the beautiful paintings and learned essays aside, most of what she had seen of her sons' lives in New York and heard of their great plans hadn't reassured her. If anything, the more time she spent with her amoral sons, the more dismayed and depressed she became.

"These 'careers' are taking too heavy a toll," Annie wrote Katharine, "and both Willard and Stanton love themselves so much better than anything in the world that there is no compassion." A short time later, after she had visited with Stanton's wife in New Jersey, she wrote again in the same vein. "[Ida] too is sacrificing her happiness, her rights, and her health for Stanton's career." A week before Christmas, Annie, Stanton, and Willard had a last dinner together at the apartment on Lexington Avenue, after which Mrs. Wright, nervous and frustrated, left for California.

Willard must have known that his mother's report to Katharine would be damaging to his cause because he felt compelled that month to send his wife an account of his progress even before Annie left New York. Willard's prediction was that, if "that hypocritical ass" Wilson didn't drag the United States into war in 1916 by way of his "moral asininities," then by the following Christmas Willard would throw in the towel or be clearly established as a major presence in the art and literary circles that counted in America. He felt that he had the drive and raw talent to assure that the result would be the latter. Doubtless this letter did nothing to calm Katharine. There was an undercurrent of a disturbing, manic energy, and Willard's digressions on the subject of the war bordered on the hysterical. "Germany has already won," he announced. "The senile old women are done for; but they are so stupid they don't even know it. If America goes into the war she, too, will be thrashed by the splendid strength of the Germans. At that, it might do her some good. . . ."

If one of the "done for" senile old women Willard also had in mind, consciously or not, was Annie, who declined to finance her sons' lives any longer while they were ignoring their marital obligations, Willard was quite wrong in dismissing her. Forced to handle her affairs without Archie, Annie was coming into her own, finding her own voice and strength. She knew that Katharine sent money to Willard on occasion, whenever she could spare a few dollars from her never-ample household funds, and Annie strongly advised her daughter-in-law not to do that anymore. She had indulged her boys long enough. It was with some guilt that she realized how painfully Katharine, Beverley, and Ida were paying for that now.

For a time it looked as if Willard's self-image might be justified. From the autumn of 1915 through most of 1916, and even into 1917, his pace was nothing short of extraordinary. Almost every month a lengthy essay of Willard's appeared in *Forum.* His novel came out in the spring of 1916, and an aesthetic treatise he and Stanton had worked on, entitled *The Creative Will,* was published later the same year. The preparation of the Forum Exhibition in the winter, entailing studio visits, work on the catalogue, and conferences with Stieglitz and John Weichsel, had meant some very full days, none of which prevented Willard from throwing himself wholeheartedly into the anticensorship campaign on behalf of Dreiser's new opus, *The Genius.* Along with Alfred Knopf, John Cowper Powys, Huebsch, and Mencken, Willard circulated petitions and drummed up support wherever he could for the man he believed to be the most significant, unjustly harassed writer of the day. In broadcasting his hatred of everything that Anthony Comstock, John Sumner, and the righteous Society for the Suppression of Vice stood for, Willard was always at his most impassioned and vitriolic. And at one point in the winter of 1915–1916 he was also taking extensive notes for a book entitled *Modern Sexual Psychology,* summarizing the recently exported and much discussed theories of Sigmund Freud, Havelock Ellis, and other Europeans concerned with sex and psychology.

One of the most satisfying things for Willard about being back in New York in good standing again was that it gave him the chance to associate with the men he felt were his natural company. It was a little like 1913 all over again. When Mencken came to town on business, now that he and Nathan were managing *The Smart Set,* he would often be by for a visit and a drink, or more accurately several drinks. There were opportunities to be back in touch with the poets and journalists he had met as a magazine editor, and—most gratifyingly—with Dreiser, who would invite him to gatherings at his house.

Not all of Willard's reunions with his pre-Europe acquaintances worked out as pleasantly as did his resumption of ties with Dreiser and Mencken. According to Stanton, Willard's last meeting with the poet Witter Bynner was far from agreeable. Willard had always held Bynner's verse in high regard and was happy enough to publish him in *The Smart Set* when he could. Bynner was a brilliant young man, a learned conversationalist whose company Willard enjoyed. But Stanton recalled being awakened one night, when he was staying over at Willard's, by a loud thump from the next room and the sound of a scuffle. "I saw Witter Bynner lying on the floor," he remembered, "with Willard standing over him cussing him in beautiful genealogical figures of speech. I naturally inquired what the ruckus was about and Willard said, 'The lousy son of a bitch cocksucker just propositioned me.' Then he threw him out."

Whatever the extent to which homosexuality is accepted in large cities or urbane circles today, it wasn't at all publicly acceptable, even in the literary or artistic world, in 1916, and Willard was no more liberal than his time or his self-consciously masculine friends. The practices of homosexuals were "obnoxious," Willard told Stanton, and that was his last word on the subject.

As his friends feared, Willard could go on only so long at the pace he was driving himself in 1916, and in the weeks after the Forum Exhibition he was stumbling again. New York proved as easy a place as London in which to find men willing to sell drugs, and men (and women) willing to join in taking them. For an addictive personality, good intentions and a relentless schedule weren't enough to keep the problem at bay. By May Willard was again in serious trouble, and his neurotic violence against Witter Bynner might have been connected to his physical instability as much as to his aversion to gay sex.

Willard Wright's hatred of weakness was legendary; it showed in his feeling for Nietzsche, in his anger at Katharine for the "weakness" of her love and dependency, in his disdain for the "weakness" of homosexuality, and in dozens of other ways. But, it seems, Willard realized at a certain point that spring that he needed help, and as usual he turned to Mencken for guidance.

The doctors Willard had consulted in New York were, for the most part, callous and unhelpful. Treatment for addiction of any kind was still an infant science, and many medical men of the day felt that the subject was out of their province. At best, Willard found, they had no advice to offer. Most, though, seemed to regard a dependency on drugs as a social and ethical matter, rather than a complicated physiological or psychological problem, and Willard was forced to endure a number of moralistic reprimands for his "weakness" and "degeneracy." He could conquer his problem if he'd only put his mind to it, he was told more than once. He also encountered a fair amount of professional ignorance: most doctors (he later wrote) overestimated the effects of opium while underestimating the catastrophic effects of heroin—the implication being that Willard had had personal experience of both drugs. Nor did most doctors have the expertise to make distinctions between marijuana and more serious drugs. It was all one to them, and for a time Willard feared that he was going to be left to grapple with the situation alone.

Mencken probably already knew about Willard's opium and cocaine abuse, as it was beginning to be talked about in New York more and more. In most matters, medical or otherwise, he felt comfortable in offering his home ground as a source of aid. He recommended that Willard come to Baltimore, and in the middle of May Willard entered Johns Hopkins for a brief stay. After his discouraging experiences in New York, he was in a mood of real desperation by the time he arrived in Maryland. What had begun as a romantic adventure in worldly decadence now had the makings of a living hell. Whatever the course of treatment, though, Willard was in much better health by July and, after a few weeks of rest at a beach resort in New Jersey, was ready to throw himself back into his high-powered life in the city.

Midsummer saw Willard full of good resolutions and cautious optimism. His novel had been released just before the Forum Exhibition and, though the critical response wasn't thunderous, he was still basking in the glow of the several fine reviews it received. He had too much to look forward to, he decided, to risk his health and sanity for what De Quincey called "the abyss of divine enjoyment . . . the secret of happiness." Enjoyment and happiness it was for Willard, a respite from the pressure to succeed, but the reality and the aftermath, stripped of any exotic aura, were too painful. Wandering the streets of Greenwich Village at night to find one's drug contact, waiting in dingy bars to make a purchase that could land him in jail, had nothing in common, as it turned out, with the opium-den melodrama of *The Picture of Dorian Gray.*

Almost as much as his drug addiction, Willard's problems with women—his tangled relationships and belligerent attitudes—made for some of the gravest complications of his life and frequently alienated him from more reasonable people. They also made his own search for personal happiness that much harder.

This antagonism toward women, worse since his return from Europe, extended beyond Willard's family circle, a context in which it was easy enough to dismiss Annie and Katharine as timid souls and conventional thinkers. Even women of spirit and intelligence could make him uneasy. Marguerite Zorach, an extraordinarily talented artist, had firsthand experience of Willard's bias. Sixteen of the seventeen painters in the Forum Exhibition, including her husband, William, were asked to contribute a short essay to the catalogue. The only artist not asked to write was Marguerite—not coincidentally, the only woman in the show. Willard's reactions to a first viewing of Georgia O'Keeffe's art, in her show of charcoal drawings at Stieglitz's gallery in 1916, was yet another example. "All these pictures have to say," he incredulously told Stieglitz, "is 'I want to have a baby.' " He couldn't imagine why his friend should be exhibiting this unknown woman's dark abstractions with their sexual undercurrents and quivering lines. (Stieglitz's answer was characteristic of him. All right, he told Willard, "that's fine, a woman has painted a picture telling you she wants to have a baby!") It took Willard several years to accept the value of O'Keeffe's art and come around to admitting that she might be an equal to Marin, Dove, and Hartley. Like Degas, a confirmed misogynist, he simply assumed that authentic creativity was a masculine trait. When an Edith Wharton or a Mary Cassatt came along, they were taken as the unnatural exception that proved the rule.

Nowhere is this side of Willard Wright outlined more clearly than in the one novel he wrote before his years as a detective writer. With *The Man of Promise*, out in the spring of 1916, Willard hoped to make the leap from the position of one who was largely known as a writer about the arts, whose job was to defend, attack, and explicate, to the rank of artist himself. In some measure autobiographical, in some measure a Nietzschean tract and a fantasy of the way in which the author wanted to perceive his life, *The Man of Promise* tells the story of a young man with grandiose ambitions, both literary and philosophical, confronted by many obstacles to his growth and worldly advancement. All of these obstacles have one thing in common. They are female. The maternal, the sensual, the marital—in whatever capacity, each woman in the life of Willard's protagonist, Stanford West, is ultimately there for the same purpose: to hold him back and tie him down. Even in a day and age in which fictional portrayals of women were often incomplete or one-sided, *The Man of Promise* is a profoundly misogynistic book, which must have had the impact of a slap in the face to Annie and Katharine—who heard nothing from Willard about the novel until it was published and he mailed them copies. Mencken, of course, looked on it simply as a dramatization of Nietzsche's plausible statement in *Human, All-Too-Human* that "women always intrigue in secret against the higher souls of their husbands. They seek to cheat the future for the sake of a painless and agreeable past."

The protagonist of Willard's "portrait of the artist as a young man," like the equivalent figure in the tales of Joyce, Mann, or Maugham, is a curious, sensitive, self-absorbed individualist with more than a few traits in common with his creator. From his childhood in a town modeled on Oneonta, his father's family's home in Upstate New York, through his early forties, Stanford West's age when the novel ends, he is engaged in a constant struggle to preserve his sense of himself as an artist, his right to cultivate extreme experiences, and his need for free time and free thought. In the end, Stanford West is defeated. Unlike Stephen Daedalus, Willard's character is forced to undergo one trial too many and finally settles into a well-ordered monogamous life that will mean the end of his best, most creative work. He assumes a safe position at the university in his rural hometown, just what his parents had wanted for him all along, and expects nothing more out of life.

"One by one, beginning with his mother," Willard wrote of Stanford West, "the women who had crossed his life had taken something vital out of it, and had replaced that vitality with a commodity which did not gratify him." After a restrictive, unhappy marriage, an obsessive affair with a femme fatale out of Gautier, a second affair with a New York actress, and an involvement with a more sophisticated but controlling mistress, West succumbs to the final snare, the trap from which he can't break loose—his daughter. His obligation to the child he never wanted his wife to bear leads him, in the last chapters of the story, to give in, end his wanderings and infidelities, put aside his antagonistic essays for more popular writing, and settle down.

In its style and plot, Willard's novel is a very unlikely book to have been produced by a man raised on the velvety writers of the fin-de-siècle. A dour, factual account in the spirit of Dreiser and Norris at their least exciting, *The Man of Promise* indicates how far Willard had traveled from his early allegiance to the Aestheticism of Oscar Wilde—a tie that would be revived later with the appearance of Philo Vance. This book was his bid for a place in company with the great American realists. But despite his critical appreciation of the new realism, Willard obviously had no flair for the creation of it, no ability (like Dreiser's at his best) to evoke the texture of urban life, doomed relationships, desperation and sadness. The best that can be said for *The Man of Promise* is that it deserves a minor place in the canon of American realist literature simply for its bluntness in dealing with its subject matter. Extramarital affairs, premarital sex, an unwed mother, abortion, and promiscuity—Willard's chronicle of the unmentionables is remarkable for 1915. If the novel failed to become a cause célèbre of the censorship debate, like *The Genius* or *Hagar Revelly*, it wasn't for want of trying on Willard's part. But the Society for the Suppression of Vice paid no attention. The book went into a second printing, and Mencken, Huneker, and Burton Rascoe of *The Chicago Tribune* gave it a reasonable press, but it didn't attract enough interest to merit banning. Nor did it make Willard enough money to get out from under his growing debts.

Helping him in that area was a new presence in his life, the only woman before the S. S. Van Dine years with whom Willard had a romantic relationship that lasted for more than a few months and with whom he seemed to have a true rapport.

Claire Burke, to judge from the little evidence that remains, was a lively, pampered, and beautiful woman. She had the sophistication that Katharine lacked, and she approved of Willard's iconoclasm, his interest in Nietzsche and advanced art, his scorn for patriotism, monogamy, and religion. She accepted that he was married and was content to live within the limits and terms of their situation. Best of all for Willard, Claire had less cause to complain when he spent the night with another woman, some new and passing acquaintance—theirs was a relationship founded on a degree of freedom, apparently on both sides. For

Claire was married herself and, undivorced, lived an amicable but largely separate life from her husband. Looked at from one angle, she had the best of both worlds: a lover who just might turn out to be someone famous and respected, and a husband (described by Mencken as "a boob") who provided a reasonable amount of money, went his own way, and asked few questions. She and Willard made a sufficiently interesting couple for Dreiser to plan a short story, unfortunately never written, based on their relationship. His single page of notes, headed simply "Willard and Claire," suggests—tantalizingly—that the material was there and that Claire's background was every bit as complicated and extravagant as Willard's.

Like Evelyn Naesmith, Stanford West's last mistress in *The Man of Promise,* Claire was well informed, knew several writers herself before she even met Willard, and "could uphold her end in any conversation." She was the first woman Willard thought enough of to integrate into the rest of his life, and she often joined him in entertaining Mencken and Dreiser. Flighty as she was sometimes, there seemed to be nothing about Claire to cause Willard any of his usual anxieties about feminine influence. In fact, for her father, Beverley Wright later observed, "Claire Burke was the only woman who wasn't the dreaded incubus." She was also ready, in a pinch, to come up with the cash to save her lover from his more demanding creditors.

The last extended period of time Willard spent with his brother, ever, was in the closing months of 1916. Early the next year, fed up with New York, Stanton was to return to California to make a new life for himself that involved reestablishing ties with his mother and finding a better environment in which to paint. Before parting, Stanton had the opportunity of seeing a book of Willard's published in which he had a special interest. *The Creative Will,* which Willard had been working on intermittently for more than a year, was published in the autumn, bringing to a total of five the books Willard had seen into print since leaving *The Smart Set.* As Stanton observed, it was beginning to seem as if there had been, after all, something fortunate in the John Adams Thayer trauma.

The Creative Will was not the definitive aesthetic treatise, the "explanation of art," Willard had been pondering since his reading of Taine in Paris, but it was the closest he was ever to come to it. Dedicated to Stanton, it should probably be considered a joint product, as the ideas expressed in the book had been discussed by both brothers in long sessions ever since the first Synchromism show. (By the 1950s, long after Willard's death, Stanton wanted to claim the book as his alone.) If reaction to the strengths and peculiarities of *Modern Painting* was divided the year before, there was a bit less cause for consternation now, as most reviewers gave *The Creative Will* little space and devoted most of that to plain summaries. The whole thing was just too eccentric to be bothered with, many people seemed to feel, and might be best taken as "an artist's book." And it appeared to Willard, in fact, that the only people who read it were the painters and writers in Stieglitz's circle or those clearly involved with the art world. From Mencken, Nathan, Dreiser, Huneker, and the usual group, there wasn't much by way of support and interest. Stanton, at any rate, thought it a good job, Georgia O'Keeffe recommended it to her own art students, and William Faulkner later referred to his reading of the book as one of the most crucial early influences on his career; he felt that it articulated aesthetic propositions, analytical attitudes, and a sense of what it might mean to be an artist that set him thinking in new ways.

Like several of Nietzsche's works, *The Creative Will* was written in an aphoristic style, constructing its chapters out of many short, provocative statements rather than lengthy, connected analyses. (That was probably Willard's most serious error with the book, making it appear disjointed and pontifical.) It touches on diverse aspects of art—meaning, by "art," literature and music as well as painting—and reiterates its themes in different ways. Among the notions Willard was at pains to disparage were the idea of art as a documentary medium, and the role of connoisseurship and personal "good taste" in judging a work of art. What he most wished to promote was the idea that there were certain eternal constants in art-making and art-appreciation, the realization of which would enable us to see art fairly and allow an art form to evolve freely and naturally. In painting, for instance, this "constant" was the artist's ability to use color to maximum effect and to create a sense of three-dimensionality, of convincing space and volumetric shapes. In literature, it was the great writer's ability to adapt his language to his subject matter, to show "a perfect mobility and plasticity."

It was, at one and the same time, an aesthetic with a strong link to physiology that Willard was establishing and a view of art that moved beyond his early beliefs in the pure sensuality of the experience. Our innate sense of balance, coordination, and movement was connected to our love of the symmetrical and dynamic in art; the rhythms of the body, Willard wrote, responded to the rhythms of the well-composed, robustly painted canvas. A static, academic painting, then, would fail to stir the viewer physically. But, *The Creative Will* maintained (in contradiction to the *West Coast Magazine* essays), "merely to feel art is to sink to the place of the primitive savage: to recognize art, by an intellectual process, attests to the highest degree of culture to which man has attained." The intellect of the viewer or critic had to be engaged to perceive the idea behind the artist's vision, the processes that led to the creation of a new style. That balance of intellectual and emotional elements in a work of art Willard labeled "poise," the universal attribute of all great art.

Fifty years before the advent of Conceptual Art, as most critics shrugged their shoulders over the fragmented Cubist still-lifes or Dada assemblages the more daring galleries were then showing, Willard was one of the few American writers to suggest that the idea behind the object had to be given equal consideration with the initial visual satisfaction (or lack of it) that the object offered. The man who had laughed at so much of what he saw at the Armory Show had become the loudest voice on behalf of the audience's duty to investigate the artist's theories and intentions. This applied to Imagist poems and stream-of-consciousness novels as well as to paintings and sculpture.

What annoyed so many readers of *The Creative Will,* though, was just that drive to extremes that marred *Modern Painting* and most of Willard's essays and reviews. Willard made the point several times in the book that great art should be seen as necessarily aristocratic and evolutionary. The implication was that it was not an experience for the great unwashed—and might even be judged by how far beyond the common taste it reached—and that modernist art was, by definition, superior to the art of previous centuries. T. S. Eliot's caution of a later time that we should not look upon art as something that improves or advances over the ages was a warning that Willard would have dismissed. It did have the potential to improve, he insisted, as it gained in complexity and intensity, just as modern life became more complex and intense, and moved toward the greater purity of abstraction.

All things considered, Willard decided after the publication of his "guide to modern aesthetics," he was off to a fair start in his pursuit of that elusive status, "man of letters." It had been "intellectually . . . a wonderful and full year," he told Katharine, and there was reason to hope that things were only going to get better. Katharine, having endured a separation of almost four years from her husband, naturally took that to mean that she and Beverley might expect to be called to New York at any time, to take their place at Willard's side.

What Willard neglected to mention in his end-of-the-year epistle was that he was deeply involved with the flamboyant Claire Burke—on the verge of falling in love—and was hoping to talk Katharine into giving him a divorce in the coming year.

CRITICS AND SPIES

"Ideas, books, seem too utterly trivial, and all the public opinion, democratic hope and what not, where is it today? Like a flower in the path of a plough."

　　　　　　　—*Walter Lippmann, on the eve of the war*

On April 2, 1917, Woodrow Wilson asked the United States Congress for a declaration of war against Germany. What had long seemed inevitable finally came about, altering American life in brutal and unexpected ways.

The immediate impact on Willard's life was quickly felt. In May, like thousands of other twenty-nine-year-olds, he learned that he was expected to register for the draft with the likelihood of being called up. Willard's reaction was one of uncontrollable panic. He first considered finding doctors to certify that his health wouldn't stand the strain of basic training, let alone combat. Though that was probably the case—between his usual nervous tension and his recent drug problems, not to mention his beliefs, Willard would never have made an adequate soldier—he could see that a medical deferment might be problematic. Even in New York, remarks about "slackers" were common, and most doctors looked askance at any young man who didn't seem eager to do his part in fighting the Hun.

When Willard calmed down long enough to consider his predicament sensibly, he realized that it was as a husband and father that he had a perfect excuse. A long, frantic letter to Katharine followed. By no stretch of the imagination, he told his wife (the wife he hadn't seen in four and a half years), were they to consider themselves as separated. When it came time for Katharine to write a letter of verification to the draft board, she must stress the fact that her husband lived in the East while she and her daughter lived in California for reasons of employment opportunities. Katharine should also point out, Willard pleaded, that he was practically the sole support of the family. Tell them how poor and desperate we are, he wrote. Of course, Willard noted, "no exaggeration is necessary in order to tell a moving story," and if worse came to worst he would declare them all in a state of bankruptcy.

Indeed, matters were getting serious in California. Annie was proving to be a less than skillful manager of what funds Archie had left, Katharine's health was weakening under the pressure of the office work she had been forced to undertake, and she and Beverley kept moving to smaller and dingier apartments. When Beverley needed her tonsils out that spring, there was some question as to whether the money for the operation could be found. In rare embarrassment over his failure to be a better provider, Willard took on a few lecturing jobs at the Art Students League that month and sent the fees directly to Katharine. For the moment, Katharine had the upper hand.

The situation with the draft board, as it turned out, was easily resolved. Willard registered, claimed exemption on physical grounds, and was never troubled to defend his claim. His relief was enormous, and he hoped to get back to work as soon as the screaming about recruitment, war bonds, and German atrocities died down again. It didn't take long to realize, though, that the atmosphere of mobilization, and all that went with it among an angry and defensive civilian population, wasn't going to pass from the scene very quickly. An ugly mood of suspicion and intolerance settled over the country.

Willard's first publication in the new year was a critical work of the kind his audience had come to expect from him. Appearing that spring under the title *Misinforming a Nation*, this small book brought out by Huebsch was a collection of essays Willard had published intermittently over the last twelve months in *Reedy's Mirror.* His subject, or target, was the Encyclopaedia Britannica, the eleventh edition of which was being advertised in dozens of periodicals and thousands of newspapers—a product of the new "hard sell" of America's newest innovation, the advertising industry.

The Encyclopaedia Britannica, a publication out of Edinburgh dating back to the 1760s, arrived on American shores in large numbers only in the 1890s, when the book-buying public in the United States began to expand dramatically and when a clever American bookseller named Edward Hooper (a true believer in the product) became involved in distribution. In the years just before the war an intensive sales campaign, of the kind Americans hadn't been subjected to before, was conducted on behalf of the eleventh edition of the Britannica, with "hard sell" ads appearing regularly in major magazines and newspapers. When the war cut sharply into sales, Hooper showed his ingenuity in 1915 by overseeing a photographic reprint of the volumes and arranging a marketing deal through Sears, Roebuck Co. Again, it was the hard sell with an ad campaign that played on the perennial American fears of intellectual inferiority and the assurance that a compilation of "world knowledge" from Great Britain had to be a culturally valuable, even indispensable product. Anxiety and snobbery played their part—what household with any claim to education could afford to be without a set?—and sales topped the 50,000 mark in one twelve-month period.

Many American writers, editors, and teachers took umbrage at the pretentious claims being made for the Britannica. Only Willard Huntington Wright took the time to plow through the books and prepare a detailed critique. The result, *Misinforming a Nation,* is an exhaustive, vituperative account of the errors and prejudices of the newly released edition. It earned Willard the praise of a few intelligent men and the scorn of a great many more.

The central charge of *Misinforming a Nation* is that the much-revered Britannica was nothing more than another chapter in "the intellectual colonization of America by England." The "assumed cultural superiority" of the British was a myth, Willard ardently maintained, and not until Americans stopped perceiving themselves as incapable of profound achievements would the nation come into its own as an artistic and intellectual power in

124

the world. Part of the problem, as Willard saw it, was America's linguistic deficiency; the inability of most Americans, even college educated ones, to speak fluently in any language but English created a tie—an unequal one—between the two countries. Another aspect of the problem concerned the aspirations of monied Americans to win British cultural approval, a syndrome Sinclair Lewis was to caricature in the Twenties. Finally, Willard blamed the universities and "the timid nobodies" who edited American magazines and "assiduously play[ed] the parrot to British opinion." The effect of all this was that Americans rushed to empty their pocketbooks on an encyclopaedia that exhibited "neither universality of outlook nor freedom from prejudice—the two primary requisites for any work which lays claim to educational merit."

Just what was wrong with the eleventh edition of the Britannica? Willard was ready to tell his readers in a specific fashion, with chapters devoted to literature, art, music, philosophy, science, religion, and every segment of life analyzed by the encyclopaedia.

As the Britannica described the world, almost any British artist or thinker occupied a more significant position than most foreigners in the same field. Thus, Walter Scott was given more space than Balzac, Hugo, or Turgenev combined, and George Meredith more than to Flaubert, Maupassant, and Zola combined. The uplifting qualities of British prose were often compared to the ethically questionable values of the French and the Germans, though the Britannica could be harsh on those native sons, like Oscar Wilde and George Moore, whose works contained some "decidedly repulsive elements." Talents recognized throughout the world, like Lady Gregory and John Millington Synge, were completely ignored, while the Irish Renaissance was treated as an aspect of British rather than Irish literature. All of this served to prove, Willard wrote, the Britannica's "tinpot evangelism" and xenophobic uselessness as a guide to "world culture."

In the pages dealing with the visual arts, the gaps were just as offensive. Mary Cassatt was never mentioned, nor any of the Ash Can painters, like Robert Henri or George Luks or George Bellows, whose reputations were secure in New York—but then, of course, they were Americans and less important than George

Frederick Watts or Holman Hunt. Worse still was the encyclopaedia's ignorance in 1915 of Van Gogh or Gauguin or Cézanne and its terse, indifferent summary of Renoir. The passages on the history of photography omitted any reference to Alfred Stieglitz (who was well known in Britain at the time) or Edward Steichen, and the pages devoted to science gave scant attention to any American pathologists, biologists, surgeons, or chemists and none at all to Luther Burbank or Orville and Wilbur Wright. The same lopsidedness existed in the areas of aesthetics and philosophy.

Though his own feelings about religious faith weren't exactly open-minded, Willard was offended too by the anti-Catholic slurs that could be found throughout the book and its wildly biased account of the Jesuit order. He noted that the editors of the Britannica seemed to think that the Anglican and Presbyterian churches represented some kind of summit of Western civilization. At the back of *Misinforming a Nation* Willard appended a four-page list of the two hundred world figures in various disciplines whose biographies don't appear in the encyclopaedia. That list alone proved Willard's argument and, as sales crossed the 100,000 mark in 1917, he could only ask if American snobbery was stronger than American self-respect.

Once again the reaction Willard hoped to receive for what he saw as a useful service was withheld from him. Newspapers that carried ads for the Britannica refused to carry ads for Willard's book, an editorial interference that substantially decreased the sales of *Misinforming a Nation.* Journals that he had expected to be behind him in his effort to expose a scholarly injustice failed to do their part. The eminent novelist Henry Fuller, writing in *The Dial,* found Willard's book "wearying and irritating," altogether too much of a tirade. Furthermore, Fuller was skeptical that the omission of names like Cézanne—or Henri Bergson, John Dewey, or Edith Wharton (naming three others who do not appear in the Britannica)—amounted to such a travesty anyway. Other reviewers agreed. This was, they felt, just another case of Willard Wright as "the boy who cried 'wolf,'" directing attention to himself and his made-up causes.

On the other hand, William Marion Reedy thought that Willard had performed "a valuable service to honest publishing" by leading a worthy attack on "a book-agenting sham." George

Sylvester Viereck and Burton Rascoe praised the book in their reviews, and Huneker wrote a note of buoyant congratulations ("How you do slam the shams!"). By far the most meaningful comments for Willard came from Louis Untermeyer. Writing in *Reedy's Mirror,* Untermeyer first acknowledged that "if Willard Huntington Wright writes four more books he will succeed in making more enemies than any one literary man of his day." (Music to Willard's ears, undoubtedly.) But he went on to observe that "a little more of [Willard Wright's] uncommon energy and enthusiasm would go far toward making a background for a culture that would be critical and creative."

Untermeyer had concisely and elegantly expressed the underlying intention of all Willard's efforts, and it was a relief to Willard to know that someone appreciated his aims. What Willard failed to grasp at the time was that more powerful forces were at work than those he and Untermeyer believed in. To attack an intellectual monument of an Allied nation in time of war, many Americans believed, especially to complain that Gustav Mahler or Max Reger had not been well served, was to play into the enemy's hands. It was almost treasonous, a few people suggested. Suspicions about Willard's patriotism grew.

In the spring and summer of 1917, Willard worked on an essay on Flaubert for *The North American Review,* an essay on Turgenev for *The Seven Arts,* an introduction to the Modern Library edition of *Beyond Good and Evil,* and an essay on drugs and drug treatment for *The Medical Review of Reviews.* The latter piece of work was Willard's only public statement alluding to his problem. Confined though it was to a small-circulation specialized publication for doctors, there is something almost noble (and uncharacteristically selfless) about this short essay; it was Willard's attempt to educate the medical profession based on his own torturous experiences. Entitled "Literary Superstition and Narcotics," the article avoids an explicit autobiographical angle, but it is clear nonetheless that the writer holds his convictions because of firsthand knowledge of addiction and the pathetic state of treatment in America. In brief, Willard urged modern doctors to see drug addiction as a medical problem, not a social or moral one. "Drug addiction is a disease," he wrote. "The fact that it is self-imposed does not alter its status."

More specifically, Willard warned that doctors often made improper distinctions between drugs (overestimating the effects of opium, underestimating the ravages of heroin), and he made a plea for the controlled, reduction method of withdrawal. Those who argued in favor of the sanitarium treatment of "cold turkey," he felt, were being harsh and dogmatic, equating punishment and needless pain with treatment. Let the medical profession look away from "moral superstition" and conduct itself scientifically and humanely.

It is unlikely that any of Willard's friends in New York or his family in California ever saw this article. But it meant enough to Willard to be kept in his files. Speaking out on such a delicate subject was paying a debt, perhaps, for an agony that he hoped was behind him.

In June Willard reluctantly took stock of his situation and had to admit that the game would soon be up if he couldn't find a full-time job. The royalties he had made from the travel book, the Nietzsche anthology, his novel, *Modern Painting, The Creative Will,* and *Misinforming a Nation*—combined—hadn't given him what would amount to a sizable full-year's salary. America obviously had no interest in supporting a cultural critic unconnected to the university or to the world of daily or monthly journalism. Nor could Willard hold out hope any longer in Stanton's commercial success and what that might mean for him. The show of "synchromies" which Alfred Stieglitz had put on at "291" in April that year made no more inroads for Stanton than had Willard's earlier attempts. Living off whatever Claire Burke would give him, borrowing occasionally from Mencken and Nathan, scrounging meals from friends, writing essays that barely paid for the week's groceries—none of it would do any longer. He began in earnest to search for a regular job.

Again, and for the last time, Willard's luck and sense of timing for jobs were with him. An opening became available that month on *The New York Evening Mail* and, with Mencken's help, Willard got the job. Still with the *Sun* in Baltimore and *The Smart Set* in New York, Mencken was soon to be writing for the *Mail* himself and knew its publisher and editorial staff well. It was a newspaper with a cloud around its name in 1917. Edward Rumely, the owner, was rumored to have taken money from the German government, and the refusal of the *Mail* to fall into line with the other New York papers in excoriating the Central Powers only fueled the rumors all the more. (In fact, a year later, solid evidence of the charge came to light, and Rumely was arrested in a scandal that rocked New York journalism.) But now that America was in the conflict, all that changed and the paper labored to be as pro-American and pro-British as they knew they had to be.

None of this mattered very much to Willard. If Rumely was a spy, it didn't mean anything to him. He had been hired as a literary editor and was happy enough to confine his attention to that page of the paper. The salary, he told a friend and fellow journalist, Stanton Leeds, "will, if I cut down on my smoking, about keep me in cigarettes." But in truth, the idea of a regular paycheck, even if it fell far short of the year of glory on *The Smart Set,* was satisfying, and it enabled him to send a few more dollars each week to California.

Willard's job on the *Mail* brought him back to the old days on *The Los Angeles Times.* His duties were remarkably similar to those he had performed for Harry Andrews. "New Books and Book News," as he called the page, was a literate mixture of book reviews, short essays, publishing announcements, and gossip. (It needs to be noted, in light of developments in a later age, that "gossip" for Willard and other literary columnists of 1917 meant what books or travels certain writers were occupied with—not the details of their family troubles, sexual foibles, or impending divorces.) This sort of work often showed Willard Wright at his best. A litterateur at heart, even more than a critic, he took enormous pleasure in helping to create a certain atmosphere among readers who wanted guidance or information, or who simply wanted to be more cosmopolitan. Ephemeral as this sort of prose tends to be, its purpose is of a higher order. As a literary editor, Willard was confident once again that he was making a difference—a difference that would ultimately see more people preferring Conrad to romance novels, more people protesting the censorship of Dreiser's novels and seeing the Britannica for what it was, more interest, tolerance, and sophistication.

In his first weeks at the *Mail,* Willard made the impression he wanted by enlisting reviews from as many "names" as he knew or could approach. On Saturdays in the summer and early fall of 1917, the readers of *The New York Evening Mail* could read book reviews by Mencken, Huneker, Louis Untermeyer, Ludwig

Lewisohn, Van Wyck Brooks, Sinclair Lewis, Ben Hecht, and Ernest Boyd about recent works or reissues by Conrad, Moore, London, Gorky, Galsworthy, Orrick Johns, Amy Lowell, and Conrad Aiken. It made the weekly literary page of the *Mail*, whatever anyone wanted to say about the paper, the most distinguished product of a daily newspaper in New York that season. The editor, John Cullen, let Willard know he was pleased, and Katharine dared to hope that her husband might be that much closer to realizing his goals which would, finally, unite them.

Horace Liveright of the firm Boni and Liveright had approached Willard earlier that year about contributing to the firm's new series of international short stories. Liveright was looking for an editor of an anthology of French stories, to complement the edition of American stories William Dean Howells had recently assembled for them and the British anthology Edward O'Brien had edited. Willard had been suggested as the best man for the job, and he accepted the assignment with alacrity. Several weeks of rummaging through the French books in his apartment, of reading his new purchases from Brentano's (where his book bills were approaching dangerous proportions), and of checking for better translations at the New York Public Library resulted in a list of stories he felt comfortable with. *The Great Modern French Stories* appeared in the fall of 1917, thus completing a three-year pattern. Since his return from Europe, Willard had published two books every year.

With a few notable exceptions, though—like Balzac's "Z. Marcas," Merimée's "The Venus of Ille," Zola's "The Attack on the Mill," and Maupassant's "Le Coup d'État"—Willard's collection, twenty stories in all, made a rather tepid anthology. If anything, the book confirms the common opinion that the nineteenth and early twentieth century wasn't a major period for the short story in France, as it was in America and England. Surprisingly, the reviews for *The Great Modern French Stories* were generally good. Most serious readers were in agreement that such a collection was long overdue—but, of course, the financial returns on it were meager. For the fourth or fifth time, Willard's publication timing was off the mark. Absorbed with news of the three-year-old war in Europe and nervous about the recent involvement of the United States in that bloodbath, Americans weren't in the mood to savor the literature of a defeated country and what seemed to be a dying culture.

The book's dedication was for Willard a particularly important one. It was to Huneker, "who has done more than any other critic in making known to America the best literature of modern Europe." In his declining years, oppressed by financial woes and perplexed by much of the new art that he had encountered in the 1910s, Huneker was touched by the dedication. For Willard, the dedication was a thank-you for all that he had gained from, or shared with, Huneker—the literary knowledge and the Pilsener binges—as well as a statement of his belief in his own place as Huneker's successor. But Huneker's assumption of the role of John the Baptist for Europe's creative talents belonged to another era entirely, the more open prewar years, and the mantle was not passed so easily. Willard was trying to assume a position that didn't exist any longer.

By this time Willard knew better than to expect to make any great sums of money on the kind of work that interested him. Ironically, in the light of what was about to happen, he was training himself to avoid bitterness and self-reproach and take comfort in a job well done and in the respect of those whose opinions mattered to him. For all his carping about philistinism and parochialism in America, Willard's work as an anthologist, essayist, editor, and aesthetic taskmaster could be said to imply an underlying hopefulness, a faith in education. America's cultural coming-of-age was inevitable, war or no war, and he saw himself as one of its guiding spirits.

Not that the immediate times inspired much optimism. Comparing New York when he first knew it in 1909 or reveled in its sophistication during his year at *The Smart Set* with the city as it appeared in 1917, Willard couldn't help feeling uneasy about any supposed intellectual progress. Everyone seemed mad with flag-waving, bond drives, spy-hunting, loyalty pledges, and hatred of the Hun. Each month it got worse. The question then became: was America actually moving backward?

Ever since the sinking of the *Lusitania,* the anti-German sentiment in the United States, which had been building since the German invasion of Belgium, had become a potent force. The British propaganda machine had done its job well, and by the spring of 1917 one risked a great deal in questioning the Allied cause or showing sympathy for the Central Powers. Men with a sense of history, even those like the President who were directing events, could see the darkness this was pointing toward. "Once lead this people into war," Wilson confided to a reporter the night before delivering his declaration of war, "and they'll forget there ever was such a thing as tolerance." It was an accurate prediction.

What surprised Willard, always the naif in political matters, was that the cultural world he cared about should have anything to do with the growing frenzy. No one was more outraged than he by the accumulating examples of America's loss of balance and civilized judgment. One horror followed another from circles that should have known better. "The Wagner cult" and "the Kaiser cult" were insidiously linked, warned one reputable New York magazine, implying that all loyal citizens would want to boycott concert halls still promoting "the Prussian spirit." The Metropolitan Opera House accordingly canceled all productions of Wagner and even Beethoven. In Boston, Karl Muck, the director of the city's Symphony Orchestra, required a police escort to get to work. Mahler and Schoenberg became unmentionables. German poetry and plays disappeared from the shelves of bookstores. Articles appeared in the art magazines discussing the need to purge American art schools of "the influence of the German technique," while several critics urged that the Metropolitan Museum of Art remove its German paintings to the basement. Even the venerable Hugo Münsterberg of Harvard suddenly became a target of harassment. By the end of 1917 few voices were raised in opposition to a stranglehold on the arts and the universities that was both official and widely popular.

Writers felt especially vulnerable to the consequences of this wave of Germanophobia once America entered the war, and not many literary men saw any point in speaking out after Wilson's war message. Huneker was vehement in denying his German roots, stressing to Mencken the Irishness of his middle name. Even the sage of Baltimore himself, whose mail was being intercepted and monitored, knew enough to lay low that first summer and autumn after mobilization. Conformity and dissent weren't laughing matters anymore. The word at the *Mail* was: "Be careful." It was against this background of panic and silence that the most significant drama of Willard's life, farcical as much as tragic, was enacted.

An obstinate man by nature and a lover of Mahler, Strauss, Goethe, and Mann, Willard Huntington Wright certainly wasn't inclined to accept an atmosphere he abhorred or find in himself the tact it called for. What was worse, or more dangerous, was that Willard refused to take the anti-German hysteria seriously when it applied to his own opinions and actions. Let others like Huneker and Mencken be solemn about it, he decided. He wasn't to be forced into lockstep. Willard's earlier fondness for Oscar Wilde's assertion about the foolishness of taking serious things seriously comes to mind. Like his mentor in adolescence, Willard had the ability to create his own more interesting world with himself at its center, unmindful of the revenge "the real world" often exacts. Well into the fall of 1917, indifferent to those who were listening closely, Willard continued to speak loudly and disdainfully about the President, the Allies, and the informant-mentality that was pervasive even in New York. Again like Wilde, Willard was to pay a large price for overlooking certain hard, crass social realities.

One individual who was paying particular attention to Willard's politics was Genevieve Matthews, the freelance stenographer he sometimes employed when he found himself behind in his work for the paper. An efficient secretary, Miss Matthews was also a vigilant patriot. In fact, "she was 'a little off' on the subject of the war," Willard later wrote to Katharine, "and constituted herself an amateur spy-hunter." At first, his secretary's humorless ideas about German evil and British saintliness tickled Willard. When she would come for an afternoon session of dictation in his apartment, he would be apt to take a break at the piano, selecting a German Lied and singing softly in the all-but-forbidden language of the Kaiser.

Genevieve Matthews was easily goaded, apparently, and none too subtle. When Willard was out of the room or left the building on an errand, she would use her break from typing Willard's copy to rifle his desk and files for the incriminating evidence of espionage she was sure she would find. Visions of heroism and delight at seeing the *Mail*'s most notorious writer in jail got the better of her. Earnest and unimaginative, Genevieve Matthews was a woman of her time, caught up in the fervor of the Allied cause.

When he became alert to his secretary's eagerness to prove his treachery, Willard decided not to dismiss her but to play along. It was just the kind of situation that appealed to him. He took to leaving odd papers on his desk to see if they had been moved in his absence. They often were. One day in early October Willard pushed the game further and dictated to Matthews a bizarre, cryptic letter hinting at clandestine meetings with unnamed persons, involving himself and two others who wrote for the paper, Stanton Leeds and Andre Tridon. The implications were that the three were in touch with German agents in the United States. At this point Willard's "amateur spy-hunter" needed nothing more definitive and, once her employer's back was turned, darted from the apartment out into the street with the letter in hand.

What followed should have been the stuff of mildly humorous recollection in later years—the material for a silly anecdote Willard might have told as an old man. Matthews took refuge in a drugstore phone booth on the corner of Lexington Avenue and 63rd Street, clutching the document while she tried to reach the Secret Service. Willard, exasperated, cornered her in the phone booth. A small crowd gathered to see what the commotion was all about, and at the cries of "German spy" someone got the police. Willard was escorted back to his rooms by two Secret Service men. By the time he was able to explain the truth of the matter, enough of a row had taken place to alert the city newsrooms. A headline in the next morning's *Times* read WRITER AND SECRETARY IN GERMAN SPY MIX-UP. The *Sun* was less benign: EDITOR IS ACCUSED BY WOMAN AS A SPY.

Rumely and Cullen were horrified. It was the last kind of publicity the *Mail* wanted. That week Willard was curtly informed that his services were no longer needed at the paper. Protestations of innocence got him nowhere, and he was told to leave the building. Living as he did from paycheck to paycheck, without any savings to fall back on, Willard very quickly found himself in desperate straits. He referred throughout October to the Matthews episode as "that comedy," but each day brought him new evidence that his joke had been a grotesque miscalculation. Professional and social acquaintances shunned him, interviews with editors at other papers were impossible to get, and even many of his old friends kept a safe distance. For that matter, not everyone in New York was convinced, in the light of Willard's writings about Germany and Nietzsche, that he wasn't in the pay of the Wilhelmstrasse.

Mencken was incredulous and reacted with a hostility against Willard that nothing could appease. The whole business was "a masterpiece of imbecility," he wrote furiously to Ernest Boyd. After this "intolerably idiotic" act, he declined to see or write his old colleague. What especially infuriated him was that Willard had involved others in the prank. Leeds and Tridon were named as the fellow "conspirators" in a few of the newspaper articles describing the infamous letter, and both were harassed by angry co-workers and neighbors for several weeks after. (It naturally crossed Mencken's mind that his could just have easily been one of the names Willard threw in for effect.) Men had been put in jail for less, now that the United States was at war. "To put such burdens upon innocent friends in such crazy days as these is an unforgivable offense," Mencken told Boyd. Henceforth he never wanted to hear from Willard, whom he dismissed as "a public menace." Nathan and Dreiser were of the same opinion. The man was selfish, probably mad, certainly not to be trusted.

Quite possibly Mencken was also tired of being hit up for money. When Willard sheepishly sent a letter to Baltimore a few weeks later, bringing up the subject of a small loan, there was no reply. By November Willard understood that his position in the East was hopeless. He was being blackballed by publishers and editors everywhere he turned. Old friends avoided him on the street. In great embarrassment, he had to let Katharine and Annie know that he couldn't send any more money and might have to return to California if a job prospect didn't present itself soon. The possibility of admitting defeat and abandoning New York after so much struggle was torturous to contemplate.

In a pathetic effort to undo the damage, Willard spent most of the early fall preparing a short companion book to *Misinforming a Nation*. He could see now, at last, that he had violated to his own detriment the sacred pro-British spirit in the country, and so he set about trying to prove his essential patriotism. *Informing a Nation*, a quickly thrown-together study taken from some of his

Mail articles praising the American *New International Encyclopedia,* aimed to show that Willard Huntington Wright was on the proper side, that the perennial complainer could find something encouraging to say about an Allied nation. Dodd, Mead agreed to publish the slim volume in a cheap paperback edition and have it out by New Year's, but it hardly mattered. No one bought the book, and few reviewers paid any attention. Waving the flag over an American encyclopedia wasn't going to help his situation. By the time *Informing a Nation* appeared in an absurdly small edition, Willard's was a name to ignore.

As the year drew to a close, Willard's spirit broke. He couldn't pay the rent. He slept fitfully and became nervous and withdrawn. The rush to edit *Informing a Nation* had worn him out, and Willard sensed the futility of the project. It was energy wasted on an insignificant book. He stopped eating, slumped into a prolonged depression and then a kind of breakdown. All the good that had been accomplished at Johns Hopkins the year before was rapidly undone, as throughout November Willard spent what money he could get from Claire Burke and others on huge amounts of marijuana and cocaine. By mid-December his body was racked by fever and tremors.

With funds for the train trip borrowed from Huebsch and Kennerley, whose generosity never wavered, Willard gave up and left New York before Christmas. He was broke, emaciated, and painfully confused about his future. Katharine and Annie awaited his arrival in Los Angeles, not knowing what to expect.

SETBACKS

"Every compulsion is put upon writers to be safe, polite, obedient, and sterile."

— *Sinclair Lewis (1926), on declining his Pulitzer Prize*

Well into her sixties, Beverley Wright could recall, painfully and vividly, the day in December 1917 she came home from school to find that her father had returned. Her mother and grandmother huddled in nervous conference in the kitchen of their bungalow, while a strange, excitable man tossed and turned in her mother's bed, talking to himself and shouting orders that didn't always make sense. Throughout the next few days, the door to that room was kept closed and Beverley caught only the briefest glimpses of her father.

En route from New York, Willard had stopped off in Chicago to see Burton Rascoe and catch his breath before the second leg of his journey. Rascoe had been shocked by Willard's stooped shoulders and haggard face. His new look—Willard had sacrificed the Kaiser moustache and was trimming his beard to a point, effecting a more French than German appearance—didn't do anything to disguise his condition. By the time he reached California after an exhausting week-long train ride, Willard could barely walk or speak coherently. The symptoms of drug withdrawal he had shown three years before on returning from

London—in particular, tremors and phobias—had returned, and the plain truth was evident to Annie and Katharine the minute they saw Willard.

The figure who confronted Beverley, a shy fourth-grader, was an otherworldly being, awesome and unpredictable. "This man I had never known in the flesh," she later wrote, "had been present with me every moment of my life, like the atmosphere I breathed." But now that she was face to face with him, she had no idea how to act, how to win his favor. To nine-year-old Beverley, in these few days after Christmas, there was something of "the monster" about this long-dreamed-of father. She later wrote of this winter as one of the most unpleasant periods of her life.

Through the many weeks of his recovery, Willard proved to be a tyrant in the Wright household. The rooms were filled with a smoky haze as he went through pack after pack of cigarettes. Every whim and every craving for food had to be satisfied, and all the normal rituals of life were changed to ensure his comfort. But aside from forbidding Beverley the use of the phonograph for fear that the noise would disturb her father, there wasn't all that much to the household to disrupt. If Willard was in any way shocked by the conditions he found his wife and daughter living in, he was too ashamed to comment on them, though he must have been amazed. Not even Katharine's most descriptive or self-pitying letters would have prepared Willard for the unrelenting bleakness of their life.

The Wrights' building fronted onto an alley more than an actual "street." The yard was weedy, unlandscaped, and overgrown. Inside, the furniture that was any good, a few heavy mahogany pieces and a glass lamp, had been borrowed from Annie. The kitchen counters had been made by Annie and Katharine out of packing crates and covered with newspaper and then linoleum. The two bedrooms were rugless, and the makeshift dressers were also just large packing crates turned on their sides. The five small rooms on Little Street had a dingy and depressed feel to them. For several days Willard didn't leave the bedroom, unable or unwilling to contemplate his future there. Yet his mental recovery was swifter than his physical rejuvenation, and quick enough to suggest that he had looked worse than he actually was.

One of Willard's first projects in the New Year, once he was able to get up and walk about, was a remarkably clearheaded letter to Alfred Stieglitz about the closing of the "291" gallery, a circumstance of wartime economics and a dwindling interest in new art. Though his own physical and mental condition was, as he described it, "abominable and unsettled," he felt as bad at that moment for Stieglitz. In a tone of almost desperate optimism, he wrote to his friend with the sympathy he reserved for men involved in artistic struggles.

> My sincere hope is that 291 is only a temporary and not a permanent loss. The more I think of the work you have done, the more tremendous it appears. Coming out to this country, where they know nothing of art, I can get a perspective on what you have done. I noticed, when last I saw you, what seemed to be a feeling of discouragement on your part at the way the world was treating you. Perhaps I was mistaken, but in any event you should harbor no such feeling. You have done the thing that had to be done and done it with no little magnificence. It has borne abundant fruit, even among those who criticize you. . . . And things will be different after the war. Intelligence is gradually coming into the world. In the new era the things we stand for will come in on the rising tide. I thoroughly believe this, and am waiting for the day.

On the verge of a deep depression, Stieglitz appreciated Willard's commiseration but was unable to rouse himself back to his own work for more than three years. (By that time he was married to Georgia O'Keeffe, busy photographing again, and ready to try his luck with a new gallery.)

For Willard, unfortunately, there wasn't anyone to offer the similar words of encouragement and gratitude he needed. On both coasts he was a man most people wanted to forget. Willard Wright was "a swine," Mencken told Ernest Boyd, and when Mencken wrote to George Sterling some time later, after Sterling had asked if a reconciliation between the two old friends might be arranged, Mencken voiced a common opinion in their circle. "I could no more have relations with him than I could with a Presbyterian," he wrote. Dreiser's comments were scarcely less generous, and many Los Angeles acquaintances kept their distance.

Worse still, that hope expressed to Stieglitz—in "the rising tide" of intelligence and culture—was to be sorely tested by postwar realities. The ignorant attitudes that had precipitated the Genevieve Matthews situation were not magically going to end with the Armistice, as Willard discovered in the early Twenties. If he fantasized about a quick resurrection and a fresh start for himself in New York, he was much mistaken.

In April Willard was able to rouse himself from the house to head downtown and look for work. At the *Times* he was anything but the returning hero now, the envied *Smart Set* celebrity, and many of the old faces at the office were gone, anyway. It was obvious that the management did not really want him around and had no intention of putting him in a conspicuous position. But, as several of the regular copy editors were on vacation, Willard was given some of their work to do. This was charity, and worse than that, it was menial labor for a former columnist and editor of a national magazine, and everyone at the *Times* knew it. However, Willard accepted the first of what would be many humiliations in a stoical fashion. As long as the war was on, he was persona non grata, and nothing could alter that.

As Willard feared it would, the strain of commuting on the crowded trolley every morning and clocking eight or ten hours of work a day undermined his health very quickly. Only a month after taking up his duties with the paper, he was a patient at the Sierra Madre sanitarium, whose sizable $250-a-month fee Annie was left to come up with. Visiting her son under these circumstances, in this setting, she found herself prey to some conflicting emotions. She brought Willard roses from her garden and homemade pudding and felt all the normal warmth and pity a mother would feel at seeing her son unable to fend for himself. But Annie also felt a growing wariness, a self-protective suspicion that she was being dragged into her boy's life in ways that would hurt her. The implicit warning Archie's will had signaled— beware of our sons and their needs—sounded clearly. So when Willard discussed his great plan with her that May at the Sierra Madre that he and Katharine and Annie move in together, with his mother taking care of the house and Beverley, while Katharine and he went to work—Annie reacted quickly and declined the "offer." She thought it best, she told Willard, that he and his wife manage on their own, while she tended to herself, giving whatever help along the way she could. Willard was stung. It was only the second time his mother had refused him something outright and in this instance, given his breakdown, it seemed to him more hurtful by far than her earlier refusal to underwrite his life in New York and Paris.

Willard's return from the sanitarium marked the beginning of the end of any semblance of normal family life at home. It couldn't work, not after all that happened since Willard's departure in 1912, not after all the accumulated bitterness that Katharine had been living with. Willard tried to establish a relationship with Beverley, but their outings had all the awkwardness of any forced relationship between strangers, one an adult with no great fondness for children and the other an uncertain, self-conscious nine-year-old. At moments, Beverley was charmed by Willard's unusual manner. When he decided to teach his daughter to play poker or bought her more boxes of chocolates than any child could possibly eat, she was able to relax and have fun with someone so unlike her practical mother and fastidious grandmother. But Willard's mind was elsewhere, and Annie began to worry that Willard's influence on Beverley might be worse if he remained than if he left again. There was also the matter of his language when he was irritated. In the six months her father lived at home, Beverley heard more casual cursing and sexual innuendos—to Annie's horror—than she had in the six years prior to his arrival.

In late June this delicate balance fell apart. Katharine was trying too hard, and in her anxiety to keep Willard now that she had him back, found herself lashing out at him. On his part, Willard was recovered enough to begin picking on his wife. The bedraggled way she looked, her bland taste in dresses, her failure to read the books that mattered to him, her lack of sophistication—all of it bothered him. At rare moments, Annie interceded, always on Katharine's behalf. When Willard angrily asked Katharine one day why she had never taken the time to learn to dance, Annie spoke for her: "You of all people should know why."

After a particularly bitter exchange, Willard would stay at the house of the one friend from the *Times* who still relished his company, Antony Anderson. Anderson was unmarried and knew plenty of available young women in Los Angeles, and Katharine rightly assumed that Willard was being fixed up with some of them. What was even more annoying to her was that, suddenly and mysteriously, Willard seemed to have pocket money beyond what Annie had given him, or at least enough to buy himself new shirts and a few suits, rent a piano for the apartment, and dine out with Anderson several times that month. It didn't take long for Katharine to learn the source of the money, a discovery which confirmed her worst fears.

All this while, since Willard's ignominious leave-taking from New York, Claire Burke had been hovering in the background. She was ready to send her lover money or, if he wanted, join him in California. In six months, she had had enough of New York City without Willard and was even willing now to divorce her husband if necessary. The money Willard had that summer came from Claire, with Anderson as a go-between. Katharine's awareness of yet one more "other woman" in her husband's life followed a similar pattern, though she sensed at once that this woman was a much more serious threat to her than any of the others from his earlier, briefer affairs or those one-night acquaintances he was meeting through Anderson.

Out of touch with Willard for a time, Claire wrote to him at the Little Street address, not knowing that he had moved out that week. Katharine opened the letter and immediately deduced the whole story. Now it was her turn, as it had been once before, to want to end the relationship. She left Beverley with Annie and went north on her own, to the town of Carpenteria. There she looked for office work and made plans for a final break from Willard. But that freedom was something Katharine didn't really want. What she wanted, urgently, was the chance to be the only partner of the only man she could imagine caring for. By midsummer she returned to Los Angeles to make one last effort, really a pathetic plea, for her marriage.

Some nasty scenes followed Katharine's return, and she made no protest when Willard packed up the rest of his belongings. She was quietly angry rather than subdued. She was also consumed with frustration at not knowing how to compete with an attractive New York rival with money. "The hysterics ... the sudden breakdowns, tantrums, slammed doors"—Beverley recalled a tense summer and a gradual withdrawal of her mother's affection, as if she blamed Beverley, the unwanted child, for her failure to hold Willard. Hurt and lonely, Beverley started to rely more on her grandmother as a playmate and confidante. Katharine seemed to assume that her marriage was at an end.

One afternoon early in the fall, Beverley came home from

school to face her second shock of the year: her mother was gone. Annie gently explained that "Daddy" had a chance for a job in San Francisco, a position that might help them all in many ways, and that her parents were going to try to work out their problems there, alone, on their own for a while. They'd send for her when everything was settled. All that mattered to Beverley, with good reason, was that both her mother and father had left without a word to her.

Stanton as usual saw the family saga in a comic light. Arriving in Los Angeles just after Willard left, he reported to Stieglitz that he hadn't seen his brother "but from what I hear he has left behind a trail of semen over the southern part of the Golden State" and was now working his way to the untried "fields in the north."

On January 18, 1919, *The San Francisco Bulletin* carried the headline FAMOUS SATIRIST TO WRITE FOR "THE BULLETIN." Beginning the following Monday, the announcement read, Los Angeles' most notorious son, author of "Los Angeles: The Chemically Pure" and one-time editor of *The Smart Set,* would be writing a weekly column for his newly adopted city, covering all its artistic events, the culture of California, and sundry topics both timely and controversial. Now that the Armistice had been signed and the spy mania ended, Willard was employable again. It was a step down for him to be writing for the *Bulletin,* but it was a minor coup for them to have him (whatever New York or Los Angeles had to say), and the paper's management went out of its way to be obliging to their new writer.

Having been talked into this futile trial reconciliation by Annie, Willard and Katharine moved to San Francisco without knowing what to expect. So they found a small apartment on Mason Street and set about exploring the city. Only a few weeks later Willard was laid up for almost two months, a victim of the influenza epidemic and his own shaky constitution, but by January he was strong enough to report for work, and he and Katharine were getting along. He liked what he saw of San Francisco that winter and, for the first time since being fired by the *Mail,* he felt a return of the old confidence. New York no longer seemed so all-important. Willard's initial impressions were similar to Mencken's when Mencken visited the West a year later and wrote of his wonder at "the subtle but unmistakable sense of escape from the United States [that San Francisco provides]— the feeling that here, at last, was an American city that somehow managed to hold itself above pollution by the national philistinism and craze for standardization."

In fact, beyond any genuine pleasure he felt for his new home, Willard was ready and eager to become a local booster. If San Franciscans wanted to feel superior to their neighbors to the south, the cultural critic of the *Bulletin,* who claimed to know London, Paris, and New York as well as anyone, was happy to tell them that they were. The sophistication of San Francisco and the provincialism of Los Angeles was an undercurrent of a good many of Willard's columns on the paper's "Seven Arts" page over the next several months. After all, San Franciscans, unlike Southern Californians, "possessed the evanescent spirit of romance and youthful buoyancy . . . [they understood] the pursuit of happiness." When Willard reviewed the exhibitions of area artists, men he would never have paid attention to before, he could be embarrassingly fulsome. LOCAL EXHIBIT EXCELS ALL N.Y. DISPLAYS was the heading for an article on Ralph Stackpole, Clark Hobart, and Ray Boynton.

San Francisco repaid in kind, and Willard became a bit of a celebrity in Bay Area circles. He was a regular at symphony and theater premieres, at gallery openings, at the Fairmont Hotel revues, and at the new cabarets, occasionally in Katharine's company but more often not. His page of the *Bulletin* was his to use in pretty much any way he wanted, and his picture, demonstrating yet another new image, adorned the top of the page. The beard gone, Willard was now sporting an Adolphe Menjou moustache, a look he thought more stylish for the "new" Willard Wright. (Not everyone was taken with it: Mencken, catty as ever, saw the picture and noted, he told Sterling, "a distinct falling-off in pulchritude.")

There was also in his San Francisco days a distinct falling-off in veracity, never Willard's strong point. When the *Bulletin* printed an interview-biography of their columnist, Willard chose to rewrite history in a few key ways, a process that he was to engage in more determinedly later in the decade. One fact Willard altered was the year of his birth. Having told a few people when he applied for the *Bulletin* job that he would turn thirty in the fall of 1918, Willard found it necessary to stand by that white lie and give out his birthdate from then on as 1888, not 1887. That deception had another, very pleasing aspect to it: it made Willard seem all the more a prodigy—*Los Angeles Times* editor at twenty, instead of twenty-one; *Smart Set* chief at twenty-four, instead of twenty-five, and so on.

To the reporter assigned to cover him, Willard narrated his "education on the run," as he called it, in appropriately confused terms. A year at the New York Military Academy became an education "in New York City private schools," never named, and the venerable Lyman Kittredge became one of his instructors at Harvard, along with Copey and Barrett Wendell. More significant than these petty fibs was Willard's account of his departure from *The Smart Set*. As the *Bulletin* reporter summarized the story he was given: "A year there [at *The Smart Set*] convinced [Mr. Wright] that he had either to compromise with his principles or break his contract. Face to face with this problem there could be no alternative, and he resigned from the magazine with his pockets empty, strong in his refusal to sanction intellectually dishonest work for mere commercial gain." No hint of the other side of the story: of being sacked by Thayer or of Ezra Pound's conclusion that Willard was the compromiser and the philistine. But who was to offer any contradiction 3,000 miles away? Willard felt free to play with the record as he saw fit.

For four months everything went smoothly. Willard recycled old pieces from *The West Coast Magazine,* made jibes in the Mencken vein at spinsters, moralists, and faddists, and carried on as he had with his *Town Topics* column, writing about the latest Conrad novel and the new translation of Maupassant, women's fashions, jazz, movies, neglected novelists, Pablo Casals' arrival in town, and "the coming woe of Prohibition." A sequel to "The Chemically Pure" was to be expected. Readers wanted it, and Willard obliged with "Los Angeles: City of Dreadful Night," a review of that region's dour habits, tasteless cuisine, and general prudishness.

Far more stimulating for Willard than his writing that spring—so much of which was a reprise of earlier work—was the new career as a lecturer he embarked on. Except for one talk on the music of Leo Ornstein given at the Palace of Fine Arts, all of Willard's lectures dealt with modern art, though now he knew better than to pretend that his brother's pictures were the beginning and the end of the story. It had been his plan to try this course since the month of his arrival from the East. In a letter to Stieglitz the year before, Willard had noted that "when I get sufficient strength, I am going to endeavor to educate this part of the country . . . to the idea of modern painting." He even remarked, though it might have been a case of whistling in the dark, that California seemed to him more promising territory for the cultivation of an intelligent audience, as it was a region where the art interests of the Academicians were less entrenched.

The four lectures illustrated with stereopticon slides given at Erwin Furman's prestigious gallery on Sutter Street, a follow-up to two art lectures Willard had given in March at Paul Elder's gallery and at the Palace of Fine Arts, were billed under the general title "What Is Art, and Why?" They dealt, respectively, with "the essentials of painting," "substance, rhythm, and technique," composition, and color, and reiterated many of the opinions expressed in *Modern Painting* and *The Creative Will.* On the whole, Willard was pleased with his performance and relished the compliments he was showered with.

Modest the talks were not. THESE LECTURES ARE THE MOST IMPORTANT ON THEIR SUBJECT EVER GIVEN IN AMERICA proclaimed the brochure advertising the four dates, a thought which must have astounded the local cognoscenti. Willard was angling, he told Stieglitz, to "do some real and practical good" on this occasion, clearly implying that he might spur his affluent, open-minded listeners on to buy their first Marins, Doves, O'Keeffes, Hartleys, Russells, and Macdonald-Wrights. Despite overflow attendance at the lectures, nothing much developed in the area of sales or ongoing curiosity. The San Francisco Art Association found Willard a sufficiently articulate and informative speaker to ask him to give a one-lecture summary of the four talks in the resplendent ballroom of the Palace Hotel later that month, but beyond that there were no results to boast of. Once again, Willard's optimism about the cultural climate of the day ran aground of some undeniable facts: the Stieglitz-circle painters he believed in mattered less to San Franciscans than the realists, Impressionists, or area talents they were more accustomed to, and in any case art was everyone's lowest priority. "Our rich people here still stick to the idea that art is trifling," one of

Willard's fellow journalists had written in 1917. "The result is that San Francisco is the worst city in the United States to sell in . . . there is a lot of talk about art [here, but] when you get down to brass tacks San Francisco is 'not there.'"

By mid-1919 Willard was inclined to agree with this sour judgment. He was stuck, he admitted, in a cultural backwater. The presence of men he respected, like the art dealer Furman or J. Nilson Laurvik, the city's museum director, didn't seem to make much difference. People simply didn't care about paintings the way that they did about their cars and homes, and no one's social standing was raised by purchasing a great work of modern art.

For Willard, San Francisco was no more a scene of stunning intellectual accomplishments than it was of marital harmony. Katharine returned to Los Angeles alone. She had found her home life on Mason Street impossible. Willard had met a younger woman he wanted to date (and even seemed to want Katharine's permission for this) and was finding it harder all the time to show any sexual passion for his wife. His physical weariness, the result of too many late nights, the foggy coastal weather, and his generally poor health, also left Willard crankier and more demanding than ever. In June he was back in a sanitarium for two weeks, recovering from extreme exhaustion and bronchial troubles, and by the end of the summer was already contemplating leaving the *Bulletin*. It was becoming a torture to churn out as many words each week as the paper expected from him. Early in the fall, Willard had to resign from the *Bulletin*, terminating the last full-time, salaried job he would ever hold. He went back to Los Angeles and asked Katharine if he might stay with the family until he found his bearings again.

A crusade for modern art in San Francisco might have been a quixotic venture, but Willard was less certain of defeat on his home ground, especially with Stanton there. After his unsuccessful show at "291" in 1917 and an equally unproductive exhibition at Charles Daniel's avant-garde gallery a year later, after months of near-starvation, Stanton had permanently given up on New York ("a city that runs to get nowhere") and had come home to live in the autumn of 1918. Reunited in Los Angeles, the Wright brothers—despite an initial wariness—bolstered one another's spirits. Within a matter of days they were making some ambitious plans.

Willard's first thought was necessarily about raising some cash. The *Times* didn't want anything to do with him nor could he stomach the thought of a regular column anymore, but in November he arranged to do a series of articles for a competing paper, the *Herald,* on nightlife in Los Angeles. These sketches of the town's cabarets and jazz joints were, in effect, a public retraction of the *Smart Set* essay and the *Bulletin* series, "Los Angeles: City of Dreadful Night." For a hefty fee, Willard agreed to rediscover the nightlife of the area, finding it, as the *Herald* management wanted it to be found, a good deal more urbane and electrifying than in days past. Willard took some ribbing from his friends and acquaintances over this about-face. But instead of feeling corrupted or hypocritical himself, he concluded that this deal simply told the whole story about American journalism, its desire to buy off good men and print what its readers wanted to hear. That "good men" allowed themselves in desperation to be bought off mattered less than the shallowness of the system itself.

Willard spent the month of December in comfort at the Alexandria Hotel in Los Angeles, a situation implying either that the *Herald* was lavish in its payment for the articles or that Claire Burke was once again sending billets-doux and, more helpfully, large checks. He was entitled, Willard felt, to live in decent quarters just then. He and Stanton were frantically busy that Christmas. Their goal was the organization of a major show of a kind that had never been seen in Los Angeles before, what they idealistically envisioned as a West Coast version of the Forum Exhibition.

Unlike his brother, Stanton had come West and landed with both feet on the ground. His own drug, money, and women problems in New York, a morass every bit as tangled as Willard's, was something he had left behind. A romantic at heart, he could nonetheless, when necessity demanded, be more practical than his brother and even more self-confident. By the fall of 1919 Stanton had involved himself in the art world of Southern California in several productive, not to say crafty ways: associating with the better, more modern artists, lecturing at local art associations, cultivating the right clubwomen and potential patrons,

148

spending time with Marsden Hartley (whom he loathed) during his stay in California, and becoming friendly with Dr. Frank Daggett, the director of Exposition Park, one of the city's principal exhibition centers. Despite its reputation for a crass, single-minded interest in commercial development and real-estate deals, Los Angeles probably was a more likely area than San Francisco for the sort of inroads the Wrights were attempting to make. Certainly Stanton felt so, and by the time Willard gave up his job and left San Francisco, Stanton had established the groundwork for his Exhibition of Paintings by American Modernists to be held at Exposition Park.

It had long been Willard's intention to try to repeat the Forum show in the West, in the hopes that another part of the country might be more responsive to the new, more colorful and dynamic work he liked, but the Los Angeles exhibition was really Stanton's undertaking, with Willard—for once—playing only a supporting role.

It was Stanton who got Daggett and his board of directors to agree to the idea over the opposition of local artists. It was Stanton who negotiated with Stieglitz the transportation of the paintings. "The better people here are alive and interested," he had told the art dealer, and he did his best to assuage Stieglitz's doubts about the public reaction and financial returns that could be expected. (J. Nilson Laurvik had written to Stieglitz hinting that an exhibition of his artists in California would meet with a lukewarm reaction, given the low level of aesthetic education and interest in the state. As a museum director, Laurvik had cause to know.) The list of participants was set by mid-January and all of the paintings arrived, miraculously, by the last week of the month. It included all of the "Forum" artists (though Stanton would have been happy to exclude Man Ray, Dasburg, and the Zorachs) as well as five who had not shown in the original exhibition: Charles Demuth, Joseph Stella, Preston Dickinson, Conrad Kramer, and William Yarrow. Georgia O'Keeffe was invited to participate but she declined, leaving Marguerite Zorach once again the lone woman of the group.

The Exhibition of Paintings by American Modernists ran from February 1 through the 29th, 1920, at Los Angeles' baroque art museum at Exposition Park. A less congruous setting for the expressive Marins and Maurers, the cubist-inspired Dickinsons, and the bright synchromies on the walls would have been hard to devise, but to some extent this worked to the painters' advantage, suggesting that the current art was in line, in a way, with tradition and "evolution in art" (Willard's recurrent point) and wasn't the complete break with the past that some critics thought it was. Privately, Stanton was surprised and disgusted by many of the paintings he and Willard hung. He felt that he had been offered the worst, not the best, examples of many of the artists' work and wondered if Stieglitz had been acting in an intentionally defeatist and condescending manner toward the Wrights' exhibition. "Irreparable detriment to the rest of us" was his fear when he contemplated the selection. But publicly he had no choice but to put the best face possible on the whole enterprise. His statement to the press exuded confidence and strength:

> We modern artists are just what our name implies; we are alive with you today—we are not animated corpses—we speak your language, the language of the hum and stir of moving things, of energy and intensity, of the aspirations of the twentieth century. . . .

Between Stanton's diligent promotional efforts and Willard's contacts, a fair amount of publicity was generated for the show. Some of the reviews were of the usual benighted level— FUTURISTIC ART SHOCKS L.A., MASTERPIECES GO TO CELLAR—spiced now with references to "bolshevistic" influences. The more conservative work, like Demuth's or Benton's, naturally received the most favorable notices, while reactions to the paintings of Stanton Macdonald-Wright were alternately negative and indignant or of the be-kind-to-the-local-boy variety. Yet, on balance, the antagonism in the press was less than what it had been in New York four years earlier, and even the ever-skeptical Antony Anderson did his best in his two articles to come to terms with the challenges Stanton and Willard were presenting him with. That the principal critic of *The Los Angeles Times* urged his readers to view the paintings with an open mind, and found flattering things to say about Zorach, Walkowitz, and Dove, represented an advance of sorts.

The trouble, though, confirming the doubts Laurvik and Stieglitz had shared, was that no one seemed eager to buy anything. A mixture of polite interest and journalistic acrimony didn't justify the time and expense of sending so many paintings all the way across the country. When at the end of the month only William Zorach's decorative "Mountain Path"—Stanton and Willard's least favorite picture in the show—had been sold, for $175, the Wrights were horrified. Erwin Furman had agreed to take the show in San Francisco the next month and yet, despite all of Willard's lecturing the year before, had no better luck in his own gallery. Furman was able to sell one painting, and there was almost no press coverage. For Stanton and Willard, the winter of 1920 represented the low point of their dreams to play a part in the artistic life of America.

Willard's own best shot at stirring the art audience of Los Angeles was an editorial he wrote for the *Times,* which the paper gave a prominent place to on its editorial page. Ostensibly about his brother's show, "Art and Aunt Maria" was a far-reaching, roundabout summary of everything that was wrong with contemporary life and its approach to the creative vision. Having had enough for the moment of playing it safe in his newspaper columns, Willard reverted briefly to his old angry self. Those obsessed with conformity, he wrote, conveniently forgot that Courbet, Monet, Pissarro, and Renoir had met with "jibes and sneers" in their time. Those engaged in mindless flag-waving overlooked the fact that the democratic mentality necessarily reduced all greatness to the lowest common level, ruthlessly seeing to it that nothing should ever make the majority feel socially or culturally threatened. Anti-intellectualism, Willard lamented, was an inherent part of American life, though not a fate we blindly had to accept. Content with having riled his readers sufficiently with these opening salvos, Willard turned to a commentary on the show and, finally, to a declaration of his usual themes: the logical and unstoppable development of Modernism, the pointlessness of representational subject matter in art, the need for a system of aesthetic judgment, the ruts into which most people fell in their reading, viewing, and thinking.

"Art and Aunt Maria" prompted some sarcastic rebuttals from a few California journalists and—no surprise to anyone—didn't help the cause of selling paintings or converting viewers at Exposition Park. Willard and Stanton judged the whole affair a fiasco. There was also a hint of strain between the brothers now. When things looked promising, Willard had been ready to claim the lion's share of the credit for the endeavor, but later when help was needed in getting the paintings to San Francisco and then back to New York, he was nowhere to be found.

"The West," Willard had written in one of his first columns for the *Bulletin*, "with its broad tolerance and freedom from precedent and tradition, is the logical place for the development of new ideas." A year later, thinking very differently on the subject, Willard was casting about for work that had nothing to do with his old professional aspirations and everything to do with what the West, or Southern California, was really all about. That meant Hollywood. In the first half of 1920 Willard became something of a classic hanger-on in the studio world, scrounging about for any kind of job, gabbing about script ideas, and trying to meet people who could introduce him to the producers and directors who counted. For a month or two he found a job writing the titles for a few silent movies of no distinction. This was the kind of hack labor Stanton deplored. Small wonder that Willard—"the illustrious brother," as Stanton was calling him now—kept his distance for a time after the Exposition Park show.

Several New York and California men Willard had known from years past, writers and editors especially, had found places for themselves on one level or another of the film business. Their example gave Willard encouragement. Julian Johnson, the former *Los Angeles Times* drama critic, was writing for the movie magazines, and Ferdinand Earle, a well-to-do artist and poet Willard knew from New York, was trying to launch a producing and directing career. Willard had renewed his acquaintance with Earle as soon as he relocated from San Francisco, and the two became friends for a while. Earle's main project that year was putting together and finding support for a film version of *The Rubáiyát* with Ramon Navarro. Ultimately he asked Willard to join him as art director and screenwriter. If *The Rubáiyát* made it into production, Willard realized, he could be sure of a respectable place in the industry.

Willard was living in an apartment in Hollywood that spring, having said his goodbyes to Katharine and Beverley. He had furnished his new quarters comfortably and was driving about the Hollywood hills in a new car. Willard even asked his mother to move in with him, but setting up housekeeping with her errant son and his mistress was the furthest thing from Annie's mind. Running back and forth between Willard and Katharine, keeping an eye on Beverley and Stanton, and having a hard time paying her own bills, had left Annie Wright fed up with the whole situation. She felt some relief mixed with her sadness when her daughter-in-law and grandchild left for Pacific Grove, where Katharine's sister and brother-in-law offered her a room in their house and a secretarial job in the husband's business.

Vigorously interested as he was in making money by some connection to the studios, Willard hadn't entirely abandoned his other passions. He told Stieglitz that he was at work on a novel, with ideas for a second one developing at the same time, and enough notes for a second book on aesthetics. The novel, enti-tled *The Mother*, was going to be "a psychological study of the New England temperament," whatever that meant. For four years this manuscript grew, though it's doubtful that anyone other than the author ever read it.

His conversations with Stanton in this period, following the Exposition Park disaster and sandwiched in between his meet-ings with Earle, were more concrete and intellectually provoca-tive. It was a remarkable feature of the Wrights' relationship that both men could be feeling awkward or antagonistic toward the other and yet ready to get together to drink, eat, and talk about art, books, exhibitions, or some new theory worth discussing. Their genuine desire for self-education and their desire to ed-ucate each other could, at times, overcome the unspoken rivalry they had struggled with since childhood.

These conversations of 1920 were responsible for the fat file of notes that produced, three years later, the promised second book on aesthetics, which Willard called *The Future of Painting*. Downcast by the feeble response to an exhibition he had labored tirelessly on and depressed by Californians' unshakable enthu-siasm for the very representational artists he most scorned, Stan-ton had started to wonder if this art form, as it then existed, was the medium he wished to devote the rest of his life to. It was bad enough that he had lost money on the show in February and that some of the private pupils he had taken on were abandoning their teacher in embarrassment. It was irksome that no gallery wanted to represent him or could sell his work. More compli-cated by far was the sense that "painting has had its say," as he wrote to Stieglitz, that the art form itself might have done all it could and be headed toward a decline.

Neither Stanton nor Willard were of a nostalgic bent. The possibility that painting was going to die of enervation in the twentieth century, the way the creation of epic verse or grand opera had come to a natural end in previous times, wasn't a staggering thought—that is, if painting was to be followed by a visual art experience of equal merit and, as Stanton specified, "greater emotional possibilities." The Wrights had never had a problem accepting change. For both men, the unknown was there to be examined. This, then, was Stanton's next avenue of study, a path down which Willard followed his brother with increasing curiosity. Though they were about to be separated for many years, Stanton's readings and speculations about a visual art "beyond drawing, beyond painting" prompted Willard to take the subject very seriously.

"The eighth art," as it was sometimes called in the Twenties, was an art of pure color achieved through the media of light and film. Even by 1920 this field had its own history and theoretical literature. For more than twenty years, men of a technical and an aesthetic background had pondered the means by which such sensations could be scientifically effected and meaningfully orchestrated. Primitive experiments along these lines had already been undertaken, and Stanton was diligent in his research of any pioneering efforts he could find out about. As far back as 1912, his friend Morgan Russell had been pondering the creation of a "kinetic light machine" and must have discussed this idea with Stanton.

For a few years after his return to California, before he resumed painting with a fresh commitment, Stanton was involved with others, all nonpainters, in the exploration of techniques designed to produce color films and abstract light shows. Their intention was not to tell a story on film but to test out various color and sound correspondences, playing music while certain supposedly "equivalent" colors were being projected on a screen. By early July of 1920 Stanton told Stieglitz that he and his colleagues were ready for a trial run of their first "picture in lights" which was to be given as a preview performance at a Los Angeles theater that month. No record of the show exists, though, suggesting that it failed to come off.

It would be a long time, Stanton realized and Willard concurred, before technology offered the means to fulfill the dreams of the "color artists," most of whom were looked upon as amusing eccentrics in the Twenties. The creation of a nonrepresentational art that also involved the elements of time, motion, and sound—something that promised aesthetic subtleties beyond even what abstract painting on canvas could achieve—would have to wait decades, they knew, to become a workable reality. But that didn't matter much to Stanton, who was beginning to see the limitations of the Synchromist dogma at the same time that its color principles connected his new projects to the old. For Willard, who avidly read the complicated literature on color/light theory over the next year, this development was to be the subject of the only book he wrote in the Twenties under his own name.

Much as he wanted to see Stanton's "light show" in July, Willard and Claire decided to return to New York at the end of May. Earle was trying to work both coasts in lining up financial support for his movie, and he wanted Willard in the East, where he was headed himself. Willard sent word to Katharine that Claire would be filing for divorce that summer and that he would see a lawyer in Manhattan about their own divorce as soon after that as he could. It was high time to end a great mistake. He would, he assured her, continue to send money back to them indefinitely. With two months' rent owing at his apartment, Willard packed his bags, left a vaguely worded note for his mother about "business in the East," and caught a train. He told his landlady that he'd mail her the rent money as soon as "his movie" was out, at which time he'd reclaim his furniture and other belongings.

Katharine didn't bother to answer or to tell Annie what was happening. She and Beverley stayed a while in Pacific Grove, later moving to San Francisco and eventually settling in Palo Alto. Subject to bouts of severe depression, Katharine had begun to drink and to brood, relentlessly, about all that had gone wrong since that magical summer in the Northwest when a young poet from Harvard had first made love to her. He'd come back to her someday when he was successful, she kept telling her sister and her daughter or anyone who'd listen, and then everything would be as it should be. There'd be no lawyers and no divorce. She was sure of that.

155

IN THE
SHADOWS

"The gods seem determined to hold me up for a time longer."
—Willard to Katharine, undated letter (1922)

Back in New York, Willard took up residence in the Alcazar Hotel in midtown Manhattan and spent most of his time with Ferdinand Earle. Barely able to contain his excitement, he saw all sorts of possibilities for turning Omar Khayyám's famous book of poetry into a cohesive film property with exotic sets and a literate script. He spoke about the movie as if it were already a resounding success. Unfortunately, Willard's euphoria was premature. Earle tried for weeks to interest backers in New York in the project before he abruptly admitted defeat and took leave of his incredulous partner. In all of his dealings in any way connected to Hollywood, it was the same: Willard took as certainties what to anyone else would have seemed obvious long shots. Later in the summer, with his money running low and a large unpaid bill at the Alcazar hanging over his head, Willard quietly decamped from the hotel and moved in with his old journalist friend from the *Smart Set* days, Randolph Bartlett, on the Upper West Side. There he spent the next few months, sleeping (rent-free) on the Bartletts' sofa, eating them out of house and home, and talking ceaselessly about screenplays, producers, and the possibilities in the cinema for enterprising young men.

Willard's whole relationship to the movie world over the next two years was indicative of his divided loyalties. He could never quite decide if he was "selling out" to a new, tawdry, popular medium or engaged in an artistic pursuit connected to a splendid art form still in its infancy. Get-rich-quick ideas were followed by admirable screenplay projects, which in turn were followed by more nonsensical plans to become a "name" in the right studio circles. And, while he was never more than a marginal figure in that strange milieu, Willard clung to the hope that Hollywood would be his means toward the secure income he desperately wanted.

At times that summer and fall Willard let his despair get the better of him and he would lapse back into some form of drug-taking. On at least one occasion Randolph Bartlett proved to be a better host than Willard had any right to expect. When Willard didn't come home one evening, Bartlett roamed from one end of Greenwich Village to the other trying to find him. Stopping at every dive he could think of, he finally found Willard passed out, gray and disheveled, after a day-long marijuana binge with some seedy new acquaintances. He took his friend home and put him to bed.

So tight was Willard's situation that autumn that, despite his promise on leaving California in May, he wasn't able to send any money West for Beverley's support. "I want to help Katharine and think of it all the time," Willard wrote, to calm his mother's wrath, "and if there was any possible way to raise a dollar, I'd send it. The tragedy of the situation hangs over my head constantly, and for weeks it has begun to keep me awake at night." Willard pleaded for his mother's help, but Annie felt as if she had been bled enough through all this "awful nightmare" of her family life since Archie's death. For that matter, her own finances were entering a precarious phase, as Stanton's divorce from Ida was at long last coming through and Annie had been tapped for those expenses. Katharine said nothing and asked for nothing. Annie couldn't even get her to return to Los Angeles, let alone the Little Street bungalow that was "the place of sad memories" she wanted to block out.

Claire Burke disappeared from the scene, for the moment, at about this time as well, proving Katharine right about the divorce. If Claire had intended to follow through on her original plan to marry Willard, she apparently didn't intend now to attach herself to a man whose prospects were declining so rapidly, whose health was again being undermined by his addictions and anxiety, and whose mood swings were becoming more volatile.

Willard's next move, giving him more than a year of stability, was to Greenwich Village. The time was when Willard would have laughed at the idea of living anywhere near Washington Square; in the old days he had dutifully followed Mencken's lead in scoffing at the whole ragtag Bohemian-Socialist-dilettante-artist set. Now he was happy to get a few rooms at 42 Barrow Street and, soon after, just as happy to get a job as theater reviewer for a short-lived weekly, *The Greenwich Villager*. The "salary" amounted to free tickets and enough cash for a few lunches a week, but his new quarters were big enough to work and entertain in, and that seemed enough.

Stanton Leeds and his wife were among the friends Willard resumed contact with and invited to visit. Leeds was a gracious man, ready to forgive and forget the whole Germany spy episode in which Willard had implicated him three years before, and his wife, Katherine, a writer herself, thought Willard good company. They were the first people to whom Willard broached the idea of someday turning out "light fiction" to pay his bills. If the time ever came when he felt compelled to do this, he told his friends, his books would be sensational, not hackwork but stories that would be entertaining and successful beyond anyone's imagining. (It is an odd coincidence, in a life later filled with name-coincidences and name-overlappings, that Willard should have first spoken of this idea to two people named Stanton and Katherine.) The thought of Willard as a writer of bestsellers seemed comical to Stanton Leeds, who knew Willard's disdain for commercial work. It seemed an even more amusing boast to Katherine Leeds, who was at 42 Barrow Street the day a man from the phone company came to disconnect Willard's phone for nonpayment of his first month's bill. Having run up a bill for a then-staggering $18 worth of phone service, Willard decided he could live without a phone. Anyone in Hollywood or the publishing world who needed to find him would have to do so by mail.

Willard wasn't averse to borrowing money from Stanton and Katherine Leeds, any more than he had been from Randolph Bartlett, from Claire Burke and Antony Anderson—and earlier from Mencken, Nathan, Huebsch, Kennerley, and so many others. He even developed the bad habit of asking people for loans whom he didn't know well enough to allow for such a request, a practice that earned him a sorry reputation in the Village. But most of Willard's acquaintances knew the futility of the loans, both for his good (it had begun to look to everyone as if he were never going to be able to stand on his own) and for the recovery of their own cash.

One man wasn't interested in declining Willard's request for money. On the contrary, he welcomed it. B. G. de Sylva was a young Broadway lyricist with plenty of ready cash. A fellow Californian who had probably heard of Willard back in Los Angeles, "Buddy" de Sylva had recently teamed up with George Gershwin and was on the verge of a spectacular and lucrative theater career. He knew Willard, who was running about town these days harassing the Shubert Alley crowd with "great ideas" for new musicals, and he was acquainted with Willard's need—his endless need—for funds. Not long after Willard settled into his Greenwich Village life, de Sylva and he worked out an intricate arrangement for a loan of $6,500. This sum, according to Willard's calculations, would see him clear for almost a year and a half. He would be able to work without any concern about finding a full-time job; by the end of 1921, or surely by the middle of 1922, Willard felt, one of his novels or screenplay ideas would have established him in a solid way. Willard signed a contract de Sylva drew up, and de Sylva handed over a check.

Willard didn't mention the loan to many people, least of all to his family. For good reason. De Sylva's loan wasn't exactly a loan—it was usury. It specified that the money was being given to Willard for personal living expenses during a period in which he would be working on two novels. All profits from the sale of the books above $6,500 were to be divided equally between the author and de Sylva; if the novels failed to make $6,500, a claim could be made on any future novels Willard wrote; no other literary work was to be published before the completion of the novels without de Sylva's permission; and, even more appallingly, Willard was to have a will made out, to be in effect until the repayment of the loan, leaving everything he owned and all future royalties to B. G. de Sylva. Each week Willard was to submit to de Sylva an accounting of his expenses. Any week that his expenses fell below $100, the calculated basis for the "65-week loan," Willard was to apply the saved money toward the next installment, which would be that much less the next week. It was a crystal-clear, breathtakingly callous document Willard signed in October 1920. His willingness to place himself in this kind of relationship to a man who was not an intimate friend suggests several things—the extent of Willard's financial desperation, his always-cavalier approach to money matters, a reckless instability, possibly some sizable drug debts, and a blind faith (or suicidal hope) in the future. It certainly didn't imply an anguished concern for Annie, Katharine, or Beverley, who never saw more than $20 a month of the money before it ran out.

To complicate matters, there was nothing like a deadline imposed by an outsider to freeze Willard's creative juices. Handing newspaper copy in on time, or preparing a review or an essay for a waiting printer, was one thing. Finishing a novel so that a twenty-five-year-old Broadway-musical prodigy could reclaim a quick investment was another. And de Sylva's contract was loaded with deadlines: Willard was to show him the completed manuscript, probably of *The Mother,* by June 1, 1921, and two-thirds of a second novel, which was going by the title "Vanderveer," by January 1, 1922. What became of these manuscripts isn't clear. They were certainly never finished. "Vanderveer" probably never existed beyond a few chapters, if it even passed the outline stage. Eventually Willard destroyed both manuscripts and defaulted on his loan. Undoubtedly to his own surprise, Willard was one day able to pay "Buddy" de Sylva his $6,500, but that time would have seemed unimaginably distant in the hard-pressed months of 1920 and 1921.

The clause in the contract that meant the least to Willard was the reference to clearing with de Sylva all other literary projects which might retard progress on the novels. What his Shylock didn't know wouldn't hurt him, was Willard's conclusion. He went ahead on a screenplay proposal with Stanton and Katherine Leeds for a dramatization of "The Fall of the House of

Usher." Fresh from their viewing of *The Cabinet of Dr. Caligari*, Willard and his friends were sure they could outdo the German Expressionist film using modernist backdrops painted by Willard's brother or any of the talented modern painters the Wright brothers knew. They spent several weeks preparing a treatment which they sent around to various studios, billing their endeavor as "an American version of *Caligari*." There were no takers. Willard refused to be discouraged, though. It was almost as if he sensed that his money would one day come by way of the movies and he needed only to be patient and determined enough. At the same time, the usual lesson about American taste was being impressed upon him: Omar Khayyám and Edgar Allan Poe might seem like plausible film material on Barrow Street, but they didn't mean a thing to Louis B. Mayer or Jesse Lasky.

Keeping himself open to any rumors of screenwriting jobs or collaborations in the works, Willard settled on movie-magazine writing as the steadiest path toward getting the attention of those in power. It was another dubious idea. How many reviewers or columnists had made the transition to studio jobs of any consequence? Nonetheless, he persuaded Randolph Bartlett, who also freelanced for some of the movie periodicals, to introduce him to the editor of *Photoplay* and he approached the editor of *Movie Magazine*, another mass-audience gossip sheet, and over the next two years took on any assignment, no matter how crass or demeaning, that those editors threw his way.

Most of Willard's writing for these two publications, which were more in the nature of fan magazines than film journals, was as trivial and ephemeral as anything he ever wrote. Throughout 1921 and 1922, though, he spent a good deal of time at the movies and was able to concoct a variety of angles from which to approach his subject. "Underworld Life at the Films" in the March 1922 issue of *Movie Magazine* looked at the feeble portrayal of criminals on the screen. "Beauty of All Ages" in the April 1922 *Photoplay* reviewed the changing standards of female beauty in painting and film. In other issues he wrote about Robert Wiene's revolutionary techniques in *Dr. Caligari*, new leading men of the day, the Valentino vogue, movie titles and background music, and Charlie Chaplin's charisma.

For several articles Willard made use of his mother's maiden name and published under the pseudonym "Frederick Van

Vranken." Sometimes Van Vranken's articles aspired to more depth than Wright's. "The Unhappy Ending" in the December 1921 *Photoplay,* for instance, analyzed the new Hollywood tendency to forsake the traditional happy ending in its better movies, indicating perhaps that the taste of postwar filmgoers (and studio heads) was improving. From *The Four Horsemen of the Apocalypse* to *Gypsy Blood,* in the deluge of war stories and in the endless adaptations of old novels, "Van Vranken" saw hope that movies were going to become adult fare in America in the Twenties, now that they had finally lost some of their sugar-coating. Some of this reads today like toadying to the studio publicity departments, who naturally expected that the movie magazines, in return for information and "star" interviews, would do their part in pushing the whole Hollywood bandwagon. Willard was even willing in this context to play the good citizen. "Chaplin's Great Secret," printed under his own name, compared the Little Tramp, the cinema's embodiment of comic warmth, to the new President, Warren Harding, that "wise and great" symbol of fatherly counsel and democratic authority. We have need of such emblematic figures, Willard wrote, and Chaplin and Harding understandably filled that need.

If Mencken or Dreiser, or Nathan or Kennerley, had bothered to glance through the movie magazines of the early Twenties, they would have been confirmed in their assumption that their old colleague had lost his way, shamefully and irrevocably. Had John Adams Thayer chanced to leaf through *Photoplay* or *Movie Magazine,* he would have been even more startled. The man who had insulted his taste and filled his magazine with Owen Hatteras' sarcasm and Ezra Pound's craziness was himself pandering to an audience bigger and crasser than any *The Smart Set* had ever known. The "wise and great" Warren Harding, indeed.

It was only a matter of time before this house of cards came down around him. In the first weeks of 1922, after fourteen months in the Village, Willard gave up his downtown apartment. Owing more people more money than he could ever imagine repaying, he made sure almost no one knew he was leaving Barrow Street. His overnight move brought him to one room on the seventh floor of the Belleclaire Hotel on the corner of Broadway and 77th Street. For the next four years, the Belleclaire was Willard's hideout, his refuge, and eventually his "base of operations" as he tried, finally, to come to terms with his life.

In the first months after he moved, Willard seldom ventured out. He slept too much, stayed in bed the better part of the day, worked in a halfhearted fashion on *The Mother* and more seriously on *The Future of Painting,* and thought about ways to reestablish his good name in New York. In April his last signed article for the movie magazines appeared. From then on, Willard decided, he had to save himself for the novel or for articles in more prestigious publications. But the best deal he could make for himself that spring was an assignment to write a short monthly art column for *Hearst's International,* an arrangement which sounded promising at first but brought in little money and lasted only five months.

Now every setback was followed by a new physical problem. As his eating habits became less regular and his nerves got the better of him, Willard found that his digestion, never very steady, was only getting worse. He became more agonizingly constipated each week and suffered a debilitating attack of colitis in October. When he entered the hospital to have a long-postponed hemorrhoid operation in December, Willard felt as if he had reached the limit of his energy and finances. As careful as he had been to stretch de Sylva's money as far as possible, he was running dangerously low on funds, had to keep the hospital and doctor waiting for their checks, and even had trouble sending Katharine the $15 or $20 a month he was averaging then.

Most of Willard's old friends in Manhattan, like Alfred Stieglitz and Stanton Leeds, assumed he had left the city once again. A few people were only too happy to spread rumors of Willard's final surrender to the drug world or untimely end at the hands of loan sharks, while those who had known him by way of *The Smart Set* didn't know or care where Willard Huntington Wright had taken himself. At this point Willard seems to have been relying on Claire once again. She reappears at mysterious and unpredictable intervals in her lover's letters of the early Twenties, while her own story never quite comes into focus. (Willard's later destruction of his letters from Claire obscures the facts and furthers the mystery of their relationship, of course.) It would seem that she had indeed gotten a divorce from her husband after returning from California, remarried sometime in 1921, and had even had a child, a girl. Willard's family later tried to piece all of this together and was under the impression, not a farfetched one given Willard's temperament, that Willard had encouraged Claire in her second marriage. Mr. Schermerhorn was rich and as a result, when she was in an indulgent mood, Claire Schermerhorn was able to treat her lover even more lavishly than in the past. This odd and mercenary arrangement was perfectly suited to Willard's needs, allowing him an aura of sophistication, the occasional cash, the uninhibited sex, and the freedom from commitment that he had always craved—none of which Katharine could provide. The price, though, was increasing dependency on a woman, a condition which didn't do much to make Willard more sensitive in his relations with the opposite sex.

Sinking into near-anonymity, almost as if fifteen years of struggle to achieve some prominence in journalism and art criticism hadn't happened, was worse for Willard than enduring any amount of hostility. And nothing proved how far his standing had eroded as clearly as Ben Huebsch's publication of *The Future of Painting*. It had been a hard book to finish, even though the manuscript had been cut to less than a quarter of its original length in the hope of attracting more readers, and Willard's feelings upon handing it over to Ben Huebsch were far from the spirit of exhilaration he had felt when *Modern Painting* was done. "I want it to stand as a kind of prophecy," he wrote to Burton Rascoe. But Willard knew the kind of traps the book was liable to fall victim to. He had confided to many friends the fear that *The Future of Painting*—his first serious work in six years—was going to be willfully misinterpreted, its conclusions taken too narrowly.

Pretty much as Huebsch expected, *The Future of Painting* had only a small impact when it appeared in March of 1923. The printing was limited to two thousand copies, not all of which were sold, and the reviews were condescending or indifferent. *The New York Times* didn't bother to review it. Paul Strand was one of the few knowledgeable readers to take Willard's speculations seriously, and in *The Bookman* he argued intelligently about which aspects of Willard's thinking made sense and which seemed to him off the mark. Lewis Mumford in *The New Republic* was more mournful, and Thomas Craven began his piece in *The*

Dial by noting that "Mr. Wright, in his periodic excursions into the science of aesthetics, has commited himself to many ill-considered prophecies," of which this was one of the worst. Willard's estimation that color, rather than drawing or figuration, was going to be, or should be, the dominant concern of future artists seemed an implausible assumption at a time when realism still loomed large on the art scene. Equally contentious were Willard's proclamation that even the best academic painting had reached a dead end, a stage of "emotional impotency," and his prediction that a new, more technological "color art" might actually divorce itself from traditional painting on canvas, allowing the two art forms to go their own way. The latter point seemed to many people an especially silly proposition, just more crazy "light theory," and hardly worth the little notice it got.

Those in the art world themselves, like Stieglitz and O'Keeffe, read the book of course, but—given the few responses he received—Willard was afraid that even most of the people who purchased it, or to whom he gave copies, hadn't troubled to read it. Few art books dealing with aesthetic issues that were important to later generations received less attention in their day than *The Future of Painting*.

It was becoming increasingly difficult for Willard to hold on to his past image as a man with something to say about the arts in America. A book review in *The Dial* the following year, a brief essay for a catalogue of drawings by Abraham Walkowitz, and an essay on the illustrational artist William Gropper for, of all periodicals, *The Menorah Journal* were Willard's final publications on art, and practically the last of his serious writing to appear under his own name. None of it meant much. By 1924 Willard was no longer a writer editors thought of for review assignments or important critical tasks.

The situation worsened over the next few years, and by the time Edmund Wilson wrote his essay "The All-Star Literary Vaudeville," surveying the American cultural luminaries of 1914 to 1926, he could only remark of Willard Huntington Wright that he was a now-unknown figure "who had once given the impression of being someone important." A reader of Wilson's article might have assumed that the writer in question was long since dead.

■   ■   ■

The world might have bypassed her father, but Beverley Wright in the early Twenties was just awakening to a serious interest in him. Once she had recovered from the shock of his presence in those wretched months on Little Street, Beverley had grown more curious about her absent father, his life in New York, his career and accomplishments. Like her mother, she still lived in the hope of a reunion and a normal family life. By the time she was fourteen, she felt old enough to write to Willard on her own. Beverley was the avid reader a literary man would want for a daughter, and Willard took care to shower her with advice. He had a horror that Beverley might take up Charles Dickens "or similar pious writers." Balzac and Conrad, Dreiser and Maupassant, Shaw and Wilde: they were the right starting points for a smart teenager, he insisted. For light entertainment, he recommended the novels of E. P. Oppenheim, which he was reading at the time.

Though Willard could finally show some concern for his child, now that she was becoming a person with a mind of her own (or a mind to be formed), there was always a carefully defined distance between them. It took Beverley a year or two of dashed hopes to understand this. If she wrote hinting about visiting New York, Willard would write back about the impossible conditions of life in the big city. When she made reference to her own growing interest in art, Willard was evasive on the subject. Most painfully, when Beverley sent some of her first short stories and drawings to her father for comment and approval, he never answered. In the midst of his anguish over his own broken career in the arts, the last thing he could bear to think about was his daughter's excitement with writing and sketching.

An especially trying time for Beverley was the beginning of adolescence. Having given up office work in a pathetic effort to start her own chicken farm on the outskirts of Palo Alto, Katharine Wright was in an unusually strained frame of mind. She convinced herself that her mother-in-law was behind Willard's aloofness and some days liked to fantasize that Beverley had been the boy they had never had, assuming perhaps that a son would have kept Willard at home or been a replacement for the husband who didn't love her anymore. Beverley was addressed in private as "Peter," the name Katharine and Willard had intended to call their first male child, and treated like a son.

She was taught to be "the young gentleman"—to hold her mother's chair at dinner, to walk on the curbside of the sidewalk when taking a lady for a walk, to open doors and give up her seat for women in public. Any show of femininity was disparaged. Masculine traits were what mattered, her mother seemed to imply. With the sexual confusion this naturally led to, in her sense of constantly failing her mother, in her perplexity over the causes of her parents' separation, and in her embarrassment at their poverty and transience, Beverley endured an agonizing early life.

Her escape was to the south for vacations with her grandmother. There physical conditions were somewhat better, and the atmosphere, especially when Stanton was at home, was much happier. At first, Annie hadn't been able to accommodate her granddaughter. Not long after Willard's departure, she had put all of her assets into a boardinghouse for single women that, financially, never quite worked out. When Stanton was at home, he slept on the living room couch. The high-strung lady boarders, whom Annie referred to as "the inmates," eventually induced Annie to give up this shaky venture, and when she was reestablished in her own small house, Beverley was able to visit. It was best when Stanton was there. Unlike her father, Stanton encouraged Beverley's interest in painting and drawing and, unlike her mother, Stanton was delighted when Beverley, at sixteen, had her hair bobbed. The least bit of rebelliousness in his timid niece pleased Stanton, whose own teenage waywardness had been of a more vigorous nature.

Stanton had started teaching at the Art Students League in Los Angeles, where he had once made a name for himself as a precocious youngster, and offered Beverley at least some sense that all the Wright talent she had heard about for so many years did mean something. He wasn't rich, but he was earning a living and developing a respectful following. He also introduced his niece to a way of life, and a kind of woman, she hadn't known with Katharine. The name of Stanton's current love—Jeanne Redman—didn't mean anything to Beverley, and neither did her grandmother nor her uncle let on, at first, that Jeanne was not a stranger to the Wright family. All Beverley knew was that Stanton's girlfriend was a delightful and exciting woman, creative and energetic; attentive to her and perfectly suited to Stanton. Jeanne was a woman of the world, while Katharine was becoming a neurotic, dreary, demanding mother.

Soon after, when Stanton married Jeanne Redman, another blow—this time a crippling one—was struck at Katharine's mental balance. She became hysterical. She refused to allow Beverley to visit her relatives and hounded Beverley for showing any admiration or affection for her new aunt. There was no escaping the past, Katharine told her daughter, but she didn't have to condone the insults heaped on her. It was then that Beverley put the pieces together and realized that her uncle had married one of the women Willard had been involved with early in his married life. Annie and Stanton could love Willard's cast-off girlfriend while his wife starved, Katharine railed. To her, this was just one more unforgivable wrong to endure and relive, one more example of the Wrights' inhumanity.

In a situation of such powerlessness, Katharine's ability to hurt Willard was slight. And, on one level, she didn't want him to suffer as deeply as she had—because she was sure, she told Beverley, that he would one day need her and they would be together again. All that Katharine could do at this time was drive Willard to distraction in little ways, and this she did religiously. She would refuse to acknowledge the checks she did receive, or wait to cash them until she had written to Willard that the money had been lost in the mail, sending him into a panic or a rage. She would alternate lacerating notes with tender letters, full of maternal concern, followed by long periods of ominous silence. She would pretend to misinterpret Willard's remarks, ask questions he had already answered, upbraid him for his failure to see his daughter decently clothed and educated, and (an old ruse with her) send cryptic messages hinting at serious illnesses. All of this had the desired effect of frazzling Willard's nerves in his weakest moments.

Willard's own epistolary strategies could be equally vicious. Writing to thank Katharine for the robe she had sewn him for Christmas in 1924, he was not averse to keeping his wife posted on the state of his relations with Claire Schermerhorn. "Nothing from Claire this year. . . . As I wrote you, I haven't seen her or spoken to her, directly or indirectly, for eight months or more. I hear she is living quite happily with her hubby. So that's that. Have contracted no other entangling alliances, foreign or do-

mestic. Age, no doubt, is coming on me. . . ." At other times
Willard took Katharine's tactics seriously. "You are punishing
me for my shortcomings as a conventional husband and father,"
Willard lashed out in one letter, but it served no purpose, he
reminded her, even if all justice were on her side. "It does not
help either you or me or Beverley," Willard noted, "for it only
makes me worry and upsets me and thus reduces my capacity to
work."

At the time of this warning to Katharine—in October of
1924—Willard still honestly believed that he was going to be able
to support his wife and daughter, even if he never lived with
them again, through his serious writing. But the moment for
decisively putting that illusion to rest was upon him.

When Randolph Bartlett paid a visit to Willard at the Belleclaire that fall, he found his friend's room full of files, books,
magazines, and cartons of papers. Willard was in a feverish,
hyperactive state, full of bravado and complicated plans. He had
given up on *The Mother,* but he was angling for a job writing titles
for some upcoming silent films, he told Bartlett, and he was very
hard at work on a reference book for writers. His *Encyclopedia of
English Usage,* a catalogue of common grammatical and stylistic
errors in writing, was going to take at least another year to
complete but was guaranteed "bread and butter money" when
Huebsch or some other publisher brought it out. Bartlett kept
his thoughts to himself but was doubtful that Willard, with his
nerves frayed and his weight dropping, had it in him to bring off
a vast scholarly undertaking of the kind he was describing. But
that wasn't all. Willard displayed his notes for *Philology and Literature,* planned as two volumes, to come out as soon as the
reference book was in print. If Mencken could write *The American Language,* the first edition of which had appeared in 1919,
Willard would outdo him in scope and linguistic learning. Bartlett left discouraged and amazed.

The situation was even worse than anyone could have known
who visited Willard in those months. Having exhausted all loan
possibilities, he was finally on the verge of emotional and economic bankruptcy. What Willard couldn't bring himself to admit
to Randolph Bartlett was that he was growing more fearful each
week that he didn't have the stamina or mental clarity to com-

plete any of these books and, even if he did, that they would leave him in the same financial limbo his writing had always kept him in. Again, the old point: without family money, or a steady university or newspaper or magazine berth, there was no hope. Cultural criticism was a luxury America did not support in the 1920s, as Willard was despondently ready to concede.

What he also failed to mention to Bartlett, and what he kept a careful secret from almost all his acquaintances in New York, was that he was preparing to point himself in a radically different direction. In May of that year, he had made his first reference to Katharine of having decided on a way "to come to the rescue." He spoke of his plan only as "his popular novel" and later as his "series of popular novels." After having devoted the better part of the last decade and a half to berating writers of fiction who put pen to paper for monetary reasons only, Willard was preparing in 1924 to do the same, to prove his earlier prediction to Stanton and Katherine Leeds—that on America's terms, he could come through if he put his mind to it.

Katharine and Annie weren't sure what to make of any of this. Willard was never explicit enough for them to have any clear notion of what this "popular novel" was going to be about. The thought that it would be a detective story would have astounded them, though they might have remembered Willard's odd mention of E. P. Oppenheim's mystery thrillers two years before. Willard's own discomfort was obvious, though. *The Encyclopedia of English Usage* and *Philology and Literature* were going to be all-important, Willard told his family, not only as educational works in themselves but to "counteract the detrimental effect of the [popular] novels on my reputation." They were also relentlessly instructed not to discuss this plan with anybody.

The most important "anybody" was Stanton. "I hope you have impressed upon Beverley," Willard wrote his wife, "not to mention, or let on, a word to Stanton about . . . the novels I am doing. If the facts got out it might hurt me a great deal; and I may use another name on the novels. In any event, he is not to be told anything. I can't explain, but it is important." What Willard couldn't explain, his family was easily able to intuit. As a result, even though Annie and Katharine urgently needed the money a bestseller might bring them, they came to share—from the very inception of the S. S. Van Dine books—an embarrassment over

Willard, circa 1907, about the time of his marriage.

The Arcadia Hotel in Santa Monica: the Wrights' first home in California.

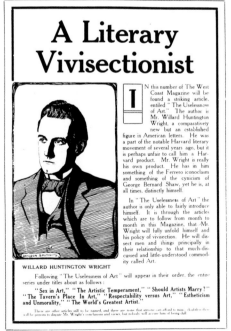

Announcing a new critic: *The West Coast Magazine*, 1909.

Willard's photo introducing him to the *Smart Set* readership in February 1913—a picture he had considerably retouched to appear older than his twenty-six years.

The last issue of *The Smart Set* over which Willard had editorial control; it contained a play by Joseph Conrad and a story by D. H. Lawrence.

Stanton's homage to Cezanne,
"Portrait of the Artist's
Brother," 1914. (THE
NATIONAL PORTRAIT GALLERY,
THE SMITHSONIAN INSTI-
TUTION)

Germanophile and
Nietzschean: Willard
in 1916 drawn by
Thomas Hart Benton.

One of Stanton's first abstract "synchromies," "Abstraction on Spectrum (Organization No. 5)" 1914. (DES MOINES ART
CENTER, COFFIN FINE ARTS TRUST FUND,
1962)

At Last—A Detective Story for the Intelligent!

THE BENSON MURDER CASE

A PHILO VANCE STORY

D. D. 19
NAME BENSON, Alvin H.
(Surname First)

ADDRESS 87 West 48th St.
CLASSIFICATION NUMBER | PRECINCT NUMBER | COMPLAINT NUMBER | DATE REPORTED
B-266 | 9 | 8427 | June 14

REMARKS Murder: Shot through head with
45 Colt automatic. Body discovered
7 a.m. by Anna Platz.

IN CHARGE Homicide Bureau and District Attorney.

New York Police Department | BUREAU OF HOMICIDE

"The Benson Murder Case" is on sale at all bookstores, $2.00, Charles Scribner's Sons.

S. S. Van Dine, who begins, in this book, to record the amazing investigations of a most unusual detective, Philo Vance, diagrams below one of Vance's bits of experimentation in his study of the Benson Murder.

Scribners' ad for the first book of the Philo Vance series, published in the fall of 1926.

Willard Huntington Wright and William Powell on the set at Paramount, 1928.

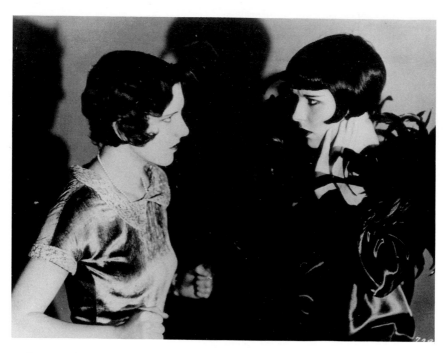

Jean Arthur and Louise Brooks in a scene from *The 'Canary' Murder Case*.

The second Philo Vance: Basil Rathbone *(right)* in *The Bishop Murder Case*, 1930.

S. S. Van Dine at home after the success of *The 'Canary' Murder Case,* 1927.

"As S. S. Van Dine Sees Himself": Willard's self-portrait, first published in *The Chicago Tribune.*

Willard with his new bride, Claire De Lisle, 1930.

Willard in his "dog phase," at the S. S. Van Dine Kennels in New Jersey, 1932.

S. S. Van Dine in the late 1930s.

Willard's prostitution of his gifts. They too wanted to avoid Stanton's bruising sarcasm. Not that Stanton wasn't interested in the good life. On the contrary, he craved it as avidly as his brother, and his marriage to Jeanne Redman, who came from a monied family, had put him on a secure footing. But it had never been in anyone's mind that a Wright would abandon art or literature to "go commercial" so publicly and flagrantly.

As Willard struggled with the plot of *The Benson Murder Case*, Stanton, living happily with Jeanne, was writing his *Treatise on Color* for private publication, becoming involved with the Santa Monica Theater Guild, and commencing his lifelong study of Oriental art that was to influence his own painting. To Willard, the contrast was excruciating.

Willard never pretended to have made the transformation from bedraggled literary man to famous detective novelist on his own. Two men, friends with whom he maintained the longest relationships of his life, helped in ways that no one else could have.

One was Doctor Jacob Lobsenz. Although he was an obstetrician, Lobsenz sometimes tended to Willard as a patient as well as a friend. He might even have been one of the many people Willard was in debt to, as Willard had averaged at least one costly illness every year—from pneumonia to an abscess to his impacted bowels—for four or five years. A tolerant and curious man, acquainted with many writers, he found Willard bright and amusing and was confident that his friend would eventually find his way out of his problems, physical, professional, and psychological. It's also likely that Lobsenz was instrumental in helping Willard to wean himself from marijuana and whatever other drugs he was still drawn to, or in steering him to the right doctors. Willard later remarked that it was Lobsenz's idea that he take a break during a period of depression by putting aside his art and philology texts and picking up some detective fiction. It seemed like a foolish suggestion to Willard but he gave it a try, to humor old "Doc Jake" as much as anything. He owed him that much.

Norbert Lederer, another gracious friend of Willard's, gave this venture a boost by opening his vast collection to him. A chemist by vocation, a serious criminologist, chess player, and tropical fish collector by avocation, he also eased Willard's initial trepidation about "wasting his time" with inferior books. Lederer had his doctorate, he was trilingual and learned in several disciplines, and he had absolutely no snobbish hesitation about well-written light fiction. In fact, he owned a staggering number of good detective novels, both American and European and, as Willard's account at Brentano's had been long since in arrears, he was Willard's means of getting his hands on some of the authors who were recommended to him.

Soon enough, this "experiment" turned into a binge, and ultimately, in typical Wright fashion, an obsession. Willard found himself enjoying a good many of the novels he read, which he thought of more as intellectual puzzles than as examples of literature, and his room filled with the kind of books "the literary vivisectionist" of Southern California had ruthlessly mocked only a dozen years before. At exactly what moment between 1922 and 1924 Willard ceased to be merely a reader and became a student of these "puzzles" with an eye on his own creations isn't clear, but it was probably by late 1923 (after the failure of *The Future of Painting*) that he was taking notes for the purpose of understanding what made some detective stories, and authors, better than others.

From Oppenheim, the lightest of the lot, Willard turned to the more accomplished H. C. Bailey and Eden Phillpotts, then to Ronald Knox and R. Austin Freeman, to A. E. Fielding and J. S. Fletcher, to Arthur Morrison and A. E. W. Mason. He read the few Americans who were said to have done anything substantial in this area, like Anna Katharine Green and Melville Davisson Post, and the young British woman everyone was curious about at the moment, Agatha Christie. Milne's *The Red House Mystery* and Phillpotts' *The Red Redmaynes* had come out in America at the same time, in 1922, and Willard devoured both of those with interest. Dorothy Sayers made her debut the next year with *Whose Body?* and Willard read that too, although he apparently didn't think any more of her than he did of Christie. All of Conan Doyle, Gaboriau, and Leroux, the already acknowledged classics of the genre like Hume's *The Mystery of the Hansom Cab,* Crofts' *The Cask,* and Bentley's *Trent's Last Case,* the Arsène Lupin tales and the Father Brown series and the Jacques Futrelle stories, and even the lesser writers like Arthur Reeve, John

Rhode, Ernest Poate, Baroness Orczy, Bennett Copplestone, and Burton Stevenson—everything, in short, that was readable, talked-about, and available in Lederer's library or from those booksellers who knew detective fiction, Willard bought and studied. Not long after Randolph Bartlett's visit, Willard put aside his manuscript for the writer's reference guide, shelved his notes for *Philology and Literature,* and gave himself up to the inevitable.

In due time Willard found his tastes developing along unambiguous lines. There was no reason, obviously, for him to be less opinionated about detective novels than he had been about other kinds of literature or about painting. To Willard's mind, Bailey, Phillpotts, Freeman, Knox, and Mason were the most entertaining and literate of the number. Too many of the "great" detective writers he read seemed to him shockingly lax. Excepting Post and Futrelle, this was especially true of the Americans. But even for the renowned Agatha Christie, who had published five books by the mid-Twenties and was already developing a loyal American audience, Willard had only limited enthusiasm. Hercule Poirot was mundane and pompous and (most annoyingly to Willard) "intuitional to the point of clairvoyance," as he later wrote. The Belgian sleuth seemed too often to solve a crime without really using those "little gray cells" he liked to jabber about. *The Mysterious Affair at Styles* and *The Murder on the Links* were reasonably engaging, Willard thought, but the famous trick of *Roger Ackroyd* was a device he hated. That kind of cleverness was something he was going to avoid, he decided, in his own detective stories, if this project he was formulating came to pass. The concept of "playing fair," something Christie didn't always adhere to, was becoming more important the longer he explored the field. Early on, it became something of a first principle.

In considering the protagonists of these many novels, even more than plot development and statements of clues, Willard was struck by the fact that there were two camps: those writers who saw the detective himself as somehow secondary to the story and the suspects, and those who believed in the creation of a vivid, ever-present, even imaginatively overpowering sleuth—a personality or temperament as memorable as the crime and the deduction itself. Christie was going to belong to the second group, though her Poirot wasn't yet amounting to much, and her countrywoman Dorothy Sayers was obviously working along the same lines with a still sketchy but striking figure, one Peter Wimsey. Conan Doyle with Sherlock Holmes, Bailey with Dr. Fortune, Chesterton with Fr. Brown, Mason with Hanaud of the Sûreté, and Post with Uncle Abner were the real leaders of that camp among the English-language writers, as their sleuths were known to anyone in America who read detective fiction in the Twenties. Indeed, they were names remembered by readers of their books who might have long since forgotten everything else about a given novel but could not forget the detective himself, with whatever flair or foibles his author had endowed him. There was sense in that approach, Willard recognized. It had both a pleasing practical and an aesthetic logic to it. This was, from the start, the group Willard felt most allied to.

An example of the risks run by a writer who paid more attention to the ingenuity of his plots or the skill of his descriptions than the liveliness of his hero was R. Austin Freeman. His were books Willard could respect, even relish, beyond anything Green, Christie, Fielding, Fletcher, or most other authors could manage, but there was still something wrong at the heart of them. For if Willard saw in Freeman's Dr. Thorndyke novels an example of detective fiction at its best—and Freeman was a master of good stories, fair and clever deductions, and fluent prose—he wasn't at all interested in creating a replica of the famous John Thorndyke. He later dismissed Freeman's sleuth as "elderly, plodding, painstaking, humorless, and amazingly dry." Nor was this detective on stage much of the time in some of the better books. In Freeman's classic *The Eye of Osiris,* Thorndyke moves to the center of the drama only in the last third of the story, an authorial decision Willard regarded as ludicrous. The detective he had in mind was going to be someone a good deal more colorful and commanding, an unusual character who would dominate the story from start to finish.

For the makings of such a character, he had only to look to himself. Little by little, as he took notes through 1924 and 1925 and gave the matter more thought, the presence of Philo Vance began to assert itself on Willard's imagination. Once established, this "presence" enabled Willard to work more rapidly and comfortably than he had in a long time. It was not the sort of work Willard would ever have envisioned himself being rejuvenated by, but that was its delightful and unexpected effect.

■ ■ ■

Whether Willard evolved a conception of his detective first, or gave attention to the construction of his plots, is another part of his development as a detective writer that isn't clear. It is true, though, that almost from the beginning Willard didn't see his authorship of a crime novel as an isolated event, a one-shot attempt at making some good money. It was too hard for a single novel, out of the tens of thousands of books published every year, to find an audience—Willard had reviewed enough of them to know that much. A new writer, or one planning to use a pseudonym, needed a more developed ploy. He concluded that he was going to have to approach a publisher with a "package," and one that seemed foolproof at first hearing. Hence, the idea for a series with a distinctive protagonist and a common style. What inroads the first novel made among the mass of detective-fiction readers, the second and third—appearing in quick succession—would capitalize on.

For the first two books Willard took two recent real-life unsolved crimes for his premise. The plot of *The Benson Murder Case,* as he called his first story, would have sounded tantalizingly similar to the much-discussed Joseph Elwell murder of 1920. Elwell, a wealthy stockbroker and noted bridge player, had been found shot to death seated in his living room chair in his locked brownstone apartment with no apparent signs of forcible entry. Despite an intensive police investigation, neither the weapon nor Elwell's murderer was ever found. Willard changed the names, invented his own cast of suspects, witnesses, and investigators, but used enough of the original crime—principally, its flavor of affluence and cunning—to interest a Twenties reader.

For the second, *The "Canary" Murder Case,* Willard turned to a more lurid and more timely episode, "Dot" King's murder in 1923. Dorothy King was "the Broadway Butterfly," a promiscuous beauty with the requisite expensive tastes and dangerous boyfriends. Her strangulation by one of her companions in her small West Side apartment still fascinated the public long after the police gave up trying to determine which man was responsible for King's exceedingly well-planned death. In Willard's version, the "butterfly" became a "canary," and he worked out an elaborate story of flappers, speakeasies, blackmail, and scandal. For the third book, *The Greene Murder Case,* with its purely fictitious premise, Willard envisioned a dark family drama of sibling rivalry and painful secrets in a nineteenth-century East Side mansion.

The stockbroker with a double life, the Broadway party girl, the Old New York family in decay: everybody's interests would be accommodated, according to this careful plan, in the three Philo Vance novels Willard hoped to have in first-draft form by the end of 1925.

Memorable names mattered as much as memorable personalities to Willard, and the naming of his sleuth required great care. Willard left few records or notes about the process, but the result is a ripe field for speculation. In its etymology, "Philo" implied, of course, the love of language in the protagonist he was shaping, whereas "Vance" was a suitably plain and euphonious match to an otherwise odd first name. Yet there was another, very minor detective writer in the business—Louis Joseph Vance— and a character, Philo Gubb, by Joseph Ellis Butler, whose pairing would serve to remind book buyers, consciously or otherwise, of other novelists they might know. (Butler himself was the first to ponder this "coincidence," wondering in a good-natured way if Willard Wright's own conscious or unconscious had been at work here.) Such a reading of the name choice makes sense: Willard had been a "borrower" since the days of his Mencken discipleship, and taking names from two men who had managed to make a living in the marketplace of commercial prose only implied, to whoever knew him well enough, Willard's ambivalence over what he was about to do.

If the name "Philo Vance" harked to the future and the new world he was entering, the name of Willard's author-narrator looked to his past. Of the "S.S.," Willard commented that the steamship abbreviation would be easy for readers (and booksellers) to remember; of the "Van Dine," that it was an old family name on his mother's side. The first point is true, but the second is not. There are no Van Dines evident in the family tree. At another time Willard remarked that he selected the word "dine" with some ironic thought to his years of living on less food than he had cared to, and there is probably more seriousness than not in that tidbit of humor. It is also the case that "S.S." was the common abbreviation for *The Smart Set*—echoes of Willard's happiest days—and that Van Dinc is very close to Van Dyck, Rubens' peer, with all the associations with painting, aristocratic living, and accomplishment that that great name reverberates.

In any event, Willard made some telling and peculiar choices concerning the role this narrator and this detective were to play in his novels. Van Dine is a noncharacter, a mute observer and recorder of events who is not allowed to speak—not once—in his own voice in the dialogue of the stories. Unlike Watson, Hastings, Polton, Archie Goodwin, or any other narrator of comparable importance before or after him, Van Dine—a lawyer and a prosaic soul—hasn't been given a trace of a personality himself. He is unmercifully silenced. Everything, but everything, was lavished on Philo Vance. But even here there was a bit of playing with mirrors, or playing with names. "Philo Vance" is actually a pseudonym, Van Dine tells his readers in the introduction to *The Benson Murder Case*, for the real genius-detective-aesthete who solved the crimes that New York's police couldn't fathom and whose name Van Dine will never be at liberty to divulge. Thus, Willard Wright the author hides behind the mask of S. S. Van Dine, a paper figure who writes about a brilliant eccentric who is hidden behind the name of Philo Vance.

This manipulation of names served a reassuring purpose. Nothing could be concrete or aboveboard for Willard as he explored this unfamiliar territory. He had too many fears to confront—that he would fail in his gamble to secure himself a fresh start, that the prize wouldn't equal the risk, or that he would succeed but suffer a mortifying, pyrrhic triumph in front of the writers and painters who laughed at corny bestsellers. It seemed safer, the more Willard pondered it, to cultivate a strict anonymity, to build symbolic layers of protection. A man who fancied himself a Leo Stein or a Hippolyte Taine couldn't be seen trying to make himself into Arthur Conan Doyle or Agatha Christie.

Yet, in spite of all the superficial signs that Willard was anxious and embarrassed about what he was doing once he had put aside his "serious" work, there is just as much reason to suspect that he was pleased, even liberated. The energy and fastidiousness with which he threw himself into the labor of writing about sophisticated murders and fantastic deductions reveal the true pleasure in the task. In fact, at thirty-eight years of age in 1925, Willard was determined to make a good job of it, not only because so much in his life depended on the project's success but because it became less of a chore, and more of a thrill, the longer he lived with it. How could writing about an amateur detective and art connoisseur who was so like himself, or his image of himself, not have been an exuberant and ego-gratifying experience? The man who was going to solve the Benson, "Canary," and Greene murders, as Willard described him, was good-looking and intellectual, snobbish and sensitive, "casual, mercurial, debonair, and whimsically cynical." A dilettante "of unusual culture and brilliance . . . an aristocrat by birth and instinct, he held himself severely aloof from the common world."

Stanford West in *The Man of Promise* had been an earnest, dour projection of his creator. Philo Vance was going to be a fantasy projection of a different kind, more demanding and more potent.

Willard's correspondence to Katharine and Annie dropped off considerably in 1925 as he spent more and more time on the detective novels, reworking clues and settings and details of character. He never went out socially anymore, he assured his wife, as every moment was given up to "the deadly delectable grind" of writing. The one and only break for him that year was a week at the beach in April, at Atlantic City, courtesy of an unnamed friend. When Katharine wrote in midsummer to say that she couldn't live any longer on her own salary and the $25 a month Willard was sending, he urged her to consider his predicament and be patient. "I am absolutely penniless," Willard wrote. "I have been ill—most of the time in bed— for over a year; I have done no writing but a few hack articles. If it hadn't been for some of my friends paying my bills—or rather part of them—God knows what would have happened."

As the end of the year approached, Willard quietly readied himself for his first move with the Philo Vance stories. He bought some new clothes and ordered a small set of business cards. "This is to impress the publishers and editors with my opulence," Willard explained to Katharine, to justify the expense. "If they think you're prosperous, they imagine you're a better writer!" He also decided that a new life required a new home and, in November, Willard left the Belleclaire, the scene of so much pain and hope for him, and resettled down the block in a large studio at 312 West 75th Street. At last, in December he was ready.

The first publisher Willard approached with his three plot summaries was Horace Liveright. The firm of Boni and Liveright had published Willard's anthology of French short stories and it had always seemed the most likely prospect. But this small company was entering a shaky period. Uneasy about his future, the usually daring Liveright was reluctant to take on the gamble he was presented with. Detective fiction by an American author was a commodity with an uncertain history. Americans tended to look to the British for their crime novels. For that matter, in this area Willard himself was an unproven commodity.

Oddly enough, Liveright's rejection didn't devastate Willard. A small publishing house could take him just so far. Another, better plan suddenly came to mind that month, with the possibility of greater financial returns. The loss, he rightly concluded, would be Liveright's.

"S. S. VAN DINE"

"When an author has been so unfortunate as to write a popular novel, it is a difficult thing to live down the reputation. Personally I have no sympathy with such a person, for there are few punishments too severe for a popular novel writer."

—*Willard Huntington Wright, 1909*

Max Perkins wasn't a close friend of Willard's at Harvard or in the years after, when both of them began working in New York. But he had followed his classmate's roller-coaster career from the *Smart Set* days through the publication of his eight books, and he certainly knew Willard's reputation. The frightening part of that reputation—the image of Willard as a high-strung, inflexible man with a tendency to undermine his own best interests—didn't worry Perkins at all. The Scribners editor responsible for nurturing F. Scott Fitzgerald, Ernest Hemingway, and Ring Lardner into print knew the extremes of the literary temperament. More to the point for Perkins, Willard still enjoyed a reputation as a fastidious writer and a methodical, almost compulsive worker. When Willard called him with his proposal, Perkins was curious.

Over lunch at the Century Club in January, Willard left the editor his three plot summaries. He tried to sound calm, optimistic, and knowledgeable about the genre he was venturing into, and he made a great point of his desire for anonymity. Perkins was suitably impressed with Willard's eagerness and understood his concern about using his own name. He promised to get back to him as soon as possible.

For three weeks, Willard lived in suspense, and then the answer came: Scribners was interested. There hadn't been much to debate at the office, in fact. Everyone, including Charles Scribner, agreed that the books were going to be sound, marketable products and the contract sent to Willard called for publication of all three novels over a three-year period. An advance for $3,000 was ready in early February. Realizing that this was more money than he had earned in the last five years, Willard was ecstatic. The turnabout had begun.

Though Perkins had read Arthur Conan Doyle in his youth, like everyone else, he had never followed modern detective fiction. Nonetheless, his instincts about Willard's project were strong; the Philo Vance stories had the right feel to them. Willard seemed to Perkins to have imagined his sleuth with a remarkable precision and vividness, and the plots were worked out in fascinating detail. Perkins also knew that he would be working with a writer he could trust, one who was in fact almost neurotically addicted to work, thorough by nature, and responsible about deadlines.

For his part, thinking about Perkins' track record and editorial expertise, Willard was able to enjoy a degree of confidence about the future such as he had not been able to feel in several years. His letters to Katharine were guarded in these months, but to friends in New York he was more relaxed and hopeful.

With $3,000 in his pocket and the promise of much more to come, Willard was ready to rejoin the world, by degrees. One of the first people he wanted to see was his old ally from the art wars, Alfred Stieglitz. In February he stopped by The Intimate Gallery, as Stieglitz was calling his new space in Mitchell Kennerley's Madison Avenue building. Beyond a few Christmas cards, Stieglitz hadn't heard anything from or about Willard in four or five years, and he was delighted to see him now. After all he had been through, Willard felt compelled in this setting to play the world-weary cynic. What excitement he was feeling about the Scribners deal, he wasn't going to share in this camp. He told Stieglitz that his only ambition was to leave America forever, that it had become a truly impossible country for a writer and aesthete to live in. But Stieglitz had heard enough talk about expatriation from his artists. "You can't escape," he gently reminded Willard. "You would find America all over the world."

Only a few art critics had come in to see the Arthur Doves on display at The Intimate Gallery that month, but the pictures arrested Willard's attention. This show included some of Dove's older, almost abstract oils and a new vein of work for the artist, portrait collages he called "assemblages," which no one bought and most viewers ignored. Dove's triumphant but unappreciated creativity was something of a reminder of a world Willard Huntington Wright was no longer at the center of, and a penurious way of life his new contract was probably going to free him from. For Dove's situation was classic, and grim: he made his paintings as he had to and wanted to, but he was barely surviving. Unlike O'Keeffe, Marin, Demuth, and others Stieglitz had sponsored along the way, Arthur Dove wasn't profiting from Twenties affluence or the growing cosmopolitan interest in new art. Willard admired the painter's stamina as much as his remarkable talent. Almost tenderly and sadly, he lingered over the paintings he recalled from earlier days. Dove's "Fishing Nigger" was "a wonderful painting," Willard told Stieglitz before he left, and the abstract "Cow" was "even more magnificent" than he remembered. Dove deserved better, Willard insisted, and went on his way.

Throughout the spring Willard worked on *The Benson Murder Case*. He saw Thomas Hart Benton a few times, and Claire more regularly, but restricted his socializing until he could gauge the pace of his writing. With this book as with all the others in the series, he proceeded through three stages: first, the 10,000-word outline, then a 30,000-word draft, followed by a final draft of 50,000 words. As the publication date was set for early October, "S. S. Van Dine" needed to be done with Philo Vance's first foray into criminal detection by midsummer. He was also acutely aware that the book had to live up to its author's lofty claims and its editor's high expectations. This Willard felt he achieved. The fictionalized story of Joseph Elwell's murder was brought to a close in late June, just when Willard promised Perkins it would be, and he then left town for a few weeks of rest at a New Jersey resort.

The strain Willard was feeling was dramatically apparent that

182

summer in a way it hadn't been in the spring. The future held out the promise of all sorts of rewards, but the present continued to be a muddle, both financially and emotionally, and it exhausted Willard. At Lake Hopatcong in New Jersey, Willard stayed with Claire and her daughter. During the week, he dined at their table at night and lounged with them on the beach in the afternoon. When Mr. Schermerhorn arrived on Friday night or Saturday morning to join his family, Willard would retreat into the background, dining by himself in another part of the hotel restaurant and making himself scarce until breakfast on Monday morning. None of the black waiters at the hotel cared to wait on Willard, as his testiness and racist language were offensive to everyone within hearing distance. The maître d' was nightly forced to seat Willard, when he was alone or with Claire and her child, in different parts of the room. No waiter would take him at the same station two nights in a row.

One evening the situation became more than a minor embarrassment. Claire's daughter brought her dog to the table with them. The waiter politely explained that dogs were not allowed in the hotel dining room and that the animal would have to be removed. Jumping up from his seat, Willard flew into a rage and demanded to speak to the maître d'. He wasn't going to "take orders from niggers," he announced hysterically to the whole room. The maître d' gave no satisfaction, and the Wright-Schermerhorn party stormed out toward the manager's office, but not before Willard overturned a whole tray of dishes and cups and saucers and hurled a few more names back at the stunned waiters and horrified guests. He demanded an apology from the manager who, in turn, asked Willard to pack and leave the hotel immediately.

This was an ugly side of himself—violently angry, bitter, irrational, more openly racist as he got older—that Willard kept carefully hidden from Perkins, Stieglitz, and most of the literary and artistic people he knew in New York. But it was there, erupting whenever he felt thwarted or, worse, patronized.

As October approached, Willard had reason to be calmer. Scribners was going all-out to promote *The Benson Murder Case*. One press release announced that "Philo Vance will inevitably find a literary niche alongside of that triumvirate of immortal sleuths, Monsieur Lecoq, Auguste Dupin, and Sherlock

Holmes." The advertising office came up with the plan of distributing 1,300 facsimile cards of a New York Police Department crime report, complete with the name and address of the deceased (Alvin Benson, West 48th Street, New York City), date and circumstance of death (June 14th, gunshot wound), and investigating officer (Sgt. Ernest Heath), an idea picked up by the design department for the dust jacket. A more than usual number of reviewers' copies had been sent out so that the first edition could be heavily "blurbed," and newspaper ads were plentiful following the novel's publication on the 8th of October.

Not long after his thirty-ninth birthday that month, Willard could look forward to paying off some of his more pressing debts and reopening his old charge accounts. *The Benson Murder Case* sold briskly (50,000 copies by early 1927), was given reasonable reviews in the dailies and in the monthly magazines, and had everyone even remotely interested in detective fiction wondering who "S. S. Van Dine" was. Even William Lyon Phelps of Yale had flattering things to say about the book, a fact that Willard chortled over, as Phelps had never thought much of Willard Wright the critic. Only two or three significantly nasty reviews appeared that winter, the worst in January, too late and too incidental to affect the novel's sales. The new critic for *The Saturday Review of Literature*, a young freelancer by the name of Dashiell Hammett, was one of the only reviewers to make the point that the identity of the *Benson Case* murderer is apparent to any alert reader right from the start. More irritating than this lack of ingenuity, to Hammett, was the strange dandy at the heart of the book, Vance himself, who had "the conversational manner of a high school girl who has been studying the foreign words and phrases at the back of her dictionary."

Hammett's wasn't a name that meant anything to Willard in 1927, nor did his crotchety opinion count for much. By New Year's Willard Huntington Wright was several thousand dollars richer and S. S. Van Dine was famous.

Willard was entering the field at the right moment. American detective fiction was at an abysmal point in the mid-Twenties. Or, it might even be more accurate to say that it had never lived up to its early promise. The genre may have originated in America, with Poe, but American writers had failed to keep pace with their British counterparts in devising effective tales of mystery, crime, and detection. Between "The Murders in the Rue Morgue" and "The Purloined Letter," the accepted starting points from the 1840s, and Anna Katharine Green's barrage of novels in the 1880s and '90s, few detective stories of any merit were published in the United States. Even after the turn of the century, the native writer who combined popularity with a modicum of craft, like Green, Mary Roberts Rinehart, or Melville Davisson Post, was a rare exception. Hackwork was expected from the Americans. It was the British who held the field. First Wilkie Collins, then Arthur Conan Doyle, and later Phillpotts, Freeman, Bentley, Bailey, Chesterton, Christie, and Sayers claimed the attention of a faithful American readership and gave detective fiction what little social acceptance it enjoyed on this side of the Atlantic.

But even the early following of the British writers was not always the most discriminating. The gap between "literature" and detective fiction was thought of as something unbridgeable. Readers of detective novels were a suspect group. That stigma of quasi-literacy remains today, of course, in certain snobbish circles, but before the 1920s the idea that academic or reputable professional critics would direct their attention to "crime novels" would have been considered farfetched. It was a mode of writing associated with pulp-fiction sensationalism and indifferent craftsmanship—necessarily "appeal[ing] to the most primitive cravings within us," as Willard had written in the *Times* eighteen years earlier. The Philo Vance novels, coming at the right time, changed all that for good. Exceeding anyone's expectations, the S. S. Van Dine series created a vast and heterogeneous market. They raised the caliber of that shaky audience and its literary standards, and they ended the British monopoly. It was Willard's achievement to legitimize and invigorate detective fiction in America and, unintentionally, to pave the way for others who would soon surpass him.

The intricacy of his plots, which had impressed Perkins, was only one aspect of Willard's accomplishment. His detective's method of deduction, described by Vance in the first book and evident in most of the later novels, was the more distinctive and entertaining feature of the series. Cases weren't "cracked" by the accumulation and analysis of clues leading to a "factual" deduction, the usual police process. Vance's method was one he liked to characterize as psychological and artistic. He would study, with a refined attention to detail, all the circumstances surrounding the murder and compile a theoretical profile of the individual likely to have committed an act of violence in exactly that manner. The suspects were then matched against the specific details of the murders, in contrast to the usual method of "logically" following the clues to the guilty individual. After all, "the only real clues," Vance tells District Attorney Markham in *The Benson Murder Case* (sounding a bit like Willard's old Harvard professor, Hugo Münsterberg), "are psychological, not material." Like an art expert determining the authorship of a painting, Vance examines not only the pigment and underpainting but "the creative personality," the unique élan, of the painter. Only one man could have painted "Night Watch," Vance intones to his friend Markham, and the true aesthete would know by the brushstrokes and chiaroscuro that it had to be Rembrandt; only one man could have murdered Alvin Benson in that particular fashion, and the alert analyst of the scene of the crime would know who that is.

But beyond the elaborate style of detection and the approach to crime displayed in *The Benson Murder Case,* and soon after in the *"Canary"* and *Greene* murder cases, it was the figure of Philo Vance himself which ensured the popularity of the books Willard was laboring over. Ultimately as famous in his day as Sherlock Holmes or Hercule Poirot, Vance was an original. Several people at Scribners who read the first drafts of *Benson* and *"Canary"* suggested that Willard tone down his protagonist's alienating smugness and countless eccentricities. Dutifully Perkins passed these suggestions on to Willard, whose reply was terse. There was no need for Vance to be likable, Willard explained. That never really mattered. It was enough that he should be memorable.

Embodying so many of his creator's interests, quirks, and frustrations, Philo Vance could only have been a character of Willard Huntington Wright's design. The long dark night of Willard's breakdown years hadn't given way to a benevolent sleuth or a gracious emissary of justice, on the order of Father Brown or Lord Peter Wimsey, but to a strange, cynical aesthete. An art student and connoisseur, Vance is a man with the intellectual skill to solve brilliantly devised crimes and serve the law better than the police but who does so only on his own terms. His terms involve firm control of the interrogations, emotional detachment from the plight of the victims, more-than-occasional bending of the letter of the law, and a healthy skepticism for circumstantial evidence and mere facts. Needless to add, despite the aggressively flippant manner of Willard's character, the murderer never escapes detection, nor are the police ever of the slightest help in solving the case.

Philo Vance leads the intellectual's ultimate fantasy life. A bachelor, untroubled by women, he lives in quiet luxury, impressing everyone with his formidable vocabulary and occupying his time with whatever scholarly pursuits interest him at the moment. Yet the world-at-large needs him. The men of practical affairs come knocking at his door. The expert help he offers the police with their toughest cases is given largely for the satisfaction of his own curiosity, for the joy of wrestling with a complicated challenge, or as a favor to Markham. So divorced is Vance from the ordinary motives of detectives and police officers that, when the criminal is particularly clever, Vance is apt to unmask him with reluctance, regretfully ending a well-suited match. His respect is often with his adversary. Only grudgingly does Vance admit the necessity of serving something as abstract and unpleasant as "the good of society." Were it not for the involvement of the authorities in each case, Vance is perfectly capable of solving the crime as he would a difficult puzzle—and then letting the guilty one go free, if he had reason to believe that the murderer would resist any further temptations to homicide. His highest regard is reserved for the murderer who commits suicide in preference to a trial and imprisonment, an act he will even tacitly assist in.

Between and during cases, Vance buys Cézanne watercolors at preview exhibitions, reads Freud and Spengler, attends afternoon concerts at Carnegie Hall, and works sporadically on his translations (never completed, as far as we know) of Delacroix's journals and lost Menander plays. Attended to by his friend and assistant S. S. Van Dine, the narrator of all the books, and by his butler, Currie, Vance makes his home in Manhattan in a town house between Park and Madison avenues on 38th Street—an address, by the end of the Twenties, as recognizable as Holmes'

Baker Street flat. The surroundings include Renoir bathers, Picasso still-lifes, Chinese ceramics, and a vast, esoteric library. An inheritance from an "Aunt Agatha" has made this charmed life possible (Agatha Christie paving the way for Willard Wright?), but Philo Vance makes no apologies for his privileged lifestyle. In the Jazz Age none was needed, as Willard had rightly concluded. A man who knew how to spend his money, a know-it-all with style, had automatic appeal.

What had become of Willard Wright the student of the French realists, the partisan of Moore and Dreiser, when he began his detective novels? He was nowhere to be found in these first enjoyable, never-credible, almost antirealistic tales. If anything, Willard had reverted to the still earlier, more deeply felt influence on his intellectual life: to his beloved Oscar Wilde and a concocted world of fable, elegance, and patrician disdain. No doubt Wilde would have recognized a kindred spirit in Philo Vance, and in 1926 a good number of readers were happy to accept the terms of Van Dine's literary game.

With *The Benson Murder Case* off to a good (though not spectacular) start, and anticipating even stronger returns on *The "Canary" Murder Case,* the Scribners publicity department lost no time in getting S. S. Van Dine before the public. Willard couldn't be produced in person, of course, as no one was supposed to know yet who he really was, but the name of Van Dine appeared in more and more ads, review reprints, and newspaper and gossip columns throughout the winter and into the spring of 1927. Scribners added to the mystery by the intentionally terse, cryptic biographical statements it released: "Mr. Van Dine is a man in his thirties," one press statement read, "who has had some legal experience, and was educated at Harvard." Willard himself, under his own name, contributed to the stir in a small way with an essay on the history of detective fiction for the November issue of *Scribner's Magazine.*

One tactic for priming the market, novel for its time, was the connection of their celebrity's name with the events of the day. When the lurid Hall-Mills case in Somerville, New Jersey, came to trial, it was one of the year's sensational news items, and S. S. Van Dine was asked by reporters to comment through his publisher's office. Willard didn't have anything remotely relevant to say about the identity of the murderer in this grisly double killing of an adulterous minister and a married female parishioner, but he used the occasion to remind those following the Somerville trial (which was every adult in the metropolitan area) of Philo Vance's "esthétique du crime." "Every murder differs from every other murder—each has its own conditions and circumstances, as well as peculiarities, which indicate the character and temperament of the person who committed it," Van Dine noted. The sensitive art lover would know a Corot landscape, he lectured his readers, without a title, a date, or a signature attached to the painting. The imprint of that artist, and that artist only, would be there for the trained eye to detect. So too was the imprint of the Hall-Mills murderer there to be read by those who could look beyond circumstantial clues for psychological imprints.

If Philo Vance was an outlandish and insufferable fantasy figure, a character who could only have found a large audience in the self-consciously cosmopolitan Twenties, "S. S. Van Dine" the author was no less preposterous. He was that new commodity on the American scene, the all-purpose public intellectual, and the press judged him, quickly and accurately enough, as solid copy. Generalities about Corot landscapes and New Jersey murderers were picked up by the wire services and reappeared in literally hundreds of newspapers, as if some wise counsel were being spread far and wide.

So confident was Scribners about the success of Willard's second novel and the whole erudite persona they were fashioning that it was decided to serialize the *"Canary"* novel in the house's own magazine. This was the first time a detective story ever appeared in the venerable *Scribner's Magazine*, a stodgy journal that had been publishing topical essays, travel and historical articles, and "literary" stories of varying quality for almost fifty years. Beginning with the May 1927 issue and concluding four months later, the magazine came out in an expanded edition, dividing the novel into four parts. That was also a departure for *Scribner's*, which usually serialized short novels over eight or nine issues, but the marketing people knew they had a good thing in Willard's story and they were eager to concentrate interest on the novel and have it in the bookstores in July. That guaranteed that even those who had been reading the installments in the magazine would be potential purchasers of the book, on the assumption that they wouldn't be able to wait until August for the unmasking of the murderer. And the perfect "vacation read" could be on the shelves for at least half of the summer.

An unexpected dividend from the advertising point of view emerged from Willard's insistence on a pseudonym, and the publicists played that angle for all it was worth. Some of the curiosity about the real S. S. Van Dine was genuine. Letters-to-the-editor pages in later issues of *Scribner's* and various newspapers were filled with guesses and grateful comments about the new author. But some of it was manufactured—excitement existing more on the pages of press releases than in reality—as most detective-novel readers wouldn't have known Willard's name to begin with, or cared who he was. Harry Hansen, the literary editor of *The New York World,* did his own sleuthing and uncovered the truth (not that hard a thing to do for anyone in circulation in New York) but was somehow induced not to spoil the fun. When Scribners announced that Hansen's choice for the honor was Edmund Lester Pearson, the noted criminologist (which wouldn't have been a bad guess), Hansen didn't deny the story. He merely commented that he knew who Van Dine actually was, and he was a learned man indeed. Pearson had been on many people's minds, though Carl Van Doren, Arthur Train, and George Jean Nathan were three other frequent subjects of speculation.

Yet still more publicity was generated that spring by an eerie coincidence. The facsimile police-report cards Scribners had sent around the country as postcards for *The Benson Murder Case* were repeated for the new crime. A card, announcing the death by strangulation of Margaret Odell, "Follies" dancer, of 184 West 71st Street, Sergeant Heath investigating, was found on a street in Toledo, Ohio, and handed over to the police there. As it turned out, a woman by the name of Margaret Odell had been missing from Toledo for some time. The Ohio police contacted their colleagues in Manhattan, who were rather mystified by the whole thing. They hadn't heard of the crime, but they knew a sergeant by the name of Heath in New York, though he had retired in 1903 and the precinct marked on the card as Heath's hadn't existed until the early 1920s. Nor was there such an address on West 71st Street. An alert reporter was able to sort out the confusion at the police station and file a good story on the mix-up. It was the last time Scribners employed this gimmick, or needed to.

However much the excitement over *The "Canary" Murder Case* might have been a product of savvy postwar Madison Avenue strategies, it clearly found its audience on its own strengths. No amount of manipulating by sales experts in and of itself could have caused the newsstand rush on the copies of *Scribner's Magazine* that followed the first installment of Willard's tale. It is always hard to account for the excessive popularity in its time of literature that seems to later generations ephemeral rather than classic. As James Hart observed in *The Popular Book*, his study of bestsellers and American literary taste, to be a runaway success at the moment of its publication a novel must often deal with ideas already in circulation or mass attitudes and feelings shaped by unique contemporary pressures. Such a book often represents a break with the past, but not too radical a break, and speaks to the newly evolving emotional needs of the present.

Hart's comment is certainly true of Willard's version of Dot King's murder. It had nothing of the tired air of British country houses or Scottish moors about it, nothing of foreign intrigue or Victorian character types. Old forms and mundane realities were just what Willard had consciously tried to avoid. Instead he dealt in character types of the modern city, specifically the side of Manhattan life that readers in the Twenties were eager to know about and were already mythologizing. This was a world of nightclubs and kept women, Broadway musicals and bootleg liquor, rich dandies and men in expensive suits with their own egotistical values (be they businessmen or criminals, or both). Willard's sprinkling of real names throughout his story or in footnotes—Odell once had a song specially composed for her by Buddy de Sylva, Philo Vance stops in at Stieglitz's gallery, various stage celebrities and cardsharks are mentioned—added nicely to the effect.

Ten years before, with *The Genius*, Dreiser had been hounded for telling a story of "ordinary" promiscuity and an unconventional artist's needs. Now, as Willard knew, that novel was dismissed by the younger generation, not as too realistic and offensive but as too banal. Readers wanted sin (as distinct from realism), glamour, aloofness, a veneer of education, and not a trace of sentiment. This was what Willard's mysteries provided. The very amorality of all the principal characters of *The "Canary" Murder Case*, including the sleuth whose view of life is more aesthetic than moral, spoke to an era, or a segment of the population, that wanted to see itself as just a bit gone-to-hell, quite knowing, and rightly removed from the pieties of the previous generation.

When Philo Vance allows the murderer at the end of the story a minute to step into a private room before his arrest, deducing that he is about to shoot himself, Willard was giving his character a flagrantly contemporary, almost Nietzschean air, an aura that the new reader was primed for. The upright District Attorney Markham is nonplussed to learn that Vance didn't try to prevent the suicide, to which his friend replies that there was after all something "rather colossal" and admirable about the deceased man. "Pray don't give way to conventional moral indignation," he tells Markham, a thought all but unprintable in America before the Great War and the new mores.

Willard swiftly accustomed himself to the exciting changes in his life. For the first time he faced the prospect of being able to support himself and his wife and daughter, and—even more remarkably—of being able to live in some degree of comfort. Whatever snobbish embarrassment Katharine felt about her husband's career as a detective novelist was mitigated by the thought of the money. Since leaving her brother-in-law's business, she had never held a job for more than a few months at a time before collapsing under the strain of some new malady, while Beverley had been compelled to find work as soon as she graduated after an unhappy few years at Palo Alto High School. For all concerned, the future looked brighter.

Willard was clever, or defensive, enough to be circumspect about his money. Instead of boasting about his triumph to those who knew he was S. S. Van Dine, he was scrupulously reserved on the subject of his new advances and imminent royalties. There were too many people, including those who had written off their loans to Willard as lost money, ready to press their claims, some of them stretching back ten years. So Willard adopted a pose, which later proved hard to drop, of never having quite as much in the bank as people assumed he did. He was able to pay Buddy de Sylva back, but he was in no rush to come up with the hundreds of dollars he separately owed to Mencken, Huebsch, Kennerley, Leeds, Lobsenz, Claire Schermerhorn, and several other people. There was always that nagging fear that all of his profits would be eaten up if he paid back absolutely everyone he had ever borrowed from. The list was too long.

With the appearance in hardcover of The "Canary" Murder Case on July 22nd, 1927, though, everything changed faster than Willard had expected. His success this time was of an order that would have been hard to obscure. The second book of the series was that happiest of publisher and author's dreams, the instant bestseller. All of the marketing office's calculations paid off as The "Canary" Murder Case passed the 20,000 mark in its first week, the 60,000 mark in its first month, and by the end of the year broke every sales record for its genre, amply surpassing (and thus renewing) the sales of The Benson Murder Case, which was still in print.

The reviewers were also far more attentive than they had been toward Philo Vance's first exploit, giving "Canary" about six times the newspaper and magazine review space of its predecessor. In December William Lyon Phelps added the book to his list of the ten best novels of the year, and the popular editor and columnist William Allen White was obliging enough to allow his own beaming photograph to be used in the ads. "[The 'Canary' Murder Case] magnificently smashed the old taboos into fine smithereens," Howard Haycraft noted in his history of the detective story. It became, in fact, "a sort of national cause." Orders to restock could hardly be kept up with. Summer in 1927 meant Mah-Jongg, crossword puzzles, King Tut, and the faintly scandalous life of Margaret Odell and her five lovers. Even the British press was kindly disposed, for once, to an American detective novel.

Not surprisingly, given all this attention, the number of fault-finding reviews for Willard's work increased dramatically as well. Several notices in prominent papers harped on Vance's excruciatingly artificial, talkative, and condescending manner and made mention of his almost accidental resolution of the crime. (At the end of The "Canary" Murder Case, Vance is convinced that he knows which of the suspects is guilty but lacks the means to prove it, until he happens, by luck rather than by his own reasoning, on the crucial evidence that has been left behind in the

Canary's apartment.) Yet, as is always the case with a well-known book, the general public intends to read regardless of reviewers' comments, the unfavorable notices served only to heighten interest in the novel and stimulate sales. Even the most well-argued reservations about America's newest detective writer didn't do anything to deter the devoted. Side by side with *Elmer Gantry, The Bridge of San Luis Rey,* and Charles Lindbergh's first postflight memoir, Willard's was the essential book that summer and fall for the thousands of readers who wanted to keep abreast of the latest publishing landslide.

Once his novel was securely lodged on the bestseller lists, Willard knew that he had actually fulfilled that idle prophecy made to Stanton and Katherine Leeds seven years earlier. On his own terms, and those of his brother and of Stieglitz, Dreiser, Mencken, Pound, and the rest of them, he couldn't "make it." On America's terms, the terms he had been fighting for twenty years, he could be at the top of the pile. At the moment, the irony seemed to Willard screamingly funny.

"There are no second acts in American lives," goes the Fitzgerald adage made famous by his own experience. But Willard's life proves otherwise. His "second act," beginning at the age of thirty-nine, gave promise to be far more extravagant than his "first act" life as a rancorous art critic and man of letters.

A NEW LIFE

"It was all rather crazy, rather splendid."
　　　　　　—Sherwood Anderson, on the Twenties

The success of S. S. Van Dine is very much a story of the Twenties, an example of nerve, excess, instant gratification, good publicity, and superb showmanship. The whole experience had a lavishness to it such as Willard had never imagined for himself. Yet in the aftermath of the *"Canary"* 's great sales, almost stunned by the doors being opened to him, Willard barely had time to enjoy the benefits of his situation.

He spent most of the fall of 1927 racing to finish *The Greene Murder Case,* a slightly longer book than the other two, in time to begin a January serialization in *Scribner's Magazine* with a March publication date. Before and after Christmas he gave interviews at local radio stations. Scribners had also brought out an anthology at the end of the year which Willard had edited under his own name, and that had taken some busy weeks of preparation. *The Great Detective Stories,* dedicated to Doctor Lobsenz, included a lengthy introduction and seventeen representative stories from Edgar Allan Poe and Arthur Conan Doyle through Arthur Morrison, R. Austin Freeman, and Melville Davisson Post to Chesterton, Phillpotts, and Bailey. *Publishers Weekly* wanted an article from S. S. Van Dine on modern detective fiction, and the author of an upcoming book on famous criminal-medical trials was soliciting an introduction. As Willard explained to Katharine in the hasty notes that accompanied his checks, he was swamped with more work than he had ever been in his life, hadn't a minute to spare for correspondence, and couldn't even manage a decent vacation yet. A week in Atlantic City over Christmas had been his only break, he maintained, since *The Benson Murder Case.*

New Year's Day 1928 saw Willard back in New York pondering that new aspect of a novelist's rise in America, his relationship to Hollywood. This was one demand on his time that felt highly desirable. After years of conniving to make some money out of movie writing, having been rebuffed and ignored to an extent that would have killed any hope in a weaker man, Willard Wright—the former *Photoplay* hack—found himself being courted by the studios. Paramount came around with the most generous terms, and on January 24th Willard signed a contract, with Max Perkins as his witness, granting that studio an option on *The Benson Murder Case* with the provision that, should the film go into production, Paramount could also buy the movie rights for both *The "Canary" Murder Case* and *The Greene Murder Case.* A better deal a new novelist couldn't have asked for. Willard's fee for the *Benson* rights alone was $17,500—at that, more than he had made on all of his art and literary writing put together.

When Willard wrote to Mencken in February, he described himself as boundlessly energetic and in a mood to square old debts. It was his first communication to Baltimore in a little over ten years, and it pleased him to be able to write a check for $400, the amount Mencken claimed was still owed. "New York is full of reports that you have made a big hit," Mencken politely responded, "and I am delighted about it."

Willard's original plan had called for three novels, a safe margin of security in the bank, and then a prompt return to the scholarly life. The writer's handbook, the philological study, *The Mother,* and other projects awaited him. Plausible as that chronology seemed to Willard and his publisher and editor in early 1926, it wasn't desirable in anybody's view two years later. The anticipation over *The Greene Murder Case* made it appear that *The*

"Canary" Murder Case hadn't been a fluke and that an audience existed, sizable beyond anyone's predictions, that could carry Willard through at least three more novels. Publishers in several non-English-speaking countries had translators on hand and were ready to sell Willard's books in France, Italy, and Eastern Europe, in Latin America, and in Japan. It also seemed likely that, if he were quick enough, Willard could have two novels on the bestseller lists at the same time. Having endured genteel poverty for so long, he was the last man to walk away from all this.

No sooner did the first installment of *The Greene Murder Case* appear in *Scribner's Magazine* than Willard was at work outlining a fourth book. His goal was to have it completed by May, with the intention that this novel would be as different from its immediate predecessor as that book had been from the Benson and "Canary" cases. Perkins had been thoroughly pleased with *The Greene Murder Case*—he had in fact stayed up till 3:30 in the morning to finish the manuscript over New Year's weekend—and was confident that Willard was far from exhausting his flair for detective plots and characters. On the contrary, to some observers in the business, it seemed that S. S. Van Dine was just hitting his stride.

The Greene Murder Case was indeed different from the other Philo Vance stories, and in some ways it was the most conventional and least plausible of the books. Dedicated to Norbert Lederer, the novel is concerned with Mrs. Tobias Greene and her five adult children and the perplexing attempts to do away with almost all the members of the family. Set in a castlelike mansion on the East River at 53rd Street, an eerie house surrounded by weeping willows and hydrangea, the story has a very un-modern feel to it. Any number of pseudo-Gothic buildings still existed in Manhattan in the Twenties, but it is more than the Greene mansion itself that seems a holdover from another era. The Greene children are less timely than the figures of the earlier books, and even the motives and methods of this story are a bit old and a bit ordinary, as if Willard were writing more in the spirit of an Anna Katharine Green detective novel from the Nineties.

This was also the first of his plots which Willard did not base on a real-life murder and the first of his stories involving multiple homicides. In a departure from the classic detective tale, which involves the analysis and solution of one or at most two well-executed crimes, Willard's novel approached the adventure mode as more and more victims fall even in the midst of the investigation. "A major massacre" was Richard Watts' summary of the plot in the *Herald-Tribune*.

The success of *The Greene Murder Case* when it appeared in serialization and then in hardcover is another illustration of the power of the well-oiled publicity machine. In the decade that began to treat advertising and mass-market manipulation as the potent tools they are, Willard was the recipient of this industry's first fruits. Had he, or Perkins or anyone at the publishing house, been so foolish as to reverse the order of the three novels, the Van Dine boom might never have taken off. *The Benson Murder Case* was needed to pave the way and give the publicists time to prepare their campaign, while *The "Canary" Murder Case* arrived at exactly the right moment to become a landmark bestseller. *The Greene Murder Case*, probably the least distinctive volume of the trio (and a book that, appearing on its own, would never have sold 60,000 copies in three weeks), simply rode a cresting wave to shore. Even more S. S. Van Dine ads were placed in regional and metropolitan newspapers than had appeared the year before, and "name recognition" took care of the rest.

Willard himself had been a little hesitant about his publisher's expectations. The plan for a 60,000-copy first printing worried him. His fear was that if the book fell short of a such a high goal, Scribners might be less interested in promoting the fourth book, which he was tentatively calling *The Cock Robin Murder Case*. But as usual the publicists knew best. The week of its publication *The Greene Murder Case* took first place on the bestseller list of *The Chicago Tribune* and *The New York Herald-Tribune*. Newspapers in Atlanta, Detroit, Pittsburgh, Milwaukee, San Francisco, and St. Louis reported it vying for the first spot, usually competing against Thornton Wilder's still-popular *The Bridge of San Luis Rey* from the year before. In April Scribners sales chief wrote to Willard on vacation in Atlantic City to let him know that not only had the 60,000 copies been sold in less than a month but that he was sure another 60,000 would go in the same or less time. With *The Benson Murder Case* still selling in its seventh printing, and the *"Canary"* in its eighth printing, there was no reason to expect to see the end in sight that year. And he was right: the Christmas ads still boasted a bestseller spot for *The Greene Murder Case*. The process by then was a self-perpetuating one.

Even those reviewers who found *The Greene Murder Case* a farfetched story tended to be pleased with it because of the more restrained presence of Philo Vance. Having painstakingly created a background and a tone for his protagonist, Willard had need of fewer digressions, speeches, and art references in the third book. Heywood Broun pronounced Vance "the most tiresome person in modern fiction," but Gilbert Seldes, Harry Hansen, and Alexander Woollcott were won over into declaring this the best of the S. S. Van Dine novels, endorsements which helped the vigorous sales drive. Likewise, President Coolidge and Secretary Hoover let it be known that they were Van Dine fans themselves.

Scribners salesmen reported that they had rarely had so easy a time placing a book and doubling, or even tripling, booksellers' original orders. You keep the stories coming, the staff at Scribners told Willard, and let us tend to the marketing.

At this point Willard still found all that was happening to him a little hard to believe. He lived with the sense that any day now the whole edifice might come tumbling down, leaving him right back where he had started. Until that time, though, he meant to do his best by Perkins' faith in him, meeting all of his deadlines and even looking the part he had assumed.

"The part," he felt, entailed another physical change: from the Kaiser Wilhelm moustache of the early 1910s to the Adolphe Menjou look of 1920 to—what else?—a Van Dyke beard and clipped moustache in the late Twenties. On occasion, at his most affected or theatrical, Willard could even be seen about town after the *Greene* royalties were in sporting a monocle and an expensive cane. To the growing number of New Yorkers who knew that Willard Wright and S. S. Van Dine were one and the same, it might have appeared that author and character were becoming confused.

At least as significant among the other rearrangements in Willard's life at this moment was the ending of his relationship with Claire Schermerhorn. If they continued to see each other after 1926, they were more discreet than they had been before, leaving no record of their affair, and more discreet than they would have had reason to be. It appears more likely that their involvement had run its course, that Claire was ready to forget Willard and that Willard was ready to strike out on his own, indebted to no one, least of all a mistress. For the first time in his life, he could afford to pay his own way and have his pick among the available women of New York.

Not surprisingly, though, Willard didn't lose himself in a whirlwind social life, not with his editor waiting to see another Philo Vance novel. Throughout the early part of the year, as Willard found a literary agent, Harold Ober, to negotiate larger advances and serialization prices for him, *The Cock Robin Murder Case* took shape. Whether the incentive was financial or creative, or some combination of the two, Willard found this novel even more pleasurable to write, a circumstance that made a difference in the final result. It is a book of more cleverness and energy than the story of the Greene tragedies and, for all its fantastic qualities, presents more varied and interesting suspects. A mathematician, a physicist, an engineer, a chess master, and an ingenue are the possible culprits for the murders committed along 75th Street and Riverside Drive, and each of these characters is given his or her own distinctive traits.

The Bishop Murder Case, as it eventually came to be called, also carried a more sinister angle to it that Willard enjoyed. Childhood innocence and the nightmarish adult world of intellect and evil overlap in his novel as Willard's criminal bases his killings on the Mother Goose nursery tales and ghoulishly leaves behind copies of the rhymes. The first title Willard used was meant to emphasize this, as the earliest victim, a man named Robin, is murdered with a bow and arrow. (Later, a victim is thrown off a wall in an allusion to Humpty-Dumpty, and so on it went.) But as Lederer and others observed, that wording was apt to lead to confusion with Eden Phillpotts' *Who Killed Cock Robin?*, a book that had enjoyed a vogue four years earlier.

Willard's second choice, *The Mother Goose Murder Case,* pleased the Scribners marketing staff even less, as they feared that booksellers might mistakenly stock the novel in the children's-books section. How much better, it was pointed out by several people, to stick to the six-letter four-word format, and so *The Benson Murder Case, The "Canary" Murder Case,* and *The Greene Murder*

Case were followed by *The Bishop Murder Case,* with the word "Bishop" pertaining to a more subtle clue planted near the end of the story.

Happy as he ultimately was with the title, Willard wasn't slow to perceive the implications of so much consultation on the matter. The more money his detective novels made, the less regard they were apt to receive as independent creative works. Here was the first sign of it. Clearly Perkins' other authors weren't ever going to be threatened by the same standardization he was, but then neither did most of them make the same income. As the Philo Vance novels were being molded into a recognizable product, with never a thought to varying the pattern of the title or the design of the dust jacket, the lack of respect Willard felt for his own achievement was, on one level or another, picked up by those around him. But having expressed approval for everything his publisher had done for him so far, S. S. Van Dine was in no position to grumble.

Willard finished *The Bishop Murder Case* in record time, and his agent worked out the terms of its serialization soon after. As the second and third S. S. Van Dine books had appeared in *Scribner's,* it was decided by all concerned that the next should be placed with a different, equally popular magazine, and a lucrative arrangement was made with *American Magazine.* The editors there agreed to begin serialization in October, enabling Scribners to set a late February 1929 date for publication. They were also willing to buy an article Willard wanted to write about himself. He felt the need now, he said, to talk about his past, the origin of his famous sleuth, and his plans for any future Philo Vance novels. *American Magazine* saw it as excellent publicity for the serialization. No one quite knew what to expect from this article—neither Wright nor the newly invented "Van Dine" were assumed to be of a confessional, autobiographical character, but Willard promised something interesting.

As the not-so-secret secret of Willard's identity as a detective writer slipped out by degrees that year, with about four different columnists claiming credit for the discovery, Willard was beginning to feel that trepidation about his name and integrity that he had brooded over at the Belleclaire.

Willard's first attempt to deal with this matter involved an effort to set his own terms for any discussion of the genre he was associated with. In all of his public statements about detective fiction, in dozens of interviews and articles, he chose to define this brand of writing in such a way as to preclude any question of literary prostitution. Simply put, Willard denied that detective or mystery fiction was "literature" at all or ever aspired to be. We didn't judge Gilbert and Sullivan by the same standards we applied to Wagner, he observed, and in the same sense detective-writing was not novel-writing as the term was ordinarily used. As a form of intellectual puzzle, it had more in common with the riddle than with imaginative literature and was best taken in that spirit. Thus, Willard hoped to sidestep the criticism that his books had psychological or stylistic weaknesses as novels by insisting that he, like Doyle and Freeman and Phillpotts, was constructing simple literary entertainments according to a few basic rules and principles. Hence, the lack of scenery and description in the Van Dine books, the charts and diagrams, and the no-nonsense first-chapter introduction of the crime or "riddle."

Willard's second and more all-encompassing way of handling the anxiety he felt about his position as critic-turned-entertainer was by that familar practice of rewriting the past. Mythmaking had always come naturally to the sons of Archie and Annie Wright. Adolescent fantasies that made the world more dramatic and romantic than it was, intensified by a passion for exotic literary images, were acted out as adult lies, reshadings of memory, the creation of more attractive self-images. This was something Willard and Stanton did constantly, almost effortlessly.

The short autobiography for *American Magazine,* written during the summer of 1928 and appearing in the September issue of the magazine, became Willard's principal vehicle of that quest. This was an opportunity, Willard had decided, to project a version of his life that would turn a mundane calculation—a poor man's desire to make some money in a clever way—into a glamorous, fateful destiny, a transformation for which he wanted to credit circumstances beyond his control. Willard's essay, which became for the rest of his life (and fifty years after) the standard account of his career as a serious writer, his collapse in the early Twenties, and his resurrection as S. S. Van Dine, was a larger and more blatant compilation of falsehoods than he had ever attempted before. It was the purest "hokum," he wrote to Katharine, but this was how he wanted it played.

"I Used to Be a Highbrow, But Look at Me Now" summarized a young man's struggle to be a literary and cultural force in his country, a fifteen-year battle that had never been tainted by compromise or surrender to commercial or editorial pressures. The result, despite several books to his name, was poverty and frustration. It had all been too much to bear, Willard wrote, and in 1923 he had suffered a complete breakdown from overwork and nervous strain. Omitted from the story was the mention of the earlier compromises or any hint of his debilitating drug problems, while a slow and sporadic deterioration was dramatically abbreviated into one final glorious collapse. Six months in a Paris sanitarium followed, according to this tale, then two years of confinement to his bed in New York. Willard told of his doctor's restriction of his reading to light novels and his own voracious reading of detective stories and novels during a three-year convalescence. When he decided to try his hand at his own detective fiction, Willard was denied permission by this unnamed doctor to begin writing before January 1, 1926. Thus, the three novels appear on Max Perkins' desk almost as a kind of miracle-birth; two years of trial and error, any normal gestation for a three-book series, is expunged from the record. Willard portrayed himself in this article as a man caught in a passion that took him beyond himself, like one of Balzac's feverish artists, ironically saved from defeat at the last minute—that fortuitous collapse of 1923—and now blessed by an ironic good fortune. Willard's contention that he was "saved by illness" was designed to make S. S. Van Dine seem all the more a child of fate. Only in discussing his reliance on a pseudonym did Willard lapse briefly, perhaps inadvertently, into honesty: "I saw no advantage, and even feared a certain disadvantage," he wrote, "in wrenching my own name from its cultural moorings and setting it adrift upon the seas of popular fiction."

The article concluded with Willard's announcement that he was committed to two more novels after *The Bishop Murder Case*, after which he would put aside the pseudonym, the detective, the excitement, the renown, and all the rest of it and return to the work that really mattered to him. Like the very title he selected for the piece, "I Used to Be a Highbrow, But Look at Me Now" was that perfect mass-magazine article with something for everyone. Intellectuals (i.e., Mencken, Stieglitz, Stanton Wright) could be assured that Willard knew that his present work wasn't the real mission of his life, while the true fans of *The Greene Murder Case* could infer that S. S. Van Dine was a happy, lucky man, able to straddle the high culture/mass culture fence in a way that few Americans could.

Only those who knew Willard best could see that this essay, for all its jauntiness, was a reflection of anything but certainty, happiness, and unambiguous good luck. Nor was the illustration that accompanied it as whimsical as it seemed. When Chicago critic Fanny Butcher, at the height of the curiosity over Van Dine's identity the year before, had dared the anonymous writer to send her a picture of himself for her newspaper column, Willard had responded with a caricature sketch he had drawn himself. He used it again to give *American Magazine*'s 2.2 million readers a glimpse of the famous novelist. With the monocle and the pointed black beard, the dangling cigarette and the exaggerated sneer, doing his best to emphasize the severity of his features, Willard looked like a comic version of the fierce "Beat the Hun" posters that had been plastered across America in 1917. Having once been called a spy for the Kaiser, the nation's favorite popular writer could have his own last laugh exactly ten years to the month after being sacked by the *Mail*.

Did anyone in 1928 other than Willard care that he had once been branded a German agent? Jesse Lasky and B. P. Schulberg certainly didn't give it a thought. The Paramount heads had announced their plans for *The "Canary" Murder Case* in the spring with understandable self-congratulation. Philo Vance was to be played by William Powell, already a favorite with moviegoers as a society roué and ripe for the transition to a social aristocrat. Louise Brooks had been signed as the Broadway "canary," and Jean Arthur as her girlfriend. A great character actor, the potbellied, frog-voiced Eugene Pallette, was chosen as Sergeant Heath, the policeman on the scene of all the Van Dine murders, and studio veteran Malcolm St. Clair was to direct. All of this seemed to bode well for the film's success, and Willard felt confident enough to hire a part-time butler (for a two-room apartment), provide himself with an expensive new wardrobe, and agree to go to Hollywood for promotional purposes.

Willard's first sight of the script, though, left him wild with anger. None of the qualities that made his novel a commercial success and a milestone in detective writing remained in the trite screenplay Paramount sent him. Lasky and Schulberg were "typical Hollywood morons," Willard complained. Like all of their kind, they were out to trivialize anything different or interesting, and he wasn't the man to work with fools whose heads were filled with "the usual porphyry" from the motion picture quarries. The studio had better come up with something better, he let it be known, or there'd be trouble.

Besieged all summer by long-distance calls and lengthy memoranda from Willard, Schulberg had dispatched Florence Ryerson, one of the company's most literate and diplomatic screenwriters, to New York to work with their irate author on a less clichéd script. She wasn't the usual studio hack (to begin with, Ryerson had actually read the book) and Willard felt comfortable with her. The sentimental love scenes Paramount wanted to add to the story, the gratuitous car chase, the stock villain—they all had to go, Ryerson agreed. She was happy to do battle with the studio bosses for her new friend and saw to it that a workable script was ready by the end of the summer. In September the movie went into production with a screenplay more appealing to everyone. St. Clair had come up with an especially effective opening, a dreamlike theater scene in which the provocative Brooks, scantily clad, swings back and forth over a leering male audience that includes some of the men she is blackmailing.

Before leaving New York, Willard experienced some anxiety over what he was getting himself into. When he had signed the contract and later agreed to do his bit to publicize the film, all he had thought about was the size of the check being presented to him. Now he was miring himself that much further in the world of popular culture. He was uncertain about how he would be dealt with in California and what his friends in the East would think of his new connections. A trip West also meant, necessarily, a reunion with his mother and brother and those other figures from the past, Katharine and Beverley. It would be a minor miracle, Willard concluded, if this all went well.

■ ■ ■

Paramount, of course, had no intention of letting its newest author feel anything less than well-honored. For S. S. Van Dine, it was the best of everything that autumn: a suite at the Ambassador, a Packard and a chauffeur at his disposal, and long, lavish dinners at the Montmartre. Arriving in California in early October, a few days before his forty-first birthday, Willard was immediately and properly impressed, flattered, and seduced. The nervousness he had felt before he left New York was dispelled by the attentions and comforts Hollywood's largest studio could provide.

A good part of the shooting of the movie was done by the time Willard got to the set. Louise Brooks had finished her early suggestive scenes, been strangled on the sofa of her West Side apartment, and departed for Germany where Georg Pabst was waiting to transform her into the even more dangerous sex symbol "Lulu." Willard was there in time to watch William Powell spar with the several male suspects and unmask the murderer, and he was on hand to be photographed observing the new camera devices that were employed to get an encircling panoramic shot during the story's famous poker scene, in which Philo Vance studies the *"Canary"* suspects in the midst of a tense, high-stakes card game.

Willard also threw himself into the frenzied social and public relations schedule that was waiting for him. He posed for pictures arm-in-arm with Powell and with costar Jean Arthur, happily submitted to dozens of interviews with columnists, reporters, and company publicists, and made sure he was seen at all the right dinners and receptions. In Beverly Hills, Santa Monica, and Laguna Beach, Willard was the guest of honor at party after party, including celebrations hosted by Ryerson and by Antony Anderson. Malcolm St. Clair even gave his author a cameo in the movie (later a cutting-room casualty), and that too made the news.

The treatment Willard enjoyed during his ten-week stay was more than flattering. For someone with his past, the whole experience began as a kind of sweet revenge. In the autumn of 1928 Willard's painfully angular face and tall, bony frame suggested something of what he had lived through in recent years. The Van Dyke beard, the pearl-handled cane, and the expensive suits were part of the attempt to forget old traumas and degradations, and the nature of the attention showered on him in his hometown was of the kind to make old enemies cringe.

Yet Willard wasn't long on the scene before he began to feel all over again an uneasiness about the less-than-gentle treatment his story was receiving. The first flush of excitement he felt in his role of visiting celebrity gave way to angry, nervous skepticism. No one at Paramount seemed able to answer his questions. At a Writers' Club dinner in Los Angeles, Willard shared a table with Dorothy Parker, Sidney Howard, and Robert Benchley. From any of them—all New York authors turned screenwriters— Willard might have heard stories enough to unsettle him about the studio system, but he had only to wait a few weeks to learn firsthand what a muddle he and his detective novel were at the center of.

Movietone "talkies" were the problem. No sooner was St. Clair done with Louise Brooks and busy orchestrating the climactic last scenes than the studio decided on a major change. Talkies were here to stay, Paramount was conceding at last, and *"Canary"* was going to be the first sound detective movie ever. That meant whole scenes had to be reshot. When Brooks refused to drop her European commitments and return from Germany to be part of the reshooting, it was decided to keep her footage and work around her. She was too good to replace entirely, and another actress was used to dub Brooks' voice. (A poor strategy: all the film's reviewers noticed the difference between the sultry actress' appearance and the low, gravelly voice that clearly wasn't hers.) Rehearsals were frantically rushed to meet the new deadline. Worse still, St. Clair, a director of silent comedies and a bit of a drinker, must have caused some concern about his own ability to handle the transition to talkies, because he was replaced in the last month by director Frank Tuttle. Willard had no idea what to expect from the final product. It was a maddening business, he concluded. But he knew enough to wear a contented mask in public and to predict a triumphant success. AUTHOR DECLARES FILM BETTER THAN BOOK, *The Hollywood News* reported.

To those in his confidence, Willard gave a more blistering account. The truth, he said, was that no one in Hollywood knew what the hell was going on. It was just as he had expected. All that the studio executives knew how to do was sign checks and

207

make promises. William Powell was "a nitwit" who was playing Philo Vance with the grace and subtlety "of a Sicilian fisherman." Willard was troubled that the movie would do so badly that it would jeopardize the filming of the other two options Paramount had bought and diminish the impact of *The Bishop Murder Case*.

At the height of his anxiety over St. Clair's replacement, the time arrived for Willard to see his family. As anyone could have predicted, the reunion with Katharine, Beverley, and Annie that month was as confused as anything taking place on the studio lot. Willard didn't want to see them. Beverley didn't particularly want to see her father. Annie was worried and hesitant, desperate to see her son and petrified that the atmosphere would be all wrong. But Katharine, more hopeful than ever for a reconciliation, still in awe of Willard and the wondrous life she imagined him leading in New York, was eager to see her husband again. When he had sent the train tickets to her and Beverley to get them from Palo Alto down to Los Angeles, she had taken that as a sign that he was ready for all three of them to be reunited permanently. But as soon as they met, Katharine realized that she had misread her husband's intentions once again. Alternately guilt-ridden and indifferent, conscious of his obligations but feeling that he had achieved his wealth with no thanks owed to his relatives, Willard was at his most garrulous and artificial the evening the Wrights gathered in Los Angeles.

Beverley's recollection fifty years later was still vivid with a sense of the awkwardness and mortification of their meeting. As she remembered it, Willard arrived with the air of "a conqueror," perfectly groomed and maddeningly charming. "I sensed he was formidable," she later wrote. "I sensed he came from a world I didn't understand." She also felt his ambivalence. As they were driven through the dark streets of the city, Willard was full of stories about the stars he was meeting and the parties he had been to. These people were stupid, he told them, but one had to go along. It was a fast, elegant world he had been admitted to, it was a vulgar and illiterate world—it was hard for Beverley to know what her father really thought of it. While her mother and grandmother were silent in the cavernous backseat of the car and later at dinner, it was painfully clear to her, though, that her father wanted to be free of them as soon as possible. His suggestion that they dine in his rooms at the hotel felt less like a hospitable gesture and more like a strategy to avoid being seen on the town with three underdressed women, especially a wife and daughter most of his friends didn't know he had. The evening ended with a cool politeness on all sides. Katharine and Beverley took the train back to Palo Alto without seeing Willard again.

With Stanton, whom he saw a few days later, Willard had even more cause to be uncomfortable. If he minded that his younger brother had married his old flame Jeanne Redman, he never said, but there were other reasons for estrangement. On the surface, everything was fine. Beneath the camaraderie and the shared memories, Willard felt the weight of his brother's example and his reserve. There was a judgment about S. S. Van Dine in every look, it sometimes seemed to Willard, and that could push him to be more defensive and truculent than he meant to be. At a meeting of the California Art Club in November at which they were both invited to speak, Willard delivered a polished talk about his own writings on modern art and then introduced Stanton with what a local reporter described as "an impertinent fling at his brother." At moments during their time together that fall, the man Willard was at heart closest to was also the person whose beliefs and opinions most oppressed him.

Some of this might have been Willard's own self-consciousness, a reading into Stanton's manner and words of more than was really there. Yet some of Willard's edginess was founded on sharp intuition. Stanton had long since concluded that Willard was only for Willard, that Synchromism in America had suffered because of Willard's penchant for offending people, and that his brother was not a helpmate to him but an undermining force. Since their last period together, eight years before, when they worked on the Exposition Park show and talked about color/light theories, Stanton had become brutally snide when mentioning his older brother and some of this must have gotten back to Willard. "He was never my press agent," he told Stieglitz, implying that all of Willard's work was, at bottom, self-advertisement. Some of Stanton's bile can be attributed to distance; theirs was a relationship that required regular contact. And some of it was simply a matter of one egotist having had enough of the egotism in his mirror-image. Still, the younger Wright was becoming more esoteric and serious about his art as he aged, and was finding ever more reason to be proud of his work as a painter and teacher, while his brother was doing no such thing.

A stronger reaction, and a more provoking threat, came from another corner: *The Los Angeles Times*. Harry Carr, Willard's friend from his last year on the paper, seemed to delight at turning his column, "The Lancer," on his old pal. More than anyone, Carr was appalled to see Willard using his talent to produce packaged bestsellers. Carr had believed in that talent and helped to nurture it twenty years before. Commenting on the most recent Philo Vance novel when it first came out, he was anything but gentle, writing that "it seems a great pity that a fine mind like Willard Huntington Wright's should be used to ooze out slush like *The Greene Murder Case*." Hearing that Willard was coming to California, Carr stepped up the attacks, noting that "it makes me laugh when I think of what [Wright] the slashing young critic would have done to S. S. Van Dine."

Perhaps it was in response to Carr's needling that Willard felt compelled to repeat the announcement several times during the three months he was in the West that he had already made in *American Magazine*. "It's all been a great adventure, and I've enjoyed it," he told one interviewer, "but by the time I've finished the last of the six Philo Vance books, I'll be more than ready to go back and gather up the loose ends of my serious interests." With his sixth novel, Willard insisted, having sent to Scribners one a year for six years, he was going to kill off his sleuth and retire permanently from the genre in which he had made his name. Neither the demands of the reading public nor of Hollywood would change that resolution. He had too many other, different projects ahead of him to consider, and besides, he noted, it was doubtful that a good detective writer had more than six strong novels in him.

On these same occasions Willard repeated the old self-justifying fables—"it was a nervous breakdown that started me [on the Van Dine books]; the doctors wouldn't let me do any serious reading or writing, so I turned to this"—and added a few desperate touches to his embellishment of the past. In Paris he had known Picasso and Matisse, he told one reporter, and to another he congratulated himself on having hired H. L. Mencken as a *Smart Set* reviewer.

No one at the studio seemed to care about all of these odd

announcements in which their "hot" author of the moment implicitly disparaged his own work, and Schulberg probably concluded that six novels by the same writer were plenty of material even for Paramount's production needs. The compulsion Eastern writers felt to bite the hand that fed them was never anything that unduly troubled the moguls. Besides, whatever steps Willard wanted to take to play down the detective-novelist aspect of his writing life didn't mean much to the larger publicity network of a Hollywood studio. Paramount used the occasion of Willard's visit to announce its plans to begin filming *The Greene Murder Case,* also starring William Powell and Jean Arthur.

Willard left California a few days after Christmas. Frank Tuttle had finished the movie. The galleys of *The Bishop Murder Case* were ready to be proofread, and various social commitments were awaiting him. But Willard was eager to get back to New York for other reasons. He had "gone sour" on Hollywood, he told Florence Ryerson. Despite the luxuries and the deferential treatment in most quarters, the experience had been even more unsettling than he had expected. There had been too many roles for him to grapple with in Los Angeles, too many conflicting desires to confront. New York afforded more control and, in its way, the anonymity he needed.

BREAK WITH
THE PAST

"The exclusive worship of the bitch goddess SUCCESS . . . is our national disease."
— *William James to H. G. Wells, 1906*

Willliam Powell and Basil Rathbone played Philo Vance very differently. In the first S. S. Van Dine movie, in Paramount's version of *The Greene Murder Case* several months later, and in its subsequent production of *The Benson Murder Case*, Powell was confident, efficient, and debonair. He looked and sounded right. Rathbone, on the other hand, a few years away from his success as Sherlock Holmes and not yet comfortable with talkies, seemed more formal and reserved in MGM's film of *The Bishop Murder Case*. Yet both actors' treatment of Willard's sleuth had one thing in common. Neither of them conveyed, or wanted to, Vance's intentionally obnoxious, arrogant, or erudite qualities. Their character's famous sarcasm and superiority, like his cultural allusions and teacherly lectures, were dropped for the screen; no American moviegoer, Hollywood knew, was going to put up with that. With Powell and Rathbone, Paramount and MGM made Philo Vance into a distinguished figure, but not the torturously learned cynic S. S. Van Dine had created. Willard had seen this emasculation of his detective coming. Indeed, as his fees rose, he had to some extent welcomed it.

Willard's lack of interest in the filming of *The Greene Murder Case,* a slapdash but remunerative picture, and his acceptance of the studio's drastic overhaul of *The Benson Murder Case* (the purpose behind the many changes in the story, screenwriter Bartlett Cormack condescendingly explained, was to make the mystery more action-packed and less cerebral) seemed odd to those around him. His sudden indifference to the whole business of Hollywood adaptations was interpreted by some friends as lordly self-confidence and by others as disgust with the commercial process he was bound to. Busy seeing his fifth novel, *The Scarab Murder Case,* into print, S. S. Van Dine extended his laissez-faire attitude even to the parodying of his creations. When Abbott and Costello included a Philo Vance spoof in one of their film routines, Willard took their humor in stride, nor did he have any complaint when Ogden Nash told the world that "Philo Vance / Needs a kick in the pance." He even seemed happy when Scribners joined in (or cashed in on) the fun with a short book by Corey Ford, *The John Riddell Murder Case.* Ford's satire, a chapter by chapter imitation of the Van Dine model, mocked Willard's elaborate use of footnotes and maps and Vance's increasingly campy dialogue. In the early promotional stages of the book, Willard made a few bookstore autograph appearances with his young imitator.

Certainly the Scribners publicity department in 1929 and 1930 had no shame in approaching their best-selling author for any outlandish news opportunities. One photo session that was picked up by several New York dailies shows S. S. Van Dine at a small table in a midtown hotel café having afternoon tea with an attractive debutante. According to the article, the novelist is trading opinions with the young woman about Manhattan's social life and the nuances of the party scene. In the same obliging spirit, when *Scribner's Magazine* decided that an article about the public's growing fascination with crime fiction and modern trials was called for, Willard was happy to dash off a piece on short notice. "The Closed Arena" in the March issue fit the bill perfectly and, in a vein that would have offended the stern young critic of 1909, flattered his audience by noting that readers of detective novels were invariably clever and curious individuals.

In return for his pliability with this "hooey," as he privately called it, Willard was able to negotiate a deal with his publisher in early 1930 that he wouldn't have had the leverage for even a year or two earlier. Since the days of *"Canary"*'s success, he had been fantasizing about a reissue of *The Man of Promise,* which had been out of print for more than ten years. His hope, now that Willard Wright and S. S. Van Dine were known to be one and the same, was to bring his first novel back into circulation, establish a place for it amid the body of realist literature for which Dreiser, Norris, Crane, Moore, and others were now honored, and—just possibly—provide its author with the nerve he needed to do away with Philo Vance and pick up the threads, or those that mattered, of the old life. It isn't likely that anyone at Scribners wanted to reprint a lackluster novel that had been a poor seller in 1916, but Perkins knew that Willard was set on this dismal idea and couldn't be fairly turned down.

At that, the last traces of the old life associated with *The Man of Promise* were fast slipping away. Willard's customary circle of friends and acquaintants, which for twenty years had included struggling painters, hard-pressed journalists, and assorted characters who existed on the fringes of the art and theater world, had been dropped little by little. They were replaced by a different, more affluent and less adventurous crowd of people. Willard avoided the galleries and the new Museum of Modern Art, where he was apt to run into old dealer, critic, and painter friends, and when he wanted to look at art, usually took himself to the Egyptian, Greek, and Renaissance rooms of the Metropolitan Museum. There, on a weekday afternoon, he could walk, alone and unrecognized, among the statues and paintings he admired, remembering his trips there with Mencken or Benton but with no fear of meeting anyone who had known him as the publicist for the Synchromists or the Forum Show impressario. Willard was more comfortable now with people who hadn't made his acquaintance before the emergence of S. S. Van Dine.

The Scarab Murder Case was out in time to be a good summer-vacation buy for thousands of detective-fiction fans, and its appearance in store windows was preceded by the usual publicity drive, this time including some staggering full-page newspaper ads. The release in the same month of the MGM *Bishop* film with Basil Rathbone was an unexpected public-relations dividend, despite the movie's mediocre reception. Inevitably,

Willard's fifth novel sold well and, as expected, it put him over the 1,000,000 mark in the total sales of the Van Dine series. It also signaled a major change in his writing and confirmed the critical view that S. S. Van Dine was falling into a rut, soon to become a creative abyss.

For one thing, *The Scarab Murder Case* was the first of Willard's books to be reviewed in a perfunctory manner. No longer were the "name" reviewers of the major papers assigned to comment on Philo Vance's deductive triumphs. By the same token, neither did the more literary journals or the better-known columnists, who had at least glanced in Van Dine's direction when the *"Canary"* and the *Bishop* stories were causing a stir, pay much attention. The public didn't care; they bought the books anyway— more than 80,000 of them by the end of the summer. Newspaper and magazine editors knew that they were dealing with a product which had already made its biggest splash, and it didn't seem to matter anymore who reviewed the novels that followed *The Bishop Murder Case*. Van Dine was "reviewer-proof," in the parlance of the trade, a status agreeable to an author's financial health but numbing to his sense of himself as a writer to be taken seriously. Ironically, one of Willard's kindest reviews came from that ardent Van Dine–hater Dashiell Hammett, who noted in *The New York Post* that the book had "several interesting twists."

In other ways at least as disturbing, though, *The Scarab Murder Case* stands apart from the first four of the series. It is the first Van Dine novel to show signs of Willard's weariness with his task. All of Vance's responses, from his fey retorts ("oh, my aunt!") to his final calculated explanations, are painfully predictable. The clues are complicated without being especially ingenious, and the plot and the principal characters have none of the flair readers were used to from the earlier stories. The Gramercy Park murder of art patron Benjamin Kyle, bludgeoned with an ancient Egyptian statuette, should have been the basis for one of the best Van Dine novels, especially as its motif played so effectively into the Egyptian craze of the late Twenties, a faddish interest that had been set off by the discovery of King Tut's tomb in 1922. All of the suspects have been involved in the archeological digs Kyle had financed, and the East 20th Street brownstone, the site of the novel's two murders, is really a private Egyptological museum and study center. The presence of Hani, the family servant from the Middle East, and a whole household full of scarabs, sarcophagi, and obelisks are meant to add a touch of the exotic. Yet this novel, making less use of its city setting than the others, is little better than mundane. It is rarely clever and never suspenseful and even descends to a hint of Western racism in its stereotyping approach to the one Egyptian character. In that respect, it has a crassness to it that wasn't a part of the other books.

Like *The Bishop Murder Case,* whose intellectual characters enabled Philo Vance to offer his own disquisitions on mathematics and physics, or like *The Benson Murder Case,* in which Vance ostentatiously displayed his knowledge of art and art history, *The Scarab Murder Case* had a kind of absurd pedagogical underpinning in its footnotes about Egyptian history and in Vance's observations about the Pharoahs and the subtleties of hieroglyphic transliterations. By now, Van Dine's audience expected learned digressions. They were part of the game. Yet Willard seemed to have gone overboard in his scholarly trappings with this novel. Any reader eager to follow the clues and make deductions is bound to share poor Sergeant's Heath's despairing impatience with Vance's arcane lectures. In fact, the book's dedication suggests the extent of Willard's newfound passion for all things Egyptian. Only the second S. S. Van Dine novel to carry a dedicatory page, it is dedicated not to any friends or family members but to three curators in the Egyptian Department at the Metropolitan Museum with whom Willard had recently become friends.

In the last chapters of the novel, Willard draws the story to a close by having the Egyptian manservant, Hani, quietly slip from the room with Vance's tacit approval to kill the murderer upstairs. The police, thanks to Vance's sleuthing, know the murderer's identity but lack the evidence to prosecute. But the ineffectualness of "the system," a recurrent Van Dine theme, is overcome by an individual retributive action. There was in Philo Vance not only a snob and aesthete, but a vigilante and a reactionary, and this too struck his readers as appealing.

With appropriate incongruity, *The Man of Promise* was published under Willard's own name four weeks later. While his potboiler had made him another small fortune, Willard's realist novel was the same resounding failure it had been fifteen years before and an even bigger critical failure. Angry as much as discouraged, Willard accepted the situation, and Max Perkins hoped that this would put an end to dreams about excavating any more Wright books of those now dead and buried.

To be sure, Scribners had done well by Willard in this pointless undertaking, and he had no cause to fault his publisher. The reprint of the novel was a respectable-looking book with an excellent preface by Perkins. The glowing reviews of Mencken, Huneker, Burton Rascoe, and others were quoted at length. The only problem was that the approving words of these critics meant nothing to the readers of 1930. The avant-garde voices of 1915 lacked urgency or influence for the new generation. Embarrassed at being thought old-hat, Willard never wanted to talk or hear about *The Man of Promise* again.

By now Willard's disdain for the standards of his society was surpassing even the cynicism of Philo Vance. That Dreiser had finally been accepted and had scored a great success with *An American Tragedy* in 1925, that a satirist like Sinclair Lewis (who would have had trouble publishing his most sarcastic material in Willard's *Smart Set* period) was a national celebrity, that D. H. Lawrence and Ezra Pound were regarded as masters by many young readers, that modern painting was claiming a place in America's cultural life—none of this struck Willard as progress, because he was not a part of it. Having made his debut as a rambunctious editor ten years too early and having been maimed by a crazy experience of the xenophobic war years, he could see America only in the light of what it had done to him. The proof of the nation's irremediable philistinism, he told Katharine, was shown in the very fact that a man of his ability had to keep on writing "bouffe opera cockeyed stories," as he called them, in order to pay his bills. As Beverley analyzed the situation, it was a matter for her father, from this point on, of just "giving the bastards what they want."

Willard's inner sustenance in these days came more and more from a new source, his first serious love affair since his breakup with Claire Schermerhorn.

In the spring of 1929, at a party aboard an ocean liner docked in New York harbor, Willard had met an attractive, well-dressed young woman who worked as an illustrator for a local paper and seemed to know something about art. She was several years Willard's junior and had the appealing name of Claire de Lisle. Willard later told the story, undoubtedly fictitious, of overhearing her in conversation with another woman disparaging the trashy novels of S. S. Van Dine. Agreeing with her vehemently, he introduced himself and asked for a date.

It was a perfect match from the start, and Claire became that rare presence in Willard's life—a woman he wanted to see more than a few times, whom he regarded as congenial as well as sexually desirable. She had some of the qualities that made the first Claire interesting to him, like her worldliness, charm, and eagerness for experience, all of which was tempered by a greater gentleness and reserve. This was an opportunity for Willard to be the unquestionably dominant one—the rich older man instead of the "kept" boyfriend—but dominant in relation to a strong, confident woman who had already made her way in the world, unlike Katharine.

For S. S. Van Dine, the self-created detective writer, there was also something intriguing about Claire's smaller efforts to construct a name and an identity for herself in New York. She had been born Eleanor Rulapaugh in Philadelphia and, with an equally adventurous girlfriend, had taken herself to Europe after high school to study art. In Paris in the early Twenties she was a student of Cubist painter André Lhote and a fairly typical young American expatriate intent on having a good time. Back in New York, she landed her newspaper job, forgot about painting and cultivated a full social life, and devised her own professional name. It must have struck Willard as amusing and ironic that a man long involved with a woman named Claire and long a resident at a hotel named the Belleclaire should find himself falling in love with a self-styled "Claire de Lisle."

With her, he was able to relax and forget the strange frustrations of his position. His new mistress, the only woman in his life in 1929 and 1930 who hadn't known Willard as an aspiring critic and editor, was content with her lover as he was—and more than content to help him spend the money that was pouring in. She wore clothes well, enjoyed dining out, was a sparkling conversationalist ("a quick study" was a friend's comment), and when Willard wasn't in one of his truculent moods while driving himself to meet a manuscript deadline, she knew how to be the perfect companion for a high-strung, witty, somewhat jaded man.

Willard did his best to keep his attachment to Claire out of the gossip columns in the interests of sparing his family's feelings. When Beverley ran off with a friend to New York and showed up at her father's doorstep late in 1929, she was quite unprepared for the tirade that greeted her and the speed with which she was hustled out of town on the first ocean liner headed back to California by way of South America. It was a case of "Machiavelli meets the milkmaid," as Beverley described it to her friends. Outmaneuvered before she even knew it, accused of all manner of selfishness, she spent most of the voyage home drinking and sleeping, stunned that she had accepted her father's offer of a larger allowance in return for a pledge to stay in Los Angeles to study art with Stanton.

Willard's reasons for wanting Beverley to share as little of his life in the East as possible went beyond his desire to keep her apart from Claire. His anger at his daughter's unexpected arrival on the eve of her twenty-first birthday was linked to his consternation about the snide press he had been receiving since returning from California: it was much easier to appear an important figure at a distance of three thousand miles. While Beverley was hinting to her father that she wanted to move in with him, Willard was still smarting from *The New Yorker*'s "Assault on Mr. Van Dine" by Alexander Woollcott, originally a fan and now a testy critic of his detective novels. Even more brutally, Gilbert Seldes picked up where Woollcott left off with a scathing article in *The New Republic*, cataloguing every complaint ever lodged against the S. S. Van Dine novels, from the pomposity of Philo Vance to the thinness of Willard's characterizations, from his tired prose style to his formulaic plots. Feeling under attack, Willard wanted no part of a needy young daughter; he wanted time alone with his mistress.

Claire de Lisle also shared with her lover a hobby that quickly became a passion and, soon after, an obsession for both of them. Since childhood, Willard had had a warm feeling for dogs, but his transient urban life never seemed suited to the owning of one. Now, in contrast to so many of the other problems that money couldn't rectify, Willard's desire for a pet was given full rein. But it wasn't only a pet Willard wanted; he wanted the best dog, or dogs, that a man of his means could find or breed.

Through the spring and summer of 1930 Willard intensively, maniacally, investigated breeds and bloodlines. He had decided on Scottish terriers—they were, he felt, the most loyal, tenacious, inquisitive, and forthright dogs in his experience—and was determined to know everything there was to know about them before embarking on his quest for the perfect dogs. By the end of the summer he had added to his growing library more than two hundred books about canine care, breeding conditions, lineage, and professional showing, he had talked to all of the breeders, trainers, owners, and authorities he could find, and subscribed to every periodical on the subject that existed. "Crashing the Dog-Breeding Gate" by S. S. Van Dine in the December issue of the *American Kennel Gazette* described the experience— the endless research, the hunt for sires—of entering the competitive, expensive, and obsessive world of prize dogs. What to a less driven person would have been a pursuit too relentless to be considered amusement or relaxation became to Willard one of the supreme joys of his life. Not toward any member of his family, not toward any friend or colleague, did Willard show the gentleness and affection he lavished on the several puppies he acquired in his first months as a dog owner.

Early in the next year Willard was in the market for his own kennels and full-time trainer outside the city, which he eventually found across the Hudson in Haworth, New Jersey. With Claire, he began traveling the length of the northeast coast from New England to Washington, D.C., to enter his Scottish terriers in all of the prestigious area dog shows. For Heather Reveller, his great champion, he reportedly paid $2,000—a news item that shocked Annie, Katharine, and Beverley. Before he retired from showing and breeding terriers, Willard saw his dogs claim all of the top prizes in the American competitions, and he came to esteem those honors as highly as his modern paintings and his Chinese ceramics.

The irony of Willard's attentiveness to his terriers, a fact about S. S. Van Dine which made its way into the human-interest columns of the California as well as the New York papers, wasn't lost on Beverley Wright. Her father was sending between $4,000 and $5,000 a year now to his wife and daughter in Palo Alto. The

220

exquisite Heather Reveller, one dog, had cost half that sum, and Willard was more interested in the health and well-being of the dog than in his family. On most days Katharine was past caring. She wasn't able to hold down a job for long stretches at a time, nor had she trained herself over the years for anything more challenging (or less taxing) than the clerical work she had always done. She spent many afternoons in bed and drank too much. But Beverley, who spent much of her time in Los Angeles living with Annie while she went to art school, cared and was hurt and angry. On her regular trips to her mother's, she tried to avoid talking about her father. It was especially painful when Katharine was in a morbidly reminiscent mood, reliving the summer she had met Willard on his way home from Harvard.

A wire from Willard in June of 1930 that he wanted to meet Beverley in Palo Alto came as a shock to her. When the three Wrights had last been together in Hollywood in the fall of 1928, Willard had made it clear that he couldn't bear their company and that a visit north to the house was out of the question. Now, though, Willard appeared and was a paragon of fatherly virtues—solicitous, tender, confidential, loaded with pocket money for his daughter. Beverley understood immediately what was going to be expected of her.

With Katharine, Willard was polite but blunt. Their marriage had been a dreadful mistake, and he was willing to take the blame, he said. There wasn't any point in prolonging the charade; Willard wanted Katharine to divorce him and told her that he was willing to continue supporting both wife and daughter indefinitely. Katharine numbly agreed. Beverley's part was to accompany her mother to Nevada for the summer, see that she established the ninety days' residence there that was required, and be sure that all of the papers were properly signed when the time came. In return, Willard promised that he would finance a year or two abroad for both Katharine and Beverley so that his daughter could study art, or whatever she wanted, in the best schools of Europe.

Beverley's alacrity in seeing her mother through the trauma of the divorce was something she soon had cause to regret. Willard had left them a few hundred dollars each for a new wardrobe, bought their train tickets to the little town of Minden, Nevada, and made motel reservations there for them. Then he departed for Los Angeles, to await word that they were properly set up and had contacted the lawyer he had secured for them. He was done with his part—and Beverley's hell began. In the broiling Nevada heat, Katharine Wright became moody and depressed. Beverley was reduced to hunting about town for bootleg liquor for her mother and was forced to listen to wrenching daily catalogues of complaints against her father who was forcing them to serve this "sentence" in the desert, alternating with flights of fancy that he would one day return and want to remarry the devoted Katharine Boynton.

When Beverley gave up for a time and headed back to California for a week's respite, Willard flew into a rage and accused her of failing to uphold her part of the bargain. He lived for the next three months, as Beverley went back and forth several times from Palo Alto to Minden, with the fear that Katharine would fall apart, drink herself into a stupor on the critical day in court, or give up and leave Nevada too soon.

On October 24th, 1930, the divorce decree was finalized. A disastrous marriage of twenty-three years and three months, during which time Willard and Katharine had lived together for no more than six years, was over. For Willard, it meant a fresh start; for Katharine, the end of everything. Three days after the divorce became final, exhausted by the anxiety but relieved at the outcome, Willard and Claire de Lisle left Manhattan to be married without publicity in Hoboken, New Jersey. Dr. Lobsenz and his wife were witnesses. By the time the marriage announcement appeared in the newspapers the following April, Katharine and Beverley were already in Europe.

With the groom's mind on money as much as romance, there wasn't much time for the Wrights to enjoy a honeymoon. On his trip to Los Angeles that summer, Willard had done more than wait to see that Katharine and Beverley were securely removed to Nevada. He had spent his time arranging two movie deals with Warner Brothers which would mean a fair amount of ready cash and a postponement of *The Kennel Murder Case*. The latter development interested Willard as much as the studio's money: he had announced so many times over the last three years that his sixth book would be the final one of the series, culminating in the death of Philo Vance, that he was ready for any plausible excuse to avoid that day of reckoning. His hope was that if he waited a year or more to hand the manuscript over to Perkins, the public might have forgotten his pledge in their eagerness for ever more S. S. Van Dine tales.

The terms of Willard's contract with Warner Brothers, signed that winter, called for his writing of an original story and screenplay adaptation for the First National Studios, a Warner's subsidiary, in Burbank. For this six-week commitment, S. S. Van Dine would collect the hefty sum of $37,000, minus any adaptors' fees should his own screenplay rendering of the story require extra work by studio script hands. A second agreement with Warner Brothers called for twelve short stories at $2,750 each, due at regular intervals throughout 1930 and 1931, for the company's series of "Vitaphone Shorts." In total, Willard would be earning almost $60,000 (a small fortune in Depression dollars) for work that would engage him only intermittently over several months, all this above and beyond his royalty checks from Scribners. Eager to make a good impression on the studio bosses, Willard decided to stick to his work during the weeks after his wedding and to spend a large part of 1931 in California.

As film commentator Leonard Maltin has noted, the Warner Brothers' Vitaphone period didn't last very long, nor were most of the films it produced any good—with the "notable exception" of the S. S. Van Dine mystery series, featuring Donald Meek and John Hamilton, "a so-so series of whodunits which at least had the novelty value, if not the quality, of the Philo Vance features which were being made at the same time." Willard's own interest in *The Clyde Mystery, The Wall Street Mystery, The Weekend Mystery, The Symphony Murder Mystery, The Studio Murder Mystery, Murder in the Pullman,* and the six other shorts he completed, all of which were released between January of 1931 and the summer of 1932, wasn't much better, but he cheerfully admitted that he was only in it for the money—an easier thing to say in the film than in the literary world. Likewise, the fate of *The Blue Moon Murder Case,* the full-length script Willard wrote for First National with Walter Huston in mind for the lead, didn't mean anything to Willard in the long run. When the studio scrapped the project and later, in 1933, resurrected Willard's story as the basis of a B-movie, *Girl Missing,* it was all the same to him. His $37,000 had already been contentedly spent.

Willard's months in Southern California in 1931, his third stay there since his apotheosis as S. S. Van Dine, were among the grandest of his life. He managed to get his ex-wife and daughter packed off to Europe by April, when his remarriage was officially announced, and spent as little time with Annie and Stanton as possible. Instead, he and Claire gave themselves up to the good life of radiant, photogenic, sought-after celebrities. There was no more worrying about being embarrassed in public by a woman like Katharine, who dressed badly and never found the right words to express herself, or Beverley, whose weight and masculinity sometimes troubled Willard as much as her earnestness and desire for closeness. With the poised and attractive Claire de Lisle, now Claire Wright, Willard felt he could make the kind of impression he wanted to, and he showed her off at every opportunity.

Florence Ryerson gave a dinner in honor of the Van Dines and treated them to a lavish weekend at Palm Springs. When Warner Brothers executives threw a spectacular garden party for the couple, Frank Tuttle, Joseph Mankiewicz, and other studio figures turned out en masse, and everyone seemed charmed, just as the beaming husband intended it, by the famous author's young wife. As a noted dog breeder, Willard asked to speak to the city's Scottish Terrier Club and judge one of their dog shows (providing the merciless Harry Carr with a few more occasions for sarcasm in *The Los Angeles Times*) and as a former student at St. Vincent's, now Loyola-Marymount, he was asked to address an Alumni Dinner. Cocktail parties, dinner parties, public appearances, studio tours, weekends at palatial beach houses, requests to meet Claire: the schedule was unvarying.

To those reporters who persisted in questioning Willard about his status as intellectual-turned-celebrity, he now felt sufficiently pampered to be cavalier about the whole thing: "I feel like the fellow who married the girl he didn't love because she had money," he joked to a *Times* interviewer, and shrugged his shoulders. He was a squirrel caught in a golden treadmill, he told several other journalists.

By the early summer of 1931 Willard had concluded all the business he had to attend to in Hollywood and had made his social mark. Yet he delayed returning to New York until September for a very particular reason. The apartment on West

75th Street was a place he loved, but it wasn't quite large enough for a couple and certainly wasn't suitable any longer for a man of his prominence and income. When he learned that the landlord of the building was eager to turn the basement into a speakeasy, he jumped at the chance to move and sent his new secretary, a devoted woman by the name of Y. B. Garden, looking about for the right property for him. He then decided, once a penthouse with the right address and the right view had been secured, that he would wait in California until Miss Garden had overseen the moving of his books, art works, furniture, and clothes.

He and Claire would then be able to return to Manhattan and, with minimal trouble for themselves, walk into their new home and proceed to do with this fabulous space whatever they wanted. Remembering his repeated returns to New York in more painful and straitened days, Willard was realizing a fantasy here that few people have the means or imagination to effect. Dazzled by his almost regal treatment in Hollywood, he was taken by the thought that he would enter Manhattan in triumph this time, to claim a position that should have been his all along.

Arriving back in New York in mid-September, Willard and Claire entered not only a new home but a whole style of living that they could never have imagined for themselves only a few years earlier. The two-floor penthouse at 241 Central Park West on the corner of 84th Street overlooked a splendid stretch of the park. From the balcony of this late-Twenties building with a vaguely Art Deco flair to it, Willard could see the Metropolitan Museum on Fifth Avenue and, to the south, the skyline of midtown. The rooms were large and accommodated quarters for the servants the Wrights now employed, principally a cook and butler. There was space in the study for the sixty-eight aquaria (built to hold more than a thousand exotic fish) that the room eventually contained, in the living room for the grand piano Willard ordered, and in the dining room for the huge dining-room set that was bought in anticipation of some grand dinner parties. Willard installed floor-to-ceiling bookcases, gratified his taste for expensive Chinese ceramics, and eventually purchased a blackjack table and roulette wheel for the amusement of his guests inclined to gambling. For getting around town and out to New Jersey to the ten-acre S. S. Van Dine Kennels, Willard and Claire now had their own car and chauffeur. In all, it was the life of a successful industrialist or Wall Street tycoon that Willard had decided to cultivate.

There was a crucial difference, though. The money that an entrepreneur could rely on, or the income from a thriving business that a company president knew would be there for the foreseeable future, wasn't something that Willard, or any novelist in the Depression, could count on. But by the end of 1931 Willard had commenced the practice of spending almost everything he made on a given book or screenplay and, most dangerously, of dipping into the advances Scribners would give for the next Van Dine novel. His restaurant and clothing bills alone were astronomical, and his home might have been more appropriate as a showplace for a great capitalist than a popular writer who never knew how much his income might fluctuate from one year to the next, but Willard was determined he wouldn't succumb to the Annie Wright virtues of prudence and economy. It was, Beverley later observed, as if the money were tainted, dirty money all of which had to be spent as soon as it was made.

The Wright penthouse was a natural subject for journalists. Every interview with S. S. Van Dine mentioned the elegance of the furnishings, the obsessiveness of Willard's collecting (the dogs, the books, later the fish), and his evident delight at his station in life—the implication being the utterly false one that America treated its writers well, that even an avant-garde art critic could realize the American Dream.

As each of the Vitaphone shorts were duly written, filmed, and released throughout 1931 and into 1932, Willard had to decide if he wanted to try to develop a screenwriting career or go back to the business of writing Philo Vance novels. The matter may have been decided for him by virtue of the fact that none of the screenplays he labored over resulted in a commercially or critically successful film. Whatever the case, by the spring of 1932 Willard had the sixth Philo Vance story, entitled *The Kennel Murder Case,* under way. He was also able to use the excuse that the Hollywood money was gone to put Beverley off. From Paris and Berlin and Vienna, wherever Katharine and Beverley were staying that month, came letters and postcards pleading for a larger allowance. But the answer was always the same. Stanton and I lived on a pittance in Europe before the war, Willard lectured his daughter, and I don't see the need for extravagance now that it is your turn to see the world.

Within a few months, his exaggerated level of comfort proved too much even for Willard to sustain. Spending money like mad throughout the first half of the year, he was angrily and reluctantly looking to make cutbacks by June. A lucrative arrangement with *Cosmopolitan* for the serialization rights to *The Kennel Murder Case* and Perkins' delight at learning that there would be a seventh Van Dine novel immediately following the sixth (and Scribners' willingness to advance more money)—none of this seemed to make a dent in the bills that were coming in. So the Wrights were forced to cut back on their entertaining for a time and put the New Jersey kennels on the market. The original scheme to make money by breeding the finest terriers in the country hadn't brought in the anticipated buyers, not in the third horrendous year of economic catastrophe, and it seemed wisest to let go of the property and the full-time manager and keep just a few of the best dogs. Then, too, Willard had already achieved his dream of showmanship and was ready to move on to another hobby, another obsession. In February of 1932 Heather Reveller had won first prize at the Madison Square Garden Dog Show, and S. S. Van Dine had appeared there, proud and satisfied.

The new hobby—exotic fish—was at first more Claire's than Willard's. It was also a good deal less costly in the beginning than dog breeding, though it eventually consumed thousands of dollars anyway, as did every pastime the Wrights enjoyed. Its justification for Willard (if one was needed) was that, just as their dog phase proved to be the inspiration behind the Van Dine novel *The Kennel Murder Case,* the passion for fish gave rise to the book that followed, *The Dragon Murder Case.*

A bad end to an otherwise reasonable year was further complicated by a visit from Stanton. On his first trip East in several years, which also turned out to be his last trip in Willard's lifetime, Stanton had asked to stay at the penthouse. Willard agreed, of course, knowing full well that Stanton's presence was going to be for him a kind of seductive torture, an occasion to reminisce and show off and yet to feel degraded, all at the same time. Stanton was coming to New York for an autumn showing of his paintings at An American Place, Stieglitz's new gallery. One brother, now a charismatic art teacher and theater designer in Santa Monica as well as a talented painter, continued to follow his bent and fight the good fight, while the other worked on *The Dragon Murder Case,* soon to be serialized in the pulp magazine *Pictorial Review*—it was a sublime incongruity, guaranteed to set Willard on edge.

Stanton found Willard in a predictably nervous, belligerent, and cynical mood that alternated with moments of tenderness. On the one hand, he delighted in showing his younger brother the level of opulence he had attained. In the midst of the Depression, Willard lived in one of the finest apartments in New York and was pleased to treat Stanton to a spectacular array of food, wine, and domestic comforts. And Stanton, who had never had any patience for romantic poverty, was suitably impressed. On the other hand, there was a subtle air of discontentment at 241 Central Park West, and it could turn suddenly overwhelming.

Willard's conversations with Stanton, especially after dinner and a few drinks, were bitter, no matter what the subject. It was always the same barrage: Didn't Stanton realize that it was all about money? Didn't he see yet that money, and money alone, was what Americans cared about, thought about, respected? So what was the point of any struggle? Hadn't they been fools in their youth? All that idealism, all those lofty ambitions. What did they think they were going to achieve? And on and on. When Stanton changed the subject, Willard could be just as menacing. Why had he married Claire, Stanton inquired, broaching the subject of his sister-in-law's flighty temperament. "I liked her legs," Willard answered, ending the conversation.

On the spacious balcony above Central Park, surrounded by shrubs and potted palms, Stanton sat with Willard each afternoon during his weeklong stay. At regular intervals, a houseboy would appear, unsummoned, to refill the snifters with Courvoisier, now Willard's favorite drink, and disappear back into the apartment. Stanton had the impression that this was a ritual with Willard now—never, during certain hours of the day, to be left without a drink by his side. The servants knew what to do without being told. Claire looked the other way. When Stanton returned to California, it was with the mournful sense that Willard had lost the will to live. Stanton kept his fears from Annie, Katharine, and Beverley, but was convinced that, for all his energy and affluence, his brother was one day going to kill himself.

KENNELS, DRAGONS, AND CASINOS

"If [the studios] want to make Philo Vance a Hungarian, or a Swede, or a Filipino—what the hell?"

—Willard, in a letter to Florence Ryerson, *1935*

Nineteen thirty-three, a dismal year for the nation, was a superb year for detective fiction. Dashiell Hammett's *The Thin Man* was published to acclaim by Knopf, Agatha Christie and Mary Roberts Rinehart each added a respectable volume to an already sizable canon, and *Murder Must Advertise,* the eighth Peter Wimsey novel, was out in both Great Britain and America—an occasion for Willard to acknowledge, finally, that Dorothy Sayers' talent and audience seemed to be growing, not declining. In the view of everyone at Scribners, it was none too soon for S. S. Van Dine to make another appearance in hardcover. The publication of *The Kennel Murder Case* in August and *The Dragon Murder Case* in October of the same year was designed to rekindle an excitement that was in some danger of dying out.

The year that saw the passing of the Old Guard in politics and the beginning of Roosevelt's New Deal—this fourth traumatic year of the Depression—was also a time in Willard's personal life of momentous change. Between the money earned in Hollywood on the screenplays, the advances for *The Kennel Murder*

Case and *The Dragon Murder Case*, the serialization rights for each, and the film rights for each ($14,000 for the *Kennel* story and $20,000 for the *Dragon* story), Willard and Claire had enjoyed a financially spectacular period. It also became evident to them then that adjusting to a less extravagant way of life, doing without the chauffeur and the box at the opera and the ability to indulge every caprice, wasn't something they were ready to confront. Too much would be lost, should Willard honor his pledge to "do in" Philo Vance. Claire claimed to be willing to follow Willard no matter what he chose to do, but she had adapted to her new life with a vitality that rivaled her husband's.

Worse still, Willard only had to look out from the balcony of 241 Central Park West or walk down the street to Riverside Park to confront the new America: Hooverville shanties dotted the city's open spaces. Breadlines and panhandlers were everywhere. A return to journalism, cultural criticism, or serious fiction, he had to admit, was out of the question, for good. The more the country's fortunes had plummeted, the more Willard had come to desire, to crave, luxury and peace. He wanted a buffer now between himself and the struggle and poverty he had known earlier in his life, and that protection could be achieved only by keeping his sleuth alive at all costs for as long as possible. In 1933 Willard completed the last of the Van Dine novels, the seventh, in which it is possible to detect even the remotest pleasure in the writing—from then on, it was a dreary, desperate, mortifying labor for cash.

The Scarab Murder Case three years earlier had touched on Willard's interest in Egyptian art and history. The next three books did more than touch on Willard's current avocations; they were actually born of those passions, none of which had anything to do with art or scholarship. *The Kennel Murder Case* was a detective story for the dog-lover in S. S. Van Dine, the man who had owned his own kennels and pored over hundreds of books on breeding and grooming. *The Dragon Murder Case* was for the fanatic ichthyologist whose collection of fish staggered guests to his apartment, filling sixty-eight aquaria. Finally, *The Casino Murder Case* (published in the fall of 1934) was for the ardent gambler in Willard. Each book was also weaker, in every way, than the one that preceded it.

The Kennel Murder Case, dedicated to the Scottish Terrier Club of America, told a reasonably interesting story of the murder of Archer Coe, an arrogant collector of Chinese ceramics and a thorn in the side of all his relatives and professional associates. Coe is found dead in the bedroom of his West 71st Street brownstone with the door to the room locked from within. The discovery of an injured terrier hiding in a closet in the Coe house, a dog not owned by anyone living there, helps Vance to evaluate the suspects—who include Coe's niece and brother, his friend and secretary, his Chinese cook, and an Italian museum official staying in the house who had been negotiating for some of Coe's ceramics—and, ultimately, to solve the puzzle. The usual Vance problem prevails at the end of this novel as it did in most of its predecessors: namely, that for all his intelligence, Willard's detective never seems quite as smart as his criminals who are accurately unmasked in the final chapter but, for want of hard and fast evidence, are almost never arrested and tried. According to the rules of the genre, the murderer can't escape, though, and in the penultimate scene of *The Kennel Murder Case* the man Vance knows is guilty is killed by a Doberman in Central Park. Strangely, none of Willard's reviewers ever made much of the fact that if it weren't for an assortment of vicious dogs, retributive Egyptian servants (as in *The Scarab Murder Case*), and other outside agents of justice, District Attorney Markham could thank Vance for solving his cases—but not for seeing the guilty parties pay for their deeds.

The reviews for *The Kennel Murder Case* were uniformly generous, and the Book-of-the-Month Club was happy to add the novel to its winter list. Christopher Morley spoke for many fans when he commented that the Philo Vance of the Thirties was a "mellowed and humanized" character, less ponderous and grating than the detective of the Benson, "Canary," and Greene novels. Yet it seems odd, looking back on Willard's success with this book, that readers and critics of the day maintained the tolerance they did for the thinness of Willard's characterizations, the hollowness of the dialogue, and the absence of any vivid description. Willard's sixth novel showed no growth at all over the work of the five previous books, and the novelty of his polished sleuth had long since worn off. Moreover, as Sayers and Christie got better, and as the market started to accustom itself to the new, more modern tone of Hammett's Sam Spade or Nick and Nora Charles, Willard's dry tales—all puzzle and no novel—must have, or should have, appeared increasingly glib and trite. Yet hundreds of thousands of readers bought the new S. S. Van Dine mystery as contentedly and uncritically as if they expected nothing better from the writer or the genre.

Even more strangely, no one commented in print on the fact that Willard Wright was violating his own tenets in making use of older detective story devices. After Gaston Leroux, Conan Doyle, and numerous others, the body found in a room locked from within wasn't an original or exciting touch. We know that a trap-door or a clever keyhole contraption is going to be discovered or dragged out in short order. The questionable use of a dog (two in this case, the terrier and the Doberman) to trap the criminal was a point Willard himself had addressed in his own essays on detective stories. "The dog that does not bark and thereby reveals the fact that the intruder is familiar" is a cheap, threadbare touch in a modern work of detective fiction, Willard had noted more than once—yet the dog in his new novel (once owned and abused by the murderer), who at the end of the story kills the criminal that the police don't have enough evidence to arrest, is every bit as silly.

If the book-buying public of the early 1930s wasn't yet as discriminating in its attitude toward detective fiction as it would become in later years, the major Hollywood producers never made any pretense of sophistication. *The Kennel Murder Case* seemed to most executives at Warner's to have solid box-office potential—unlike *The Scarab Murder Case* (one of only two Van Dine novels not made into a film immediately after publication), the story of Archer Coe's murder had action and outdoor scenes—and the agreement for the rights was settled long before publication. The fact that William Powell had moved over to Warner Brothers in that company's "raid" on Paramount's talent roster in the early Thirties made the quick filming of *The Kennel Murder Case* all the more desirable. When the movie was released in October, the very week that *The Dragon Murder Case* arrived in the bookstores, the opening title proclaimed WILLIAM POWELL RETURNS AS PHILO VANCE, and everyone involved with the project sat back to count their money. The screenwriters had fumbled one element of the plot in a remarkably inept way—by changing the residence of the murderer from the house next door to Coe's own building, the final explanation of the crime makes no sense at all (another glaring fact reviewers failed to comment on)—but none of that really mattered, to judge from the press clippings. The movie, directed by Michael Curtiz, just wasn't very engrossing, and interest in Powell's Philo Vance was wearing out. The revenues for *The Kennel Murder Case* fell far short of Jack Warner's expectations, and Powell soon left the company for greener pastures at Columbia and later MGM. Within a year, he had revived his career in spectacular fashion as Nick Charles in MGM's *The Thin Man.*

October of 1933 should have been an embarrassing month for Willard Huntington Wright. Between 1928 and 1932, he had gone on record some two dozen times announcing that Philo Vance was to retire or be killed at the end of his sixth exploit so that the author could go back "to writing the books one starves on." That sixth intellectual adventure had come and gone, the seventh was out, and Scribners was announcing that S. S. Van Dine was hard at work on the last chapters of his eighth book, *The Casino Murder Case.* There was no more pretense about giving up the role of prosperous detective novelist, the exemplar of popular culture.

Willard dealt with his chagrin in three ways. First, he continued to avoid those people from the art and literary worlds who might make him uncomfortable on this sorest of subjects. He lived exclusively among those friends who enjoyed the good life as much as he did—and who particularly enjoyed the Wrights' dinner parties with games of roulette or blackjack in the playing room after dessert, with cocktails in the study surrounded by the aquaria and the dazzling colors of the fish—and who didn't care where Willard's money came from. At the Belmont or Jamaica racetrack, in the city's nightclubs, at his favorite restaurants, he found plenty of congenial, uncritical company. Second, he made an excuse of the common problem of the day, the economic slump that ate into the nest eggs even of the well-to-do. While Willard had in fact lost some money in 1929 and the first years of the Thirties, he had never invested very heavily in the stock market. But he let on that he had, and didn't contradict the stories in the New York press that year that he was really continuing the Philo Vance series because of grave and unexpected financial reverses. Lastly, Willard turned with more fervor than ever to a romanticizing of the past, a dramatic distortion that would make the present, so comfortable but mundane, more bearable.

When he would talk now about his early days in California, New York, Paris, and London, Willard didn't portray himself merely as a friend to James Gibbons Huneker, Alfred Stieglitz, Leo Stein, and Thomas Hart Benton. Rather, he was the man who had helped Mencken and Pound find themselves, advised Picasso about the failings of Cubism, conferred with Stravinsky, dined with Gertrude Stein, shared notes about the West with Ambrose Bierce. The aura of Willard's past life was such that no one who hadn't known him then was quite sure which anecdotes were the honest ones and which the fabrications, and in time Willard seemed to convince himself that he had actually met Picasso, Stravinsky, Stein, and Bierce. Anyone who insisted on the narrow truth, on any small-minded adherence to mere facts, was a bore and a fool, one of the "goddamn morons" Willard scorned in this increasingly acerbic period. By 1933, devoted to making money, he had less control over his life than at any time before—and more need to define and redefine his self-image to better manage the gap between the past and what loomed ahead. The older Willard became, the grander the lies and the greater the abuse showered on anyone who suggested a different version of the truth.

A reminder of that supposedly happier past made an unexpected appearance at about this time, in the figure of Burton Rascoe. Rascoe was the Chicago–New York journalist who had been Willard's staunchest ally in the press, a true believer in his talent since his reading of *The Man of Promise* in 1916. Always full of energy and goodwill, he had decided now, with *The Smart Set* reduced to the level of a pulp-fiction magazine, to prepare a history and an anthology of the journal for the younger generation that wouldn't have known the great days of the magazine, from 1910 to the early '20s. He also wanted in his account of the rise of *The Smart Set* to literary eminence to give Willard his due as one of the great American editors, a reputation (he felt) obscured by the private grudges of Mencken and Nathan. When Rascoe stopped by the penthouse to confer with Willard, it was a tender moment for S. S. Van Dine, exhilarating and somewhat awkward. Mencken had gotten wind of the project and was refusing to have anything to do with it, even to the extent of denying Rascoe permission to use any of his work in the anthology section. Some part of Willard must have seen this as his golden opportunity, a chance to feed Rascoe his "line" on the events of 1913 without any interference from Mencken. But the potential for old flare-ups, for more acrimony from Baltimore, was there, Willard knew, and he waded into the murky waters of reminiscence with mixed feelings. He gave Burton Rascoe his version of the magazine's history and his role in publishing its better "finds" and waited to see what Rascoe would do with it.

Max Perkins was pleased with *The Dragon Murder Case*, or so he said, and as usual saw no need for extensive revisions. Scribners pushed it in the fall of 1933, along with Hemingway's *Winner Take Nothing* and a new John Galsworthy novel, as hard as any of the earlier Van Dine books. Ads were everywhere, and with William Powell's face on the posters for *The Kennel Murder Case* movie at exactly the same time, the firm anticipated large sales. Those hopes were realized and the novel made a fair number of the country's bestseller lists. Yet all signs weren't positive.

For the first time, the better-known newspaper reviewers started to turn a bit snide. Their reactions didn't have much effect on sales figures, and certainly didn't bother the publicity and marketing people very much, but it was irritating to Willard to read in *The Boston Transcript*, which had usually been kind to him, that Philo Vance was "the same egregiously conceited ass" as always. It was annoying that Bruce Catton thought his book a dismal failure, that Gilbert Seldes mocked it as subliterate entertainment, and that G. K. Chesterton sidestepped any comment on its merits in his ticklish review. Gone were the days when S. S. Van Dine was seen as an original force revitalizing a stagnant literary genre, a popular author that even intellectuals should take note of.

These responses hurt most particularly because Willard had tried in *The Dragon Murder Case* to stir himself to a new freshness. Dedicated to Claire and inspired by their passionate interest in tropical fish, this novel was the first Philo Vance story removed from his traditional setting of midtown Manhattan. The Stamm estate in Inwood, the one area of northern Manhattan still undeveloped in the 1930s, was Willard's setting for the murder of Sanford Montague, Bernice Stamm's fiancé. The title's reference to a "dragon" alluded both to the bizarre fish collection kept by Rudolf Stamm, Bernice's brother and a noted aquarist, and to the manner of the victim's death. Montague disappears while swimming in a pool of water amid a rock formation on the grounds of the estate, only to be found a day later, mutilated, in a hole near the watery caves of that area of Manhattan. Fears of an underwater "monster" dominate the story from the start. Unfortunately, Willard's success with a new setting and an intriguing (if somewhat hokey) premise was the beginning and the end of the book's power: the identity of the murderer is obvious from a rather early point in the novel, as only one person of the crowd of guests wasn't at the pool at the moment Montague vanished in the water. An even more serious failing is that the suspects and secondary characters, an assortment of friends of the Stamm family, are as banal a group as any Willard ever wrote about. Willard's lack of interest in creating fully rounded characters, an outgrowth of his monomania with Vance and Vance alone, was finally reaching its logical outcome. He was creating stories too unconnected to the outer world and the desires and drives of real people.

Clearly Max Perkins was in an odd position. It is hard to imagine that an editor working at the time with Hemingway on some of his best stories and with F. Scott Fitzgerald on *Tender Is the Night* could have regarded *The Dragon Murder Case* as a fine piece of fiction for mature readers, but what was he to say to Willard?

Jack Warner's situation was similar. With William Powell's departure from the studio after *The Kennel Murder Case*, none of the executives at Warner Brothers was overjoyed that the studio was stuck with the film rights to Willard's latest novel. They had no Philo Vance and for a while, it seemed, no director. Curtiz had had enough of S. S. Van Dine with the *Kennel* movie and declined the offer, as did the next three directors that Hal Wallis, Warner's production head, approached. Not one of the available directors the studio wanted—Archie Mayo, Mervyn LeRoy, or Alfred Green—thought the novel or the screenplay good enough or anticipated a sufficiently strong box office to make the job worthwhile. The unwanted task of directing *The Dragon Murder*

Case finally went to H. Bruce Humberstone, who hated the book and had to be brutally strong-armed by Jack Warner before rethinking his position.

> You're going to make this picture [Warner told Humberstone]. Do you think it matters that it's lousy? That picture, with my theater chain, is going to make me fifty thousand dollars, good story or not. So, you're going to make it for me. Or . . . you're never going to direct another picture in this town.

Humberstone agreed to direct the picture.

Ironically, Humberstone's handling of the story was more serious and inventive than any of Warner's or Wallis' earlier choices would have managed, and the film was a help, not the expected hindrance, to Humberstone's career. (He later worked on the popular Charlie Chan series.) The obviousness of the murderer is less apparent in the screen version, Warren William did a creditable job as the new (the third) Philo Vance, and some of the more skillful shots of the tropical fish in Stamm's aquarium added an effective touch to the story's macabre aura. Indeed, a small-scale "fish craze" swept the country after the film's release, with specialty shops offering exotic fish springing up on both coasts. Most importantly for Willard, MGM was sufficiently impressed with the public response to *The Dragon Murder Case* to make an offer on Willard's next two novels, indicating a willingness to buy as soon as S. S. Van Dine was ready to flesh out a plot.

At this point, Willard in effect ceased writing for Max Perkins and began composing his stories with the movies in mind first and foremost. An S. S. Van Dine tale in a Scribners hardcover was from then on only a stopover en route to its repackaging in the screenwriting offices of Southern California. As Willard's luck would have it, *The Dragon Murder Case* was also the last movie of the Van Dine books to be a popular or critical success.

While Willard saw the *Kennel* and *Dragon* novels and films through to completion, and while he finished work on *The Casino Murder Case* and began the next book, he did his best to think about Katharine or Beverley as seldom as possible. From his perspective, he had bought them off at a rather high price and, while he and Claire made a solid new life for themselves, wanted to hear as little as possible about them. But regularly, and vociferously, Katharine wrote to Willard from Europe, keeping her ex-husband informed about Beverley's doings, commenting on life abroad, and insinuating that she now recognized her grand old love as a sadist, an unnatural father, and a Scrooge.

The escape from Palo Alto after the anguish of her months in Nevada had been a rejuvenating experience for Katharine Boynton Wright. She hadn't left the West Coast once in her married life, and the great world she had missed in her youth both delighted and repelled her. She and Beverley spent a year in Paris, several months in Berlin and Stockholm, and even longer in Vienna and Salzburg. In each city they would find a moderately priced apartment or room-for-two in a pension and spend their days taking in the sights, studying the language, or looking for work or art classes for Beverley. They made side trips to Italy, Switzerland, and Czechoslovakia, ultimately seeing much more of Europe than Willard had. For several productive months Beverley studied theater design at Max Reinhardt's school in Germany, a development that led Katharine to hope that her daughter had at long last found a professional calling. Her suggestion that Willard might find work for Beverley in New York in this line elicited only grim warnings from 241 Central Park West to the effect that the theater was dead in New York and that "the happy wanderers" would be better advised, once they were done with this "spree" on the continent at Willard's expense, to look for more sensible work back in California.

If it galled Willard that Katharine showed signs of a new liveliness and feistiness (not all of it very cosmopolitan—many of Katharine's letters read like a Sinclair Lewis parody of tourism), he was visibly dismayed by the thought of Beverley coming into her own in the arts. Rather than feeling any paternal pride, or even curiosity, over Beverley's accomplishments in the famous Reinhardt school, he took an offended tone, as if such news were beneath his notice. His daughter's success at her production drawings for *Hedda Gabler* was not something he wanted to hear or comment about. By the time the travelers returned to America at the end of 1934, they knew enough to dock in New York and head West without attempting any visits with the terribly busy, cranky, and aloof S. S. Van Dine.

Willard might also have excused himself from meeting Katharine and Beverley that fall on the legitimate grounds of his anxiety over Claire's health. A normally vigorous and dependable woman, Claire had been losing weight and showing signs of fatigue for some time. Willard was used to being fussed over by the women in his life, and it was a new and distinctly unpleasant feeling to have to worry about his partner. When vaginal bleeding began, Claire consulted various New York doctors but finally, at a close friend's urging, settled on a Baltimore physician at Johns Hopkins. Though Willard's letters are extraordinarily discreet on the subject, it appears that Claire's trouble was a uterine cyst or tumor, and she was advised to undergo surgery in the Maryland hospital as soon as possible. But for many weeks Claire refused to discuss the possibility.

Aggravations followed Claire's illness in quick succession. *The Casino Murder Case,* published in September, had sold only moderately well, given the standards Willard had set for himself in the Twenties, making very few bestseller lists. This didn't necessarily trouble Willard, as the book's summertime serialization in *Cosmopolitan* had amply made up the difference in income, while he had enjoyed a few profitable weeks in Chicago that summer writing mystery radio scripts for an area station. What did worry Willard were two different but related matters: that a negative pattern of sales was in place and would gain momentum, and that MGM's treatment of the novel and its author were not what they should be. At moments during the last months of 1934, Willard felt as if the studio were making fun of him, and that was an intolerable sensation.

Even before *The Casino Murder Case* was in the bookstores, MGM had announced that it was going to bring back William Powell as Vance with Myrna Loy as his sidekick. The allusion to the recent film of *The Thin Man* was obvious and embarrassing. Willard hated Dashiell Hammett's book and his "plebian" sleuth, and any comparison between himself and Hammett usually infuriated him. Shortly after the Powell idea was dropped, and gossip columnist Louella Parsons let it be known that Powell was only too delighted to be done playing that flippant bore with the pretentious British accent, the studio announced that it was considering a female lead for the role of the detective. (The part was finally given to Paul Lukas, whose Hungarian accent made him the strangest-sounding Philo Vance.) Adding insult to injury, MGM admitted in its press releases that it was trying to lighten up Willard's novel, to give it the brisker tempo of the newer crime movies the public seemed to want. To this end, slapstick comic Ted Healy was hired to replace Eugene Pallette as Sergeant Heath, and screenwriter Florence Ryerson was told to write in a part along the lines of Myrna Loy's urbane Nora Charles.

For a while, Willard tried to convince the studio production people and Ryerson that their thrust was a mistake—even a commercial more than an artistic miscalculation—but he eventually gave up in frustration. If anything, it seemed to him that Hollywood had gotten worse, grown less rational, since the arrival of talkies. So do what you want with Philo Vance, he told Ryerson— make him a Hungarian (a reference to Lukas' accent), a Swede, or a Filipino, give him a funny sidekick, a girlfriend, or a harem of girlfriends, so long as I get my money. As Willard sadly told Claire, the role of high-priced prostitute was not an easy one to cast off.

In many ways, *The Casino Murder Case* was the least likely of Willard's detective novels for any studio to tamper with, especially for pointless comic effect. It was a taut, sensible story that, while not particularly dramatic or compelling as a novel, was ripe with potentially cinematic touches. The opening scene takes place in Kinkaid's Casino on Riverside Drive and 73rd Street, a resplendent private gambling club of the type that flourished in Manhattan from the Nineties to the early Thirties, a locale Willard was very familiar with. Vance is at the casino because he had been anonymously warned that a wealthy young male acquaintance, Lynn Llewellyn, will be in grave danger there that night. When Llewellyn is poisoned, though not killed, at Kinkaid's in full view of a crowd of gamblers, the mystery begins, ultimately resulting in two other poisonings. Like the Greenes in Willard's third book, the Llewellyns are "old money" in Manhattan, and much of the novel takes place in their Park Avenue town house, another favorite Thirties film site. The Park Avenue life, a suspenseful scene in a darkened hunting lodge in New Jersey, an attempt to shoot Vance, Van Dine, and District Attorney Markham, and a last-minute nighttime rescue back in the abandoned casino are all elements that hint that Willard had the movies very much in mind when he outlined his story. Even

Vance's expostulations on the fine art of gambling take second place to the momentum of the poisonings, false clues, and final unraveling.

None of this was good enough for MGM. The studio wanted a funny movie with a little suspense and a little sex appeal, not a serious detective piece, no matter how appealing the settings. Starlet Rosalind Russell was brought in to play a wisecracking feminine love interest, though even she came to the film under protest. As conscious of making the right career moves as anyone in that business, Russell knew a B-movie when she saw one and wanted nothing to do with *The Casino Murder Case*. As an actress under contract, though, she wasn't left with much choice. Reluctantly, under Edwin Marin's direction, she played opposite an awkward Paul Lukas, taking on the part played by narrator Van Dine in the novels.

Another reason, unknown to his public, that Willard might have been particularly offended by MGM's desire to turn his eighth novel into a farce was his use, conscious or otherwise, of his own family patterns. Lynn Llewellyn is the spoiled elder child of a possessive mother, a widow who controls the purse strings for both of her indulgent children. A socially impeccable woman, Mrs. Llewellyn devotes herself to duty and good causes while one child devotes himself to pleasure, particularly gambling, and the other to art. In this case, the art student–sibling is a younger sister, Amelia Llewellyn, rather than the male that Stanton was, but the antagonism between the two is as real as it often was between Willard and Stanton. Even Katharine is given a place in this psychohistory: Lynn had married beneath his class and intelligence and is forced to spend his adult life trying to ignore his youthful mistake. A supreme egoist, Lynn lives only to satisfy himself, though his oedipal attachment to his mother is strong indeed. Surely a story, the MGM production head told Willard, that could use a few laughs.

Burton Rascoe's *The Smart Set: An Anthology* was published in November of 1934 and was widely reviewed. The absence of any Mencken material in the volume severely undercut the book's claim to authority and most reviewers commented on this lapse. (No matter how many times Rascoe tried, Mencken had been adamant about not granting him permission to use any of his old pieces from the days of Thayer & Co.) For all of the attention the book received in the papers and the monthlies, though, the whole messy problem of sorting out the belated honors of the past seemed to interest people a good deal less than Rascoe (or Willard) had hoped it would. Rascoe's glorification of Willard as a literary adventurer and guiding light of American letters and his dismissal of Mencken in his introductory essay might have had some truth in it, it might have been woefully lopsided—no one really cared one way or the other to debate a minor point of literary history twenty years after the fact. What mattered was that Mencken's was the big name now, not Willard's, and so it would remain. Moreover, even Mencken's reputation as a crusader for American literature was undergoing its own natural devaluation in the Thirties as his politics became more conservative and his mood more somber. Within a few years, the whole generation of pre-Twenties critics would seem a crowd of old fogeys to most young writers and readers.

Nonetheless, it could have been a pleasant, if not a vindicating, moment for Willard. But it assuredly wasn't. Mencken let it be known that he was not pleased with Willard, and all the old hurts were reopened on a small scale. When it became obvious that Claire had to have the operation the doctors had been urging on her, Willard had no choice but to bring her to Baltimore, to Johns Hopkins, just after Rascoe's book was out. He then made a polite but uncomfortable social call on the Menckens. (H. L. Mencken, the confirmed bachelor, had been married to everyone's surprise in 1931.) Deeply depressed, he spent as little time in Maryland as possible and took Claire home as soon as the doctors pronounced her fully recovered.

Christmas of 1934 and New Year's of 1935 weren't celebrated at the penthouse, as Claire was still bedridden. She required a nurse's care and took a long time to regain any strength at all. Frustrated, overtired, and anxious about his wife and his career, Willard caught the flu himself that winter, moped about the apartment in feverish self-pity, and didn't even bother to see the film of *The Casino Murder Case* when it opened a few weeks later.

He wasn't alone in that, however. The reviews were terrible and audiences were bored. One reviewer offered the opinion that the film "must have been made while Irving Thalberg was out fishing." When Willard finally did see the movie later that spring, he described himself as "entirely flattened and utterly speechless." MGM, he felt, had made a pseudo-comic monstrosity out of his most straightforward story. Even Rosalind Russell was embarrassed by the picture. For years afterward, as Russell herself later remarked, her maid would jokingly hold the threat over her head, "Be good or I'll remind people you were in that *Casino Murder Case*." As Willard knew, it was only going to get worse.

THE LAST
YEARS

"Every man wears a mask, and wise is he who knows it."
—Arthur Schnitzler, PARACELSUS

Theh persona Willard had created for himself with the invention of S. S. Van Dine in 1926 had seemed foolproof at the time. The whole foray into mass-market fiction was supposed to be taken as a lark by those who knew the author, as a clever, profitable diversion on the part of a cultivated literary man. Yet at the same time that the Philo Vance phenomenon was billed as a short-term enterprise (ending with the fourth, or the fifth, or the sixth novel), it was designed to be a thing brought off with such panache that even snobbish intellectuals could admire the style and craft of the stories. And, for a while, Willard's intricate endeavor had worked, and he had held on—however precariously—to his self-respect.

By 1935 the situation was different. In a brief note to Mencken that March acknowledging their recent visit, Willard described his life as "uneventful and depressing of late." To others, he indicated that he was slipping into a serious depression. Claire's inability to rally from her surgery troubled him, the embarrassment of being associated with a film like *The Casino Murder Case* was annoying, and his lack of excitement over the novel he was finishing, *The Garden Murder Case,* was a source of looming anxiety. Even more ominously, Willard was pondering hard the direction of his career and what looked to be an inevitable decline just ahead. He lived in these weeks with a feeling that his life was about to come apart at the seams. This troubling reality might not have been apparent to the general public, to the columnists like Walter Winchell and O. O. McIntyre who still lightheartedly mentioned Van Dine's social affairs in their pages, or even to all of the Wrights' friends. To many people, he was still the man who had it all. Yet Willard was ready to acknowledge that no one believed the old public-relations ruse anymore, the tale of an intellectual temporarily sidetracked by quality detective fiction. His original plan might have been otherwise, but he felt on the verge of being exposed finally for what he was, a writer who turned out an increasingly formulaic product for money and who was on the verge of losing even the undiscriminating audience that still cared for him. It was a grotesque, humiliating feeling, and before the year was over, he would have tangible proof that old friends were talking about him in just that way.

From California, meanwhile, came letters from Beverley filled with hope and excitement. She and her mother had returned from Europe to go their separate ways, Beverley to the south to live off and on with Annie, and Katharine back to her small house in Palo Alto. Fresh from a gratifying experience at Max Reinhardt's school, Beverley threw herself into various local theater projects in Southern California and seemed on her way toward making a living, if only a tentative one, as a set designer.

Willard's reactions to his daughter's first serious theater ventures were just further signs of the depth of his discontent. On the one hand, he seemed to want to reestablish a rapport with Beverley, as some stirrings of guilt over more than twenty-five years of neglect were awakened in him by her letters, but that urge never quite led to anything. His statements of interest and support for her theater work, usually sent as postcards or short notes, were unfailingly polite but never much more than that. Something always prevented the expression of tenderness he seemed close to making. Impossible to overlook, for Willard, was the fact that Beverley wasn't the docile child safely at home with mother while Willard Huntington Wright, the precocious critic and adventurer, made his way in the world. Instead, she was taking her turn as an apprentice in the arts with a reasonably promising future before her. The situation might have been less disturbing had Beverley's work not been of such an earnest character. But the Pasadena Playhouse, where she landed her first steady job, took itself seriously. Beverley's productions included plays by O'Neill, Hauptmann, Pirandello, and Strindberg. To hear of his daughter designing sets for *Anna Christie* or *Miss Julie* only served to remind Willard of the literary tradition he had abandoned for a far less imposing one.

Sadly, Beverley could never quite figure out what she was doing wrong. Willard's reserve on the subject of her career baffled her, as her need for his encouragement clashed with her sense that she was ultimately going to have to make it on her own without any parental goodwill. For a while, the latter feeling won out and sustained her. "I'm just not going to be downed by an unwilling father," she wrote to Katharine in one of her more determined moments that year.

In July Willard gave Heather Reveller, his beloved terrier and greatest prizewinner (the dog that had cost him $2,000), to his former kennel master in New Jersey, William Prentice. It was an act of uncharacteristic generosity for Willard, though his feelings for Prentice, who had skillfully tended to the dozens of terriers the kennels once housed, had always been strong. While he still kept other dogs in the apartment as cherished pets, Willard was done with the world of showing and breeding, all of which had proved too expensive. A blissful era in his life ended when he said goodbye to Heather Reveller. Yet at the same moment a new hobby was consuming Willard's free hours, a pastime that both represented and reinforced his concern with quick money and the unpredictability of his life.

For several years Willard had enjoyed gambling, though never with particularly large sums, in Manhattan's private clubs. *The Casino Murder Case* was a reflection of that interest. By 1934 he and Claire were taking their pleasure that way from another, somewhat similar avenue as they became regulars at the track. Once she had recovered enough to go out, Claire joined her spouse in outings to all of the racetracks within driving distance of their home. Twice they traveled south to attend the Preakness. They had a regular bookie, subscribed to all of the racing papers and digests, and got to know some of their favorite trainers and jockeys. Their latest hobby allowed for a new group of friends and, on the whole, cost less than owning kennels and acquiring unusual fish.

Racetrack gambling also provided the convivial background for the novel Willard handed over to *Cosmopolitan* for serialization in June, to Scribners for publication in October, and to MGM for adaptation that same fall. It was Willard's hope that the betting element, complete with a foldout racing form that Philo Vance uses in the course of the story, would set a jazzier tone for his detective's life. Vance's scholarly interests, amusing five or ten years before, were plainly boring Van Dine's current readers. Disquisitions on Cézanne watercolors or Egyptian scarabs were out, and something new—a bit more in line with the self-consciously masculine flavor of the Thirties fictional detectives—was required. Portraying his hero as an avid (and of course brilliant) follower of the horses added the touch Willard wanted.

Beyond that, Willard had decided on another more striking change in his old patterns, and that was the inclusion of a fleeting love interest for Vance. A romantic awakening for his sleuth was a flagrant violation of one of Willard's published principles for writing detective fiction ("to introduce amour is to clutter up a purely intellectual experience with irrelevant sentiment"), but by this time those stringent guidelines, formed and aired in a more complacent period, didn't mean much to their harried creator. Besides, Nick Charles had Nora, and Peter Wimsey was obviously warming to Harriet Vane with each new Dorothy Sayers book. It might have been acceptable for Sherlock Holmes in the Nineties to live a bachelor's life with a male friend, but it was about time, Willard joked, that Philo Vance's sexuality was cleared of suspicion.

The title for this, the ninth book, came from Willard's secretary. Miss Y. B. Garden had been pleasantly and efficiently handling Willard's clerical affairs, both personal and professional, for the better part of five years. She appreciated her employer's sense of humor (having worked for Edna Ferber, Miss Garden was familiar with the acid tongues of literary types), accepted his mood swings, and was willing to work long and irregular hours. At some point after *The Scarab Murder Case* Willard had decided to dictate his books to his secretary, in part or in whole—an authorial quirk that accounts perhaps for the plainness of style of *The Kennel Murder Case* and the novels that followed it. According to Garden, she was allowed to interject her own plot or dialogue ideas about the lines while she was typing her notes after each first-draft writing session. "I was free to do this at any time," she claimed, "and of course he was free to accept or reject such suggestions." In honor of this close working relationship, Willard named the story he was working on *The Garden Murder Case*.

Dedicated to Annie Wright, *The Garden Murder Case* is as much a story of family entanglements and alienation as it is a racing tale. Vance is present to listen to the racing results at the apartment house of Professor Ephraim Garden and his wife and son, along with a whole congregation of racing enthusiasts, when Garden's nephew is murdered. In the course of piecing together the plot against the affluent Garden family, Vance becomes infatuated with one guest, Zalia Graem, and learns about the unpleasant underside of the family relationships and friendships he has been exposed to in his visit. With his usual finesse, Vance at the end of the novel tricks the murderer into making an attempt on his life by pushing him from the balcony of the apartment while the police secretly film the murder attempt. In a carefully prepared daredevil feat of acrobatics, Vance has actually plunged to safety one floor below, and the murderer, unmasked, leaps from the balcony as the police close in.

What struck most readers of *The Garden Murder Case* was the changed Philo Vance who walks through the pages of this workmanlike novel, a character who is doing his best to be more robust than he had been in the past, a little less remote and overpowering. We are meant to feel something for him in his unrequited passion, as the beautiful Zalia Graem marries young Floyd Garden and makes a life for herself with her own fashionable set, and to see him more as a recognizable person than the forbidding intellectual of *The Benson Murder Case*. This dilution was the price S. S. Van Dine was willing to pay to hold his readership.

There were plenty of the expected constants in this book, though: the difficult mother who gives her children, particularly sons, a hard time (in this case the truculent lady is killed off, poisoned in her bed), the forty-eight-hour format for the whole process from first murder to solution, the second death, the uselessness of the legal authorities, and the inevitable suicide of the murderer. *The New York Times* thought the novel one of the best of Van Dine's recent books, while *The New York Post* reviewer announced that Vance's "fascinating dope" on the history and intricacies of horse racing was "alone worth the price of admission."

MGM saw *The Garden Murder Case* simply as a decent plot premise and eliminated most of Willard's story, pushing the romantic element for all they could and altering both the manner of Vance's deduction and the identity of the killer. The studio had in mind the good-looking Edmund Lowe for their new Philo Vance and Virginia Bruce for Zalia Graem, and so it was inevitable, with such an attractive starring couple, that a love interest would be advanced in the screenplay far beyond what Willard had included in his own. No unrequited love for MGM's Depression era audiences. What surprised Willard when the film was released (the following February) was that the screenwriters had also rejected his thriller ending: to the author, Vance's ostensible leap from the balcony—a psychologically suggestive touch for a writer actually living in a similar high-rise apartment—had seemed to him the most filmable moment in the whole story. The studio thought it silly and did away with it altogether, substituting a hypnotizing scene in which the murderer tries to induce Vance, supposedly in a trance, to leap to his death.

The Garden Murder Case enjoyed a moderate success and better reviews than any of the film versions of Willard's novels had received in some time. But Willard knew not to put too much faith in any momentary upturns in his fortune, and he was right. *The Garden Murder Case* was the last S. S. Van Dine novel brought out first in serialization and then in book form and subsequently bought by Hollywood. Willard's accurate instincts told him that his free ride was over and that the moment had come to get out of the business altogether or to devise new strategies.

In its November 2nd, 1935, issue, *The Saturday Review of Literature* published an article about S. S. Van Dine entitled "A Man of Promise." Illustrated with a recent *Daily News* photo of Willard at the track (his hair and beard streaked with gray), the piece was written by Randolph Bartlett, whose hospitality Willard had taken advantage of in the darkest days of his poverty. Like most of his other work, Bartlett's essay was a well-written reflection by a competent journalist on a subject he knew well: in the years before "S. S. Van Dine" appeared and abruptly dropped him, Bartlett had been a particularly reliable friend and a colleague who believed that Willard was capable of serious, lasting accomplishments. The turn of events since *The Benson Murder Case* dismayed and angered him. Nor did he like what he heard about Willard's haughty manner and pretentious anecdotes about his "illustrious" past. Bartlett's intention in writing his article, then, was twofold. He knew he had a fair, newsworthy topic and the right moment at which to address it, and (as he later told Mencken) he was ready for some "sweet revenge." That Bartlett achieved. When Willard read the article, he was as angry as he had ever been in his life.

"A Man of Promise" reviewed the spectacular potential Willard had shown since his great days at *The Los Angeles Times*, described his pathetic down-and-out period at the Belleclaire, and, in effect, asked what had become of the fellow so many people had rightfully expected so much from. Bartlett took more than one swipe at *The Garden Murder Case*, calling Willard's ninth Van Dine novel "the ninth stitch in [the author's] literary shroud," made fun of Willard's old habit of announcing as ready for publication books he had never finished, and described him finally as a man trapped in "a mummy case of his own making." Willard Wright might be "one of the most interesting enigmas on the American literary scene," as Bartlett phrased it, but the implication of the *Saturday Review* article was that he had been brought down by all of the usual snares that society sets for the weak-willed and intellectually lazy—those traps laid for men who put money and an easy life before artistic quality and self-respect. Bartlett suggested that Van Dine's next book be entitled *The Wright Murder Case, or What Happened to the Creative Will?*

Being discussed in public in these terms wasn't a new experience for Willard. Alexander Woollcott and Gilbert Seldes, among others, had taken the same line more than once before. But this time the attack was different. This time the critical eye was that of an old and dear friend, not a professional reviewer, and the arrow hit the mark. There wasn't anything libelous in

Bartlett's commentary, which didn't even hint at some of the questionable aspects of Willard's life that Bartlett was personally familiar with, like his drug-taking and promiscuity. Yet the effect was worse for Willard than if Bartlett had gone all-out to smear his reputation. The very reasonableness of the tone increased the sense of being condescended to and laughed at. "I hear that he was like a maniac for a week [after reading the article]," Bartlett proudly told Mencken.

Bartlett's timing couldn't have been better suited to confirm his point that Willard was just another sellout. The month before, Willard had agreed to do his first product endorsement, a form of financial prostitution he had avoided until then as beneath his dignity and the dignity of any writer. The very week the *Saturday Review* issue was on the newsstands, *Collier's* began carrying full-page ads showing S. S. Van Dine at home enjoying and recommending his new four-foot General Electric radio console, an ad campaign that was to appear in the pages of *Saturday Review* itself and several other magazines in the first months of 1936. (Eventually Willard would do advertisements using his picture and his name for Goodrich Tires, Parker Brothers board games, and several brands of liquor.) This bind was a trap from which there was no release: Willard found that he couldn't decline any job that paid enough, least of all something as easy as posing by the radio in his study. He simply had to have money. Yet he couldn't make himself indifferent to the opinion of men like Bartlett, Mencken, Nathan, Harry Carr, and their kind, who obviously scorned mystery potboilers and writers crass enough to endorse commercial products. From urging his countrymen to honor Dreiser, Conrad, Nietzsche, and Cézanne to extolling the virtues of G.E. radios was a distance not even Willard Huntington Wright could rationalize away.

While still in an emotional upheaval over the *Saturday Review* embarrassment, Willard had to cope with the news from Max Perkins that the royalties on *The Garden Murder Case* were going to be less than originally projected. The following week Annie Wright suffered an attack of peritonitis that nearly killed her, a situation that left her eldest son in a panic. Her recovery was slow and her hospital bills, sent to Willard, were large.

Willard's last, faint hope for a decent end to the year was tied to an odd venture that, incongruously, involved President

Roosevelt and the former editor of *Liberty* magazine. Early in his administration FDR had had a much-reported conversation with Fulton Oursler, then editor of *Liberty,* in which he speculated about the possibility of a man of means choosing to disappear with enough of his own money to sustain him throughout his lifetime but without leaving behind a hint of his whereabouts or his new identity. Oursler encouraged the President to develop his fantasy situation into a short detective story, but when Roosevelt admitted that he couldn't come up with a satisfactory ending to his plot premise, Oursler proposed that the story be handed on to several well-known mystery writers who would each offer their own conclusions in the pages of *Liberty.* Willard joined John Erskine and several other writers in offering narrative solutions, none of them very good, to Roosevelt's puzzle. The serial began appearing in *Liberty* in November and, as *The President's Mystery Story,* was published by Farrar & Rinehart on December 27th. S. S. Van Dine's chapter included his characters Heath and Markham but not Philo Vance. Reviews were brief and scattered, and its reception among mystery fans wasn't anything to rouse Willard out of his winter doldrums.

The next book Willard turned his attention to in the new year was his last actual "novel." Originally named, rather feebly, *The Purple Murder Case,* the story was eventually given the more marketable title of *The Kidnap Murder Case.* It proved to be a hard book to write, clearly more of a chore than any of the other novels had been, yet the end result wasn't the failure, or the same kind of failure, that the Casino and Garden stories were.

At the beginning of *The Kidnap Murder Case,* Philo Vance is returning, melancholy and unrefreshed, from a trip to Egypt following his successful conclusion of the Garden murder case. Van Dine describes him as speaking with a weary voice in a distracted undertone "with a tired look in his wideset grey eyes." Only when District Attorney Markham asks his aid in investigating the abduction of playboy Kaspar Kenting from his West Side home, known as "the Purple House," does Vance come to life again. And come to life he does—in a way that the original Vance, tranquil and reflective, never would have. For what Willard attempted in this story was a blatant remolding of his detective in the more modern late-Thirties mold of tough talk and virile action. It was an effort to let his character bestride both worlds, much as Willard himself (aesthete and gambler, critic and racetrack regular) tried to do. Before the murderer has finished, one person is dead and another kidnapped, and Vance has spent a night in Central Park in a tree waiting for the alleged abductors to collect their ransom, has been brutally attacked in a tenement apartment in the Bronx, and has had to shoot and kill three men in self-defense. Though this story remains more readable than many of Willard's books from the Thirties, these developments are something in the spirit of Miss Marple engaged in a shoot-out car chase or Father Brown in a drunken fistfight—unthinkable to detective-fiction buffs, artistically and psychologically wrong.

Yet at the same time that Willard was pandering to current tastes in popular fiction, he managed to tell a more compelling story than he thought he could. There is less of a true Manhattan ambience to *The Kidnap Murder Case,* but there is also less pointless "learned" discourse from Vance. There is an absence in the book of the distinctive texture that defined his earliest novels, but the reader is also spared much that made those novels so mannered. And while there is a more than usually limited number of plausible suspects—the gravest flaw of the book—the premise of the initial abduction (a kidnapping that appears at first to be a ruse designed by the victim to get money from his family) is clever and interesting. In the hands of a Chandler or a Hammett, the real "tough guy" writers, the story might well have been a forceful one.

As publication time neared, Willard began to feel anxious and to drink more than usual. *Cosmopolitan*'s serialization of the book in its August through November issues hadn't elicited any strong reactions one way or the other. Indications were that the reviews wouldn't be encouraging. Nervous about a poor hardcover sales showing, with the economy getting no better and more readers waiting for book-club discounts, Willard agreed with the marketing people at Scribners to go out of his way to stir up some interest in his novel. He wrote a piece for *Reader's Digest* entitled "How I Got Away with Murder," recounting the origin of his career as a detective writer, and oversaw the organization of a deluxe anthology of the three books preceding *The Casino Murder Case.*

A measure of Willard's agitation in the days before *The Kidnap Murder Case* was released can be found, as always, in his reactions to Beverley. He coolly informed her that he was discontinuing her allowance now that she was twenty-eight and of age to take care of herself. Beverley was upset at the thought of doing without the money, as her theater work barely paid enough to cover the rent and food bills, and the temporary secretarial jobs she found from time to time never seemed to make much of a difference in her budget. But, as she wrote to her father, if with all of his contacts he was willing to help her find a job with one of the Hollywood studios, as a script reader or synopsis writer, she'd consider everything settled fairly enough. What astounded and enraged her was Willard's decision to offer no such help at all, ever. Most people in the studio offices she approached found it hard to believe that she was Willard Huntington Wright's daughter. After all, why wouldn't he just give them a call to say something on her behalf? A word from a man of his position would open doors for Beverley that women of her age and inexperience couldn't hope to pass through.

Beverley finally landed a low-paying job as a synopsis writer for Twentieth Century–Fox, no thanks to her father, and remarked to Katharine that she would scrub floors before taking money from Willard again. "I think his daughter is just as important as tropical fish or 50 scotties," she wrote. When Willard intimated that he would renew his financial assistance if Beverley would move in permanently with Annie and take care of her grandmother, she lashed out at him as someone who "can manipulate all the inquisition devices known with perfect skill." According to Beverley, Stanton advised her to sue her father for some share of his wealth.

Willard ignored all of this enmity. Three thousand miles distant from his family, that was easy to do. They had never understood him or sympathized with his dreams, he felt, and he was tired of being drained for support. Becoming testy even with Claire now, he anxiously awaited the reaction to the Scribners anthology and to the publication of *The Kidnap Murder Case*. It was, he felt, a critical moment for him.

The *Philo Vance Murder Cases* was a marvelous S. S. Van Dine collection that should have been a big seller but wasn't. It was a fat volume that reprinted three of Willard's novels—the Scarab, Kennel, and Dragon stories—along with pages of supplemental material and photos of all the Philo Vances of the screen (Powell, Rathbone, William, Lukas, Lowe) and several good artists' renderings of the detective. The fact that the book failed to sell surprised its author, who belatedly calculated—to his horror—that the recent attempts to keep his name before the public might detract from rather than enhance the sales of *The Kidnap Murder Case* that month. He was correct, though the glut of Van Dine material in the bookstores that fall probably didn't affect his overall sales for the novel one way or the other. The Philo Vance series was in "a slump," as *The New Yorker* charitably observed, and the meager dramatic offerings of the tenth novel only confirmed everybody's feeling that S. S. Van Dine was washed up. The end-of-the-year figures on *The Kidnap Murder Case* justified the middling ad campaign Scribners expended on it (Philo Vance was always a reasonable Christmas gift), but the royalties Willard could anticipate were not enough to pay the yearly bills for a penthouse, domestic staff, car, chauffeur, and all the other trappings of the high life. More importantly, to Willard's amazement, not one Hollywood or foreign studio expressed the slightest interest in making an offer on the book's film rights.

That winter, for the first time, the Wrights cut back on their entertaining and their evenings out, and Willard let his agent know that he was ready for more product endorsements—any product, any sponsor, for a few thousand dollars.

Almost as if to deny the obvious signs for which he had been preparing himself, Willard tried to proceed for a while, in a professional sense, as if nothing had changed, as if Max Perkins or Irving Thalberg were truly interested in another book from the pen of S. S. Van Dine. A stern work pace had been his usual response to self-doubt in the past, and now Willard reacted in the same industrious way. He began sometime in 1937 dictating to Y. B. Garden a novel he intended to call *The Powwow Murder Case,* a crime story that was (in the narrator's turgid words in the opening chapter) to shock "New York as no other case had done, with the possible exception of the fantastic crimes which came to be known as 'The Bishop Murder Case.'" The story was presumably going to involve mysticism and ritual, as the cabala is mentioned in the early pages, and Willard had some idea of his cast of characters and the murder that was to spark the investigation. But he was never able to finish the novel or, evidently, to advance the manuscript beyond its first few chapters. Nor does it seem that Willard was able to bring himself to tell Perkins right away about his block, a paralysis which he feared was going to be permanent.

At this point Willard's penchant for announcing publications far ahead of time came back to haunt him again. Acting on their author's statements that he was going to finish the novel by the following summer, Scribners had printed up a dummy cover and table of contents for *The Powwow Murder Case,* the kind of promotional device the firm's salesmen used to circulate on their bookstore rounds when placing early orders. Once the cover, dust jacket, and table of contents were ready, though, Willard collapsed in exhaustion and gave up the whole project. All that remains today of *The Powwow Murder Case* is that cover and some four pages of the story, a bizarre collector's item that sold for $2,500 in 1981.

It is possible that Max Perkins himself ultimately precipitated Willard's abandonment of the book. In the spring of 1937 he had sent a letter to Willard hinting that the future for S. S. Van Dine at Scribners did not look favorable. It must have been a torturous letter for Perkins to have to write, and his message is couched in the gentlest, most euphemistic terms. Still, its meaning is perfectly apparent. Times were bad, Perkins noted, and it only made sense for Willard to continue the series if his agent could ensure decent serialization agreements before Scribners went out on a limb to publish anything more in book form. That was going to be a problem, as both Perkins and Willard knew. *Cosmopolitan* had taken three of the novels and was probably ready to end their involvement with Philo Vance. The other magazines weren't interested in paying Willard's old prices or publishing any more of his stories with so many other writers to choose from. In 1927, who besides Willard was writing original detective fiction in America that anyone wanted to read? Ten years later the field was crowded with exciting newcomers, with Rex Stout confidently leading the pack. So the decision to put *The Powwow Murder Case* aside might well have come after consultation with Harold Ober's agency and the realization that six months of labor, time spent imagining a story, dictating a draft, and rewriting, didn't stand a chance of being profitably repaid.

In April Willard appeared in the pages of *Life, The Saturday Review of Literature,* and *Collier's* testifying to the superb quality of Goodrich Tires. He had decided not to think about the future. It seemed best to go back to spending whatever he wanted and assume that fate would settle matters as it chose. In spite of his doctor's increasingly strong warnings, he continued on the eve of his fiftieth birthday to drink staggering quantities of brandy at all hours of the day and to eat the rich foods and heavy desserts he had come to love. His face grew puffy. The circles under his eyes deepened. As Jon Tuska, a friend of Stanton's, later observed, Willard was living in these last years not dangerously, as his adored Nietzsche advised, but desperately. Denial, anger, and fear were overshadowing the splendor of the penthouse and the sedate public image.

On some level Willard must have been contemplating his own death, whether or not he was secretly courting it as Stanton firmly believed. His actions in regard to Claire's future were too calculated to suppose otherwise. Beginning in 1937 more and more of their money was transferred from Willard's bank account to one that had been set up for Claire. It was a logical decision from a man supposedly indifferent to practical considerations. In the event of her husband's death, Claire would be spared the loss of funds through inheritance taxes, and in accordance with this plan Willard thereafter never kept more than $20,000 in his own account at any one time. He also began his remarkably thorough and systematic attempt to thwart any future interest in his life story by destroying files of correspondence and early unfinished manuscripts.

Much of the rest of this grim year was devoted to spending the money *The Kidnap Murder Case* had brought in, along with the few hundred dollars he received from Grosset & Dunlap for an anthology that firm brought out. *The Philo Vance Weekend* brought together the "Canary," Greene, and Bishop cases but included no new material. When Claire suggested that they had been betting too much at the track, Willard got rid of the last of the aquaria and took to selling his books, three or four hundred at a time. With the few thousand dollars that one of these periodic housecleaning projects netted him, he could go back to the track with a clear conscience, though he told Katharine—incredibly—that the day was approaching when she would have to look out for herself, alimony agreement or no alimony agreement. He even intimated to Beverley that he and Claire were discussing giving up the penthouse sometime in 1938 and moving to a smaller, less costly apartment in the same building. Pure bluff, was Beverley's assessment of this forecast. From her boardinghouse room in California, she found it hard to feel sorry for a man living as comfortably as her father seemed to be.

The sole piece of work Willard brought himself to do in the final months of the year was also the last piece of writing he published under his own name. The Modern Library series, inaugurated under Albert Boni and Horace Liveright in the 1910s, had continued to attract readers throughout the Twenties and Thirties, and in 1937 a reprinting of Nietzsche's *Beyond Good and Evil* was being prepared. Willard was asked to write a short biographical and critical introduction to the volume, a task that he found refreshing, both for the happy remembrance of things past it provided and the rare chance at an intellectually stimulating exercise.

Willard's Nietzsche had always been a figure of his own devising, to some extent. Few philosophers have been as variously interpreted as Nietzsche, as used for different, even conflicting purposes. So it isn't surprising that the tone of Willard's introduction is more in line with his own mood of belligerence toward his family and disdain for the world. It isn't Nietzsche's tough-minded affirmation of life's pain and struggle, his call for a fierce and accepting joy, that Willard stressed, but his pride and righteousness. "The hardier human traits, such as egotism, cruelty, arrogance, retaliation and appropriation, are given ascendancy [in Nietzsche]," Willard approvingly wrote, "over the soft virtues, such as sympathy, charity, forgiveness, loyalty, and humility, and are pronounced necessary constituents in the moral code of a natural aristocracy." How ludicrous the thought of his place in a Nietzsche-inspired natural aristocracy must have seemed now, to a man who wrote for *Reader's Digest* and *Cosmopolitan*. But to an individualist who wanted a literary justification for his own lack of sympathy, charity, forgiveness, loyalty and humility, those detestable "soft virtues," Nietzsche would always be the easy source of quotation and allusion.

Having completed his task for Modern Library, Willard in effect sat back, in a fatalistic rather than a curious or hopeful sense, to see what the future would bring. He knew that his ability to arrange his destiny, like his control over his income or reputation, would be minimal from this time on. He had no plans or expectations of anything promising ahead. On some days it was, he told Max Perkins, only the brandy that kept him going.

The immediate way out, the new route Willard realized that he would have to follow if he wanted to maintain his income for at least a few more years, was suggested to him just before Christmas in 1937. It was then that he was contacted by a Paramount executive who had, he told him, a great idea that was going to make his studio and S. S. Van Dine a fair amount of money. Willard was eager to hear the scheme; anything lucrative at this point, now that he was done with novel writing, was worth looking into. Like the weary Vance, who perked up only when the trail of a murder was presented to him, Willard could be brought out of his depression only by the thought of a financial venture. The angle brazenly presented to him by Paramount was—outright parody. The vehicle for the proposed satire, comic actress Gracie Allen.

Whatever Willard really thought of teaming Philo Vance up with the costar of the popular Burns and Allen radio show, of seeing his once-cherished creation remade in the spirit of screwball comedy, he never revealed for the record. And while S. S. Van Dine was not exactly a stranger to the satirizing of his detective—he had helped Corey Ford with *The John Riddell Murder Case* spoof in 1930, and the several parodies that had appeared in the intervening years had struck him as fair and amusing—the idea submitted to him was something vastly different. He would be agreeing to a level of self-abasement beyond his worst fears when he visited Hollywood in 1928 and pronounced the whole studio world too ignorant to take seriously, or when he began his own detective screenwriting for Vitaphone in 1931 and felt that he was calling the shots. It seems, though, that Willard didn't hesitate to accept the studio's offer for a Gracie Allen–Philo Vance story as the contracts were drawn up with dispatch, and Harold Ober was able to report that he had secured an easy $25,000 for his client.

All that was asked of Willard for that money was that he prepare a plot outline of 3,000 words to be "used as the basis for the development of a more detailed treatment" which would follow a few months later. The "detailed treatment," a fully developed story or novel didn't matter in the least to the studio. Their interest was in a plot line with the name of S. S. Van Dine attached to it. But the agreement allowed for Willard to hand over a completed novel (really a novelized screenplay)—and a very short one, as it turned out, of some 20,000 words—for Scribners to publish. Scribners was quite willing to handle the book knowing that its sales would be directly linked to a movie version with a star like Gracie Allen. Willard had only to agree that Paramount could make any changes with *The Gracie Allen Murder Case* it wished in the ultimate transformation from synopsis/novella to screenplay.

Willard saw George Burns and Gracie Allen for lunch in New York early in 1938, the only time he met the two performers. The whole idea sounded fine to them, and it was concluded that parts would be written in for both of them. "And that was all there was to it, as far as we were concerned," Burns later recalled. "He retained all the rights, and we took advantage of the publicity."

No more care was expended by Willard on the writing of his plot outline, or the novella that eventually emerged from it, than Paramount later expended on the screenplay. In Willard's own words, *The Gracie Allen Murder Case* was "a flop," a mortification of the first order. In the view of George Burns, who was a character in the novel but who had decided not to be in the film after all, the fiasco of the movie version was reason enough for Gracie not to appear on screen again without him.

The Gracie Allen Murder Case was written, not as an original work of fiction like the ten Philo Vance books that preceded it, but in consultation with people at Paramount. The first instruction to Willard had to do with the title, as his tradition of a four-word title with the second word always of six letters had to be abandoned in order to accommodate Gracie's first and last name. In every other way, the book reads like the makeshift contraption that it is. Its virtue, if that is the word for it, is the fidelity with which Willard captured Gracie Allen's daffy style of speech, which entertained a large audience in the late Thirties, while its failings are too numerous to list beyond noting that, as a "proper" detective novel, it is a stillborn venture. The story involves gangsters and a threat on Markham's life; the confusing murder of a young man in a Manhattan café owned by under-world figures; the wooing of Gracie Allen, a sweet but dopey factory worker, by her co-worker at the plant, George Burns, who is also a suspect in the case; and Allen's desire to assist Philo Vance in his investigation of the crime to clear her boyfriend's name. Even Paramount's script department found the book a rambling and undramatic narrative and changed the plot con-siderably when it passed into their hands.

The one character of interest in the novel is a somber, intel-ligent mob leader who is one of the men involved in the murder and a figure who might almost be seen as Vance's doppelgänger and a reflection of the novel's author. "Nothing has the slightest importance," this character, Dominic "Owl" Owen, philosophizes in a private moment with Vance. He complains that his temper-ament has drawn him in too many directions at once, leading him to waste his energy in life, and only now, late in the day, does he recognize "the rotten futility of all things—the futility of do-ing anything, even of thinking." The "instinct to achieve" has driven Owen to be a criminal "big shot," and it is that drive to make a mark in the world that he sees as the real problem, or tragedy, of life. "We learn its worthlessness only when it has devoured us," he tells Vance.

For once, Philo Vance seems to have met his equal. He is mesmerized by Owen's fatalism, his calmly expressed bitterness, his scorn for the manner of most men's lives. Suffering from a bad heart, knowing that his time is very short, Owen is unafraid of death. The affinity between the two world-weary men, one working for the law, the other for himself, is such that Vance actually agrees to allow "Owl" Owen the opportunity to pass out of life neatly and quickly should the occasion arise, a kind of spiritual compact Vance has never made in any of his other cases. At the end of the story, Vance even suggests to Owen the means by which he might speedily commit suicide before the police arrive.

Nothing about Owen, the philosophical gangster, struck Paramount as worth preserving when Willard's scathingly reviewed novel came out in the spring of 1938. (Interestingly, *The Powwow Murder Case* was still listed as "in preparation" on the front page of *The Gracie Allen Murder Case*—a bizarre quirk of optimism on Willard's part.) The Hollywood screenwriters were soon at work radically altering the story to their purposes, giving Gracie a bigger role than Vance's in the sleuthing, writing out George Burns, who didn't want to be in the movie, and adding more corny comedy. Even in the debased form Willard had written his story, Van Dine was still too "highbrow" for Paramount's purposes. Mercifully, Willard was dead by the time the film was released in 1939. He was spared the brutal humbling of Philo Vance, whom the forgetful Gracie calls "Fido Vance," and the sight of Warren William and William Demarest walking through their parts as Vance and Heath.

Willard's choice of an epigraph for this "novel," the last work he completed, is a line from Cromwell—"One never rises so high as when one does not know where one is going"—and would seem to be an allusion to Gracie's scatterbrained help in solving the case. Yet the line also rings true as a statement about the path of Willard's life since his Century Club luncheon with Max Perkins when he nervously handed over his plot outlines for a series of three detective stories. Not quite sure of where he was going then, he had traveled both higher and lower than he had expected.

In an advertising campaign for Hiram Walker gin that began appearing in various magazines in April of 1938, the photographs of S. S. Van Dine that the publicists used show a startling change in Willard's appearance over the last two years of his life. In his light suit, dark tie, and hat, with a flawlessly trimmed beard turned almost white, he might have been a plump, well-preserved man of sixty-five or seventy. No one unfamiliar with the famous author in the ad would believe that the aging dandy in the picture (who looks indeed as if he enjoyed his Hiram Walker gin) was only six months short of his fifty-first birthday. Willard was a man growing old rapidly, almost deliberately. His immaculate style of attire, which had only grown more precise over the years, couldn't disguise what the lines of the face and the exhaustion of the eyes registered, a consented drift toward death.

If Stanton's presentiment of his brother's condition and fate wasn't accurate in 1932, it was certainly true six years later. Cynical, fastidious, and resigned, like his strange character "Owl" Owen, Willard was just waiting for the end.

AN ORDERLY
END

"There must be no pebble thrown. We must cut through this shadow clean. . . . Accounts, a house-cleaning, temporal orderliness. No ripples to follow me for all time. Cleanliness—beyond . . . you understand?"

—*"Owl" Owen, on the proper way to die*
(THE GRACIE ALLEN MURDER CASE, *1938*)

O n March 13th, 1939, Willard read in *The New York Times* of the death of Antony Anderson. The former Los Angeles art critic had been like an older brother to the arrogant twenty-one-year-old he met in 1908 in Harry Andrews' newsroom, taking him to the theater and introducing him to California painters and writers (and available women) in those first great days on the job. He had also been his welcoming host when Willard returned triumphantly to California in the late Twenties as S. S. Van Dine. And now he was gone, one more piece of the past brushed aside.

Willard learned of Anderson's death while he himself was recovering from what seemed at first to be a mild heart attack. Two weeks earlier, at the end of February, Willard had been stricken at home. He was well enough to be released from the hospital in less than a week and outwardly gave signs of a quick return to a functioning state. The reality of his condition was otherwise. Claire did her best to appear pleased with her husband's progress and told Willard that everything was going to be back to normal very soon, but the doctors had privately warned her that Willard's chances of living out the year were slim. If he did live for an extended time, she was told, he would be an invalid subject to recurrent blood clotting and more heart trouble. Coronary thrombosis was the ominous term the cardiologist was using now, and the prognosis was bleak. If Willard suspected the truth, which is likely, he seems to have tacitly agreed to maintain the fiction that would be easier for both of them to bear. He returned to the penthouse to be fussed over and tended to by Claire, his valet, and a full-time nurse.

The six months before Willard's attack had been a strangely full, almost intense period after a lull of several months. At the end of the summer, long after *The Gracie Allen Murder Case* was out in book form and in the hands of Paramount's rewrite people, Willard had heard from another old California friend, Julian Johnson. Johnson had been the third member of that critical triumvirate on *The Los Angeles Times*, covering drama while Anderson reviewed art and Wright took on the literary world, and his path had crossed Willard's on numerous occasions later—when Willard published Johnson's stories in *The Smart Set*, when Johnson as *Photoplay* editor had published Willard's movie magazine pieces. Since the early Thirties Johnson had been head of the story department at Twentieth Century–Fox and, hearing in 1938 that the competition had tapped S. S. Van Dine for a movie-novel idea tailored to a particular star, he had decided to try to arrange for the same kind of deal.

Willard was open to Johnson's overture for a detective story to highlight a new Fox actress, the professional ice-skater Sonja Henie, but the studio was reluctant to meet Willard's asking price of $25,000 "up front." Darryl F. Zanuck, head of production then, was eager to come to an agreement but had a hard-and-fast rule about paying advances sight unseen. To keep everybody happy, an elaborate system of staggered payments was worked out whereby Willard was paid $2,500 for a basic story idea of no more than a few pages, another $2,500 for a 6,000-word outline, $15,000 for the novella itself (about the length of *The Gracie Allen Murder Case*), and $5,000 for any changes Willard was asked to make by the studio. Scribners could then pick up the property once the studio had decided it was their kind of story. After Willard's yearly ritual of a few weeks' visit to Atlantic City in September, the contracts were signed in October and S. S. Van Dine went to work.

Early in November two previous films of Henie's were screened for Willard at Fox's New York office, so that he could have some idea of the young woman's dramatic strengths (slight as they turned out to be) and considerable limitations. Not that Willard was bothered by the thought of writing a part for someone of less than high-caliber acting talent: from Louise Brooks to Rosalind Russell to Gracie Allen was a descent that spoke for itself. But it quickly became apparent that Van Dine and Twentieth Century–Fox were working at cross-purposes on this project.

Having been stung by Paramount's insinuation that his efforts with *The Gracie Allen Murder Case* hadn't been quite what they expected (too much Philo Vance, not enough Gracie Allen), Willard wanted to be sure that he got it right this time. He bombarded Julian Johnson and Harry Joe Brown, an associate producer at Fox, with questions about the story and clarifications about just what they wanted from him. Willard's obsequiousness and tentative manner left both men at a loss, and it surely must have been most uncomfortable for Willard's old colleague Johnson. "We want your ideas on what the story should be, what the characters should be, what the location should be," he wrote to Willard after Willard had offered to mail the studio a questionnaire to better understand their wishes for Henie and intentions for the picture. When Willard learned that Fox didn't even care if Philo Vance were included in the story at all (Fox's sole interest was in being able to attach the name "S. S. Van Dine" to a script), he must have felt that he had come to the end of the line.

All about him there was an aura of respect—hefty sums by Depression standards dangled before him, a veneer of deference, an agent to negotiate terms for him, gossip columnists always ready for an item about him. Yet, when left alone to consider his situation, Willard knew there was nothing left to respect. "S. S. Van Dine" was a product valued for the name only, a commodity long since run to ground. Willard himself had become, at last, the kind of man he had mocked in his youth, a John Adams Thayer, a blight on the culture he had once planned to elevate and open to new artistic influences.

With a clear, almost stoical awareness that this would be the last thing he would ever write, alerted by his cardiologist to the fact that if he kept working and drinking as he did he would be dead within a year or two, Willard pressed himself to finish the story he decided to call *The Winter Murder Case*. (He drew the line at Johnson's thought that they could call it *The Sonja Henie Murder Case*.) It is an aptly named novella. The story is wintry in both its setting, an Upstate New York mansion in January, and in its gray mood. Vance is old now, and his investigation of the murders on his friend Carrington Rexon's estate and the theft of Rexon's jewel collection is perfunctory and uncomplicated. His long-time allies, the District Attorney and the Sergeant, have been retired from the field of action for the most part. Markham appears only briefly at the beginning of the book. At the center of the story is the simple character written for Henie (given her full share of ice-skating scenes), who is the daughter of the estate's caretaker. She is one of Willard's few innocents in all of his work, and her love for Rexon's son provides the drama's only sense of youth and future life. She is a Cinderella figure in the story, raised from obscurity to wealth by the attentions of a rich and handsome young savior, a man who can appreciate her qualities in the midst of a circle of more urbane and shallow friends.

The Winter Murder Case was completed, at least in its 20,000-word stage of the process, in the third week of February. Y. B. Garden saw that it was typed and left on her employer's desk for his inspection. He did not live to reread it.

Before Christmas Willard had made out his will, leaving everything to Claire. All during the autumn and winter, whenever he wished to take a break from the writing, he had seen to the sale of those of his more valuable books or ceramics. That money he put aside for Claire. This tending to "accounts . . . housecleaning . . . temporal orderliness" that "Owl" Owen had spoken of was executed by Willard in these weeks with scrupulous care and eerie determination, almost as if he knew that the time left was even shorter than those around him thought. Then came the first attack, the week in the hospital, the return to 241 Central Park West and confinement to bed.

On the 11th of April, a cold and cloudy day, Willard died. Claire described that afternoon to Max Perkins a few weeks later. "We had a happy time together Tuesday," she wrote. "He seemed so much better and talked of getting up soon. I was helping the nurse with his dinner and he joked about various things—and made some comments on some news I had repeated to him. Suddenly he relaxed against the pillows and he was gone—quietly and painlessly."

Willard was cremated two days later, as he had requested in his will, without any ceremony ("we must cut through this shadow clean"). Obituaries, most of them long and filled with all of the anecdotes and misinformation Willard had carefully planted over the years (including the inaccurate birth year of 1888), appeared in every major newspaper in the country, and Claire was comforted by an impressive pile of cards and letters of condolence. *The New York Times,* honoring Willard with both an obituary and an editorial, wrote that "his was a curious, various, and ample life, comparatively short as it was" and praised Willard as "a master of his form."

In June the disastrous film of *The Gracie Allen Murder Case* was released and passed quickly from the scene, while a few months later *The Winter Murder Case,* the twelfth and shortest S. S. Van Dine novel, was released by Scribners with a brief preface by Max Perkins. Perkins was his usual gracious, charitable self, though his remarks about what he described as Willard's essentially gentle, anguished nature shed no light on the real man or the failed artist. This eulogy from his editor was merely the replacing of one false image, the one Willard had concocted himself, with another. As expected, the sales for *The Winter Murder Case* were meager, and the film version as Willard had conceived it never materialized. Reworked into the B-movie *Sun Valley Serenade,* the story of the Rexon murders became a dismal vehicle for Henie's skating that omitted Philo Vance altogether and retained only the Cinderella motif of innocence rewarded and rags-to-riches.

Despite Willard's lavish obituaries, which Claire collected into two fat scrapbooks, the decline of his name into obscurity began soon after his death, with more people remembering the eight or nine bad novels of the detective series and fewer people remembering the earlier, more worthy achievements. Almost no one in the Forties and Fifties, it seemed, thought that Willard's pre–Van Dine career merited any attention. (Both Mencken and Nathan declined to talk about Willard at any length, or with any honesty, with their myriad interviewers of those decades.) Alfred Kazin's 1942 classic *On Native Grounds* made mention of Willard's role in America's coming-of-age in the 1910s, as did Henry May's book *The End of Innocence* in 1959. In *Modern American Painting and Sculpture* of the same year, Sam Hunter was one of the few authorities of the museum and art-historical community to write about Willard as a seminal force in America's introduction to modern art. Beyond that, it was as if Willard Huntington Wright had never existed while Philo Vance still retained a hold on the popular imagination.

By the 1960s, though, both Willard and S. S. Van Dine (and his sleuth) were pretty much forgotten in American cultural histories, a situation which both Claire and Stanton had done nothing to arrest. Fearful of revelations about her husband's drug addiction, Claire discouraged any serious inquiry into her husband's life throughout the 1940s and '50s and eventually destroyed many letters. Stanton, too, did little to encourage serious biographical work. He came in time to think more warmly of his difficult brother, but he must have felt some satisfaction in outliving Willard to become a respected professor at UCLA, an affluent painter, and a much-interviewed old Modernist.

Claire Wright survived Willard by seventeen years. Having given up the penthouse within a year of his passing, and having auctioned off most of their grand furnishings and almost all of Willard's thousands of books, she lived in comfort in a smaller East Side apartment until her death in 1956. Annie Wright benefited from a small allowance from Claire until her death in her late eighties in 1949. She died with only a few hundred dollars in the bank.

A prominent figure in the California art world, Stanton died in 1973, not long after a full-scale retrospective of his work in Washington, D.C., at the Smithsonian. Synchromism itself had to wait until 1978 for its serious revival at the time of a major color-abstraction exhibition at the Whitney Museum in New York. Today, with abstraction long since established as a main current of modern art, a major Synchromist painting would sell in the six-figure range (a fact that both Wrights would relish). The scholarship about Synchromism continues, Willard's art criticism has been written about more extensively in the 1980s, and the first retrospective of Morgan Russell's work was held in 1990.

Beverley Wright outlived her father by forty years, though the happiness and professional success she hoped for, connected as it was to her father's approval, always eluded her. She remained unmarried and, as she grew older, became a difficult, demanding woman—her father's child at the end. Working at a succession of jobs, Beverley never quite found her way in life. Her last years in Oakland, California, were a financially strained and unhappy time. Before entering a nursing home, she was forced to sell the few drawings of her uncle's that she owned. Katharine, devoted supporter and earliest victim of Willard's needs, died in the late 1950s, almost completely dependent on Beverley. Drinking more heavily after Willard's death and unable to hold a job, impoverished and dismayed that all of Willard's money had been left to Claire and none to her or Beverley, she gradually lost touch with the world around her. After a collapse brought on by her alcoholism, she returned, Beverley wrote, "to the fairy tales and dreams of her childhood and never left them again."

Finally, in an ironic touch Stanton and Willard would have appreciated, the early "Portrait of the Artist's Brother" from 1914—Stanton's homage to his best critic, now renamed "Portrait of S. S. Van Dine"—remained in family hands, seemingly unsellable for decades. In 1987 it was bought by the Smithsonian. There it lines a corridor of the National Portrait Gallery on F Street near the Smithsonian's portraits of Hemingway, Fitzgerald, Wolfe, Ring Lardner, Dashiell Hammett (and Stanton), and so many others of his generation. Thanks to Stanton's artistry and Willard's devotion to his brother's quixotic cause, Willard Huntington Wright finally has the place he merits among that gallery's collection of American originals. His life is not a tale of undeterred accomplishment and impeccable aspirations, to be sure, but it is still a very American story of ambition, struggle, and "success" on a large scale, with some sense of the complications and costs of that pursuit of James' devouring "Bitch Goddess." It is appropriate that Stanton's fine painting, echoing the colors and style of Cézanne, suggests not the later, defeated side of his brother's life, but the earlier, brighter moment of confidence in his own and in America's future.

Source Notes

ABBREVIATIONS

U.Va.   University of Virginia: Willard Huntington Wright Collection (family letters, many undated)

Pr.   Princeton University Library: Willard Huntington Wright Correspondence or, principally, Willard Huntington Wright Scrapbooks (dated but unpaginated newspaper and magazine clippings)

SS   *The Smart Set*

LAT   *Los Angeles Times*

PREFACE

xvi   "whose books seem not to be affected . . ." Kuehl, 167.

xvi   "all booze and erections . . .": WHW letter to Florence Ryerson, 1/16/35, Pr.

xvii   "I'm so glad for all the brandy I've had . . .": Berg, 364.

xix   Wright's last visit to Perkins before Christmas: Ibid.

xx   "complete to the last comma": Perkins, Preface to *The Winter Murder Case*, ix.

xx   "a kind of subtler splendor . . .": *New York Times*, 4/13/39, 22.

xxi   "a great liar . . .": Forgue, 434.

xxii   "a gallant, gentle man . . .": Perkins, op. cit., xiii.

4   "a token of vigorous experiment . . .": Kazin, 166.

6   "just plain dopey": WHW letter to Katharine Wright, undated (1913), U.Va.

6   "We believe no literary critic . . .": SS, February 1913, 160.

7   "This month I have surrendered my column . . .": SS, March 1913, 160.

7   "I believe that this is the day . . .": Ibid.

7   Wright's article on Los Angeles: SS, March 1913, 107–114.

9   "If only some eminent divine . . .": WHW letter to Katharine, undated note (spring 1913), U.Va.

10   "It seems incredible . . .": SS, April 1913, 159–160.

12   "all American literature seems to be written . . .": LAT, 5/19/09, Pr.

14   on WHW and Terhune's stories: Terhune, 196–198.

15   "a conscientious hack": LAT, 1910 clipping, Pr.

15   "as if he had just left . . .": Boyd, 8.

16   "our ballyhoo bard": LAT, 1/8/11.

16   On Willard and Pound's visit: Paige, 59.

17   "Wright thinks me a bit cracked . . .": Read, 24.

18   "The Night Romance of Vienna" appeared in the October issue of the magazine, 103–110.

20   "If Thayer lets [Willard] alone . . .": H. L. Mencken to Harry Leon Wilson, 7/4/16, Mencken Letters, Beinecke Library, Yale University.

THAYER'S REVENGE

22   "You don't know what it is . . .": WHW to Katharine, November 1913 note, U.Va.

23   "Be careful with the sexual stuff . . .": Manchester, 68, and Bode, 66.

26   "Glorious stuff . . .": Read, 19.

26   "that brute in New York . . .": Ibid., 24.

28   "Of course I have a contract with [him] . . .": WHW to Katharine, undated letter (autumn 1913), U.Va.

29   WHW's refusal of "The Death of a Hired Hand" and Pound's reaction is described in Weintraub, 315–316.

32   "entertain, amuse, thrill . . .": SS, March 1914, 160

33   "It's a Presbyterian paper . . .": WHW to Katharine, 2/5/14, U.Va.

33   "There is no smell of Broadway here . . .": H. L. Mencken to WHW, 3/2/14, Mencken letters, Yale University.

BEGINNINGS

35   "I was born in Virginia by accident . . .": undated clipping, newspaper interview, Pr.

36   "a manure and dust bonanza in dry weather . . .": Kean, 12.

37   "A man of silent mien and devout habits . . .": *The Man of Promise*, 4.

37   "Willard matured very young . . .": Crawford, 4.

38   On Stanton and Willard's relationship in childhood: interview with Jon Tuska (a friend of Stanton's), Portland, Oregon.

41   He told his friends of running away . . .: this tall tale appears in all of the literature about Stanton Wright and many of the interviews he granted in the 1950s and '60s.

43   "If you want a real portrait of Willard . . .": Macdonald-Wright/Jon Tuska correspondence (undated letter to Tuska from the 1970s), Portland, Oregon.

43   "hale, clear-eyed, and conspicuously able": *The Man of Promise*, 19.

43   "a rare exhibit": Schallert, "Men Whom Made the 'Times,' " LAT, 4/29/48, *Los Angeles Times* Archive, employee file.

44   "a well-kept orchard": Simonson, 6.

45   "drifted in" to Cambridge . . .: Ibid., 10.

46   Irene Brenner affair: *The Man of Promise*, 88–126.

46   "The desire for sensation . . .": Ibid., 78.

46   "the crowded glamour . . .": Ibid., 93.

47   "Our undisciplinables . . .": Kahn, 118.

47   "to get out into the world": B. S. Hurlburt to WHW, 3/21/07, Harvard University Library.

47   "supremely happy days": Jay Dinsmore to WHW, letter from 1922, U.Va.

49   "a clever and rising young poet": newspaper clipping, July 1907, family papers, U.Va.

THE SCHOOL OF MENCKEN

52   "Huntington did not recognize . . .": Carr, *Los Angeles, City of Dreams*, 347.

54   "an overworked, sedentary style": LAT, 11/29/08, Pr.

54   on Dickens: *LAT*, 4/11/09, Pr.

54   on Walpole: *LAT*, 11/29/08, Pr.

55   "the ne plus ultra of 'The Ladies Home Journal': *LAT*, 5/30/09, Pr.

55   "The raucous and tautological atrocities . . .": LAT, 3/6/10/, Pr.

55   "He has nothing to supply . . .": LAT, 8/8/09, Pr.

56   "Mystery yarns are at best sad affairs . . .": LAT, 8/28/10, Pr.

56   "The woods are full of detective stories . . .": LAT, 2/3/12, Pr.

57   "The most uncompromising and zealous literary critic . . .": Carr, LAT, 3/8/31, Pr.

61   "I find here in the East . . .": WHW to Katharine, 10/24/09, U.Va.

62   "I got into Baltimore about 4 p.m. . . .": WHW to Katharine, 10/25/09, U.Va.

62   "When the time comes . . .": Forgue, 7.
62   "Believe me . . .": Ibid.

THE BIRTH OF SYNCHROMISM

68   The four postcards from the Armory Show are in the University of Virginia Wright Collection.

70–72   Much of this information comes from a typescript of Macdonald-Wright's European journals, U.Va.

73   "capable of moving people to the degree that music does": Levin, 16.

74   "the palpitation or undulation": Ibid., 18.

74   Sonia Delaunay insisted . . .: Ibid., 19.

75   "[its] subject is deep blue": Ibid., 23.

76   "a rippling surface movement": Abramson, 122.

76   "eddies of mist . . .": Ibid., 124.

78   "the heart of [his] development . . .": Levin, 22–23.

79   Salmon's and Kahn's remarks: quoted in Baker, 85–86.

80   "full of picturesque blasphemy": Benton, *An Artist in America*, 39.

85   "left floundering . . .": *New York Evening Mail*, 3/7/14.

85   "artistic Barnums . . .": *Town Topics*, March 1914.

BATTLING FOR MODERN ART

86   "I'm glad to be near Stanton . . .": WHW to Katharine, 3/25/14, U.Va.

87   "that fat Dutchman from Baltimore": WHW to Huebsch, 5/4/14, B. W. Huebsch Papers, Library of Congress.

88   "When I want to satisfy . . .": "The Sex Impulse in Art," *West Coast Magazine*, October 1909, 287.

90   "Don't worry over me . . .": WHW to Katharine, 3/25/14, U.Va.

91   "They take debt much more seriously . . .": WHW to Katharine, summer 1914 letter, U.Va.

92   "having Willard by the neck": Forgue, 152.

93   "I had hoped never to see [America] again . . .": WHW to Katharine, 4/10/15, U.Va.

93   "The only intelligent people left today are the Germans . . .": Ibid.

93   "Wright used to try to convince me . . .": Bode, *The New Mencken Letters*, 116.

95   "prejudice, personal taste . . .": *Modern Painting*, 32.

95   "A true appreciation of art . . .": Ibid., 7–8.

96   "Synchromism embraces every aesthetic aspiration . . .": Ibid., 227.

96   "a young Lochinvar . . .": WHW's *Modern Painting* Scrapbook, Pr.

96   "all the credulous eagerness . . .": Ibid.

97   "The average spectator . . .": *Forum*, January 1916, 34.

98   "clinging to a musty and unvital past . . .": *Forum*, January 1916, 41–42, and March 1916, 333.

98   On Winslow Homer: *Forum*, December 1915, 661–672.

98   the attack on his fellow art critics: *Forum*, February 1916, 201–220.

99   "Mr. Wright goes through . . .": *Reedy's Mirror*, 11/5/15, 312–313.

99   "tired of chasing art up back alleys": Benton, *Artist in America*, 47.

100   "America the damnable . . .": Stanton Macdonald-Wright to John Weischel, undated (winter 1916?) note, *Archives of American Art*.

101   "the divided character of early American modernism": Knight, "On Native Ground," 167.

102   "I strive to divest my art . . .": Forum Exhibition catalogue.

102   The exchange with Coady is recounted in Harrell, 10–11, and Baker, 229–239.

103   "It was a magnificent show . . .": Alfred Stieglitz to Paul Haviland, 4/19/16, Stieglitz Collection, Beinecke Library, Yale University.

A MAN OF LETTERS

105   "of all the smug moralists, the lousiest": WHW to Katharine, 3/15/15, U.Va.

105   "full of hallucinations and phobias . . .": Ibid.

106   "The physical austerities I can bear . . .": WHW to Katharine, spring 1915 note, U.Va.

107   "I don't know how in hell . . .": WHW to Huebsch, 6/18/15, B. W. Huebsch Papers, Library of Congress.

109   "In a very real sense, it is the philosophy of Nietzsche we are fighting": quoted in Melvin Drimmer, "Nietzsche in American Thought, 1895–1925," Part II, 535 (Ph.D. thesis, University of Rochester, 1965).

109   "strength, confidence, exuberance . . .": *What Nietzsche Taught*, 12.

109   "taking haughty attitudes . . ." Benton, *Artist in America*, 46–47.

110   "These 'careers' . . .": Annie to Katharine, 10/1/15, U.Va.

111   "Germany has already won . . .": WHW to Katharine, 12/11/15, U.Va.

113   "I saw Witter Bynner lying on the floor . . .": Stanton Macdonald-Wright to Jon Tuska, Portland, Oregon, undated letter from the 1970s.

115   "All these pictures have to say is 'I want to have a baby.' ": Lisle, 75.

116   "One by one . . .": *The Man of Promise*, 276.

118   "a boob": Forgue, 152 (Forgue misreads Mencken's reference to "C" as pertaining to Katharine rather than Claire).

118   "Willard and Claire": Dreiser's sketchy notes for a story about the

couple are in the Dreiser Collection, Van Pelt Library, University of Pennsylvania.

118   "could uphold her end . . .": *The Man of Promise*, 272.

118   "Claire Burke was the only woman . . .": an unpublished and incomplete autobiographical sketch written by Beverley Wright in her old age, 16, U.Va.

119   William Faulkner's interest in *The Creative Will* is documented in Martin Kreisworth's *Arizona Quarterly* essay, among others.

120   "merely to feel art . . .": *The Creative Will*, 288.

121   "intellectually . . . a wonderful and full year": WHW to Katharine, 6/8/16, U.Va.

CRITICS AND SPIES

123   "no exaggeration is necessary . . .": WHW to Katharine, 5/10/17, U.Va.

124   "the intellectual colonization of America . . .": *Misinforming America*, 1.

125   "the timid nobodies . . .": Ibid., 3.

125   "neither universality of outlook nor freedom from prejudice . . .": Ibid., 9.

126   "wearying and irritating": clipping, WHW's "Misinforming a Nation" Scrapbook, Pr.

126   "a valuable service . . .": *Reedy's Mirror*, 1/26/17, 48.

127   "How you do slam the shams!": Huneker note to WHW, 8/12/17, Huneker Letters at Beinecke Library, Yale University.

127   "if Willard Huntington Wright writes four more books . . .": *Reedy's Mirror*, 5/25/17, 342.

127   "Drug addiction is a disease . . .": *Medical Review of Reviews*, June 1917, Pr.

129   The salary "will, if I cut down on my smoking . . .": WHW to Stanton Leeds, 6/21/17, Wright Letters, Beinecke Library, Yale University.

132   "Once lead this people into war . . .": Vacha, 172.

133   "she was 'a little off' . . .": WHW to Katharine, 11/30/17, U.Va.

135   "a masterpiece of imbecility" and other comments to Boyd: Forgue, 109–110, 112–113.

SETBACKS

138   "This man I had never known in the flesh . . .": Beverley Wright's sketch, 2, U.Va.

139   WHW's letter to Stieglitz: 1/4/18, Stieglitz Collection, Beinecke Library, Yale University.

139   "I could no more have relations with him . . .": H. L. Mencken to Stanton Leeds, 6/17/18, Mencken Letters, Beinecke Library, Yale University.

141   "You of all people should know why": Beverley's sketch, 6.

142   "The hysterics . . . the sudden breakdowns . . .": Ibid., 11.

143   "but from what I hear he has left behind a trail of semen . . .": Stanton Macdonald-Wright to Alfred Stieglitz, late 1918, Stieglitz Collection, Beinecke Library, Yale University.

144   "the subtle but unmistakable sense of escape . . .": quoted in *New York Times*, 7/15/84, E3.

144   "possessed the evanescent spirit of romance . . .": LAT, 2/9/19, Pr.

144   "a distinct falling-off in pulchritude": H. L. Mencken to George Sterling, 6/10/19, Mencken Letters, Beinecke Library, Yale University.

145   "A year there . . .": *San Francisco Bulletin*, 6/2/19, Pr.

146   "when I get sufficient strength . . .": WHW to Alfred Stieglitz, 1/4/18, Stieglitz Collection, Beinecke Library, Yale University.

146   "Our rich people here still stick to the idea . . .": quoted in Baker, 261.

147   "a city that runs to get nowhere": Stanton Macdonald-Wright to Alfred Stieglitz, 10/12/18, Stieglitz Collection, Beinecke Library, Yale University.

149   "The better people here are alive and interested": Ibid.

150   "Irreparable detriment to the rest of us": Ibid., 2/3/20.

150   "We modern artists are just what our name implies . . .": from Stanton's foreword to the catalogue for his show, quoted in Baker, 277–278.

151   "Art and Aunt Maria": LAT, 2/27/20.

152   "The West . . .": *San Francisco Bulletin*, 2/22/19.

153   "painting has had its say": quoted in Baker, 298.

IN THE SHADOWS

157   "I want to help Katharine . . .": WHW to Annie, 1920 note, U.Va.

158   WHW's conversations with Stanton and Katherine Leeds: Katherine Leeds, S. S. Van Dine obituary, *Greenwich Times*, 4/15/39.

159   The contract with de Sylva is in the David R. Smith S. S. Van Dine Collection, Pasadena, California.

164   "I want it to stand as a kind of prophecy . . .": WHW to Burton Rascoe, 1923 note, Rascoe Papers, Van Pelt Library, University of Pennsylvania.

165   "Mr. Wright . . .": clipping from *The Dial*, WHW's "The Future of Painting" Scrapbook, Pr.

165	"who had once given the impression . . .": Wilson, 318.
166	"or similar pious writers . . .": WHW to Katharine, October 1922 letter, U.Va.
168	"Nothing from Claire this year . . .": WHW to Katharine, 12/30/24, U.Va.
169	"It does not help either you or me . . .": WHW to Katharine, 10/12/24, U.Va.
169	Bartlett's visit: Bartlett, 10.
170	"counteract the detrimental effect . . .": WHW to Katharine, 8/27/24, U.Va.
170	"I hope you have impressed upon Beverley . . ." Ibid.
173	"intuitional to the point of clairvoyance": WHW's introduction to *The Great Detective Stories*, 20.
174	"elderly, plodding, painstaking . . .": Ibid., 17.
178	"casual, mercurial, debonair . . .": *The Benson Murder Case*, 19.
178	"I am absolutely penniless . . .": WHW to Katharine, 7/25/25, U.Va.
178	"This is to impress the publishers and editors . . .": WHW to Katharine, 12/19/25, U.Va.

"S. S. VAN DINE"

182	"You can't escape . . .": Seligmann, 42.
183	The Lake Hopatcong incident: conversation with retired professor James Butcher of Washington, D.C., who was a busboy at the hotel that summer.
183	"Philo Vance will inevitably find . . .": 1926 Scribners press release, Wright "S. S. Van Dine" Scrapbooks, Pr.
184	Dashiell Hammett's review: *Saturday Review of Literature*, 1/15/27, 510.
188	"Mr. Van Dine is a man in his thirties . . .": 1927 Scribners press release, Wright "S. S. Van Dine" Scrapbooks, Pr.
189	"Every murder differs from every other murder . . .": clipping (autumn 1927), WHW's "S. S. Van Dine" Scrapbooks, Pr.
192	"Pray don't give way to conventional moral indignation": *The "Canary" Murder Case*, 343.
193	"[*The 'Canary' Murder Case*] magnificently smashed the old taboos . . .": Haycraft, 1965.

A NEW LIFE

196	"New York is full of reports . . .": H. L. Mencken to WHW, autumn 1927 note, Mencken Letters, Beinecke Library, Yale University.
197	Perkins had been thoroughly pleased: Berg, 122.
198	"A major massacre": undated clipping, WHW's "S. S. Van Dine" Scrapbooks, Pr.
199	"the most tiresome person in modern fiction": clipping, WHW's "S. S. Van Dine" Scrapbooks, Pr.

205   "typical Hollywood morons . . .": WHW to Florence Ryerson, 6/19/
       28, Pr.

207   "Author Declares Film Better Than Book": *Hollywood News,* 10/12/
       28.

208   The description of William Powell: Beverley's sketch, 24.

208   The awkward family visit: Ibid., 20–25.

209   "an impertinent fling at his brother": undated clipping, December
       1928, Pr.

209   "He was never my press agent . . .": Stanton Macdonald-Wright to
       Alfred Stieglitz, spring 1923, Stieglitz Collection, Beinecke Library,
       Yale University.

210   "it seems a great pity . . .": LAT, 7/8/28, Pr.

210   "It's all been a great adventure . . .": *Los Angeles Herald,* 10/15/28,
       Pr.

       BREAK WITH THE PAST

215   "several interesting twists": *New York Post* clipping, WHW's *Scarab
       Murder Case,* Scrapbook, Pr.

217   "giving the bastards what they want": Beverley's sketch, 22, U.Va.

218   "a quick study": a conversation with William T. Beatty III, New
       York City.

219   "Machiavelli meets the milkmaid": Beverley's sketch, 27.

223   Leonard Maltin's remarks on the Vitaphone films: Maltin, *The Great
       Movie Shorts,* 23.

224   "I feel like the fellow . . .": LAT, 3/8/31, Pr.

226   It was, Beverley later observed: an observation repeated more than
       once in her sketch, U.Va.

227   Stanton's visit to New York: conversation with Jon Tuska and
       Tuska, *The Detective in Hollywood,* 27.

       KENNELS, DRAGONS, AND CASINOS

232   a "mellowed and humanized" character: clipping, WHW's *Kennel
       Murder Case* Scrapbook, Pr.

234   "to writing the books one starves on": Ibid.

236   "the same egregiously conceited ass": clipping, WHW's *Dragon
       Murder Case* Scrapbook, Pr.

238   The Humberstone–Jack Warner anecdote and information about
       The Dragon Murder Case: Tuska, *The Detective in Hollywood,* 39–41.

242   Rosalind Russell's reluctance to be in *The Casino Murder Case:* Rus-
       sell, 65.

242   MGM's interest in comic relief: WHW to Florence Ryerson, 1/16/
       35, and 2/15/35, Pr.

243   the film "must have been made while Irving Thalberg was out
       fishing": clipping, WHW's *Casino Murder Case* Scrapbook, Pr.

| 244 | "entirely flattened and utterly speechless": WHW to Florence Ryerson, op. cit. |

| 244 | "Be good or I'll remind people . . .": Russell, 65. |

THE LAST YEARS

| 245 | "uneventful and depressing of late": WHW to Mencken, 3/10/35, Mencken letters, Beinecke Library, Yale University. |

| 247 | "I'm just not going to be downed by an unwilling father": Beverley to Katharine, 9/18/36, U.Va. |

| 248 | "to introduce amour . . .": WHW's list is reprinted in *Philo Vance Murder Cases,* 74. |

| 249 | According to Garden, she was allowed . . .: Tuska, *The Detective in Hollywood,* 45. |

| 250 | "fascinating dope": clipping, WHW's *Garden Murder Case* Scrapbook, Pr. |

| 251 | "sweet revenge": Randolph Bartlett to H. L. Mencken, 11/17/41, Mencken Papers, New York Public Library. |

| 251 | Bartlett's article: *The Saturday Review of Literature,* 11/2/35, 10. |

| 252 | "I hear that he was like a maniac for a week . . .": Bartlett to Mencken, 11/17/41, Mencken Papers, New York Public Library. |

| 255 | "I think his daughter is just as important . . .": Beverley to Katharine, undated letter (mid-1930s), U.Va. |

| 256 | "a slump": *The New Yorker,* 10/24/36. |

| 257 | Times were bad, Perkins noted . . .: Perkins to WHW, 1938 note, Perkins Letters, Scribner Archive, Pr. |

| 258 | Willard was living in these last years not dangerously . . .: Tuska, *The Detective in Hollywood,* 46. |

| 259 | "The hardier human traits . . .": Introduction, *Beyond Good and Evil,* Modern Library, 1937, xiv. |

| 261 | Willard saw George Burns . . .: Tuska, *The Detective in Hollywood,* 46. |

| 262 | "Nothing has the slightest importance . . .": *The Gracie Allen Murder Case,* 166. |

AN ORDERLY END

| 268 | The writing of *The Winter Murder Case* script is recounted in David R. Smith's essay on the subject in Tuska's chapbook, "Philo Vance: The Life and Times of S. S. Van Dine." |

| 269 | "We had a happy time together . . .": Claire Wright to Max Perkins, 4/26/39, Perkins Letters, Scribner Archive, Pr. |

| 269 | "his was a curious, various, and ample life . . .": *The New York Times,* 4/13/39, 22. |

| 271 | "to the fairy tales and dreams of her childhood . . .": Beverley's sketch, 40. |

BIBLIOGRAPHY

Adams, Henry. *Thomas Hart Benton.* New York: Knopf, 1989.

Adams, J. Donald. *Copey of Harvard.* Boston: Houghton Mifflin, 1960.

Agee, William C. "Synchromism." Exhibition catalogue, Knoedler Galleries, 1965.

———. "Willard Huntington Wright and the Synchromists," *Archives of American Art Journal,* Autumn 1985.

Angoff, Charles. *H. L. Mencken: A Portrait from Memory.* New York: T. Yoseloff, 1956.

Baigell, Matthew. *Thomas Hart Benton.* New York: Abrams, 1974.

Baker, Marilyn. "The Art Theory and Criticism of Willard Huntington Wright," Ph.D. thesis, University of Wisconsin, 1975.

Bartlett, Randolph. "A Man of Promise," *Saturday Review of Literature,* November 2, 1935, p. 10.

Benton, Thomas Hart. *An American in Art.* Lawrence, Kans.: University of Kansas Press, 1969.

———. *An Artist in America.* New York: Robert McBride, 1937.

Berg, A. Scott. *Max Perkins, Editor of Genius.* New York: E. P. Dutton, 1978.

Bode, Carl. *Mencken.* Carbondale, Ill.: Southern Illinois University Press, 1969.

——— (ed.). *The New Mencken Letters.* New York: Dial Press, 1977.

Boyd, Ernest. "Willard Huntington Wright," *Saturday Review of Literature,* April 22, 1939, p. 8.

Brown, Milton. *American Painting From the Armory Show to the Depression.* Princeton, N.J.: Princeton University Press, 1955.

Bruccoli, Matthew J. *The Fortunes of Mitchell Kennerley, Bookman.* New York: Harcourt Brace Jovanovich, 1986.

Butcher, Fanny. *Many Lives, One Love.* New York: Harper & Row, 1973.

Carr, Harry. *Los Angeles: City of Dreams.* New York: Grosset & Dunlap, 1935.

Churchill, Allen. *The Literary Decades.* Englewood Cliffs, N.J.: Prentice Hall, 1971.

Crawford, Walter. "Willard Huntington Wright: Aesthete and Critic," M.A. thesis, Columbia University, 1947.

Davidson, Abraham. *Early American Modernist Painting.* New York: Harper & Row, 1981.

Dolmetsch, Carl. *The Smart Set: A History and an Anthology.* New York: Dial Press, 1966.

Einbinder, Harvey. *The Myth of the Britannica.* New York: Grove Press, 1964.

Forgue, Guy (ed.). *The Letters of H. L. Mencken.* New York: Knopf, 1961.

Forum Magazine, 1912–1917.

The Forum Exhibition of Modern American Painters. Exhibition catalogue, Anderson Galleries, 1916.

Francisco, Charles. *Gentleman: The William Powell Story.* New York: St. Martin's Press, 1985.

Gelman, Barbara (ed.). *Photoplay Treasury.* New York: Crown, 1972.

Gilmer, Walker. *Horace Liveright, Publisher of the Twenties.* New York: David Lewis, 1970.

Harrell, Anne. *The Forum Exhibition: Selections and Additions.* Exhibition catalogue, Whitney Museum of American Art at Philip Morris, May 18–June 22, 1983.

Hart, James. *The Popular Book: A History of America's Literary Taste.* New York: Oxford University Press, 1961.

Haycraft, Howard (ed.). *The Art of the Mystery Story.* New York: Carroll & Graf, 1974.

———. *Murder for Pleasure.* New York: Carroll & Graf, 1984.

Hearst's Weekly Magazine, 1921.

Hertz, Elizabeth. "The Continuing Role of Stanton Macdonald-Wright and Synchromism in Modern Art," Ph.D. thesis, Ohio State University, 1968.

Hoffman, Frederick; Charles Allen; Carolyn Ulrich. *The Little Magazine: A History and a Bibliography.* Princeton, N.J.: Princeton University Press, 1946.

Homer, William Innes. *Avant-Garde Painting and Sculpture in America, 1910–1925.* Exhibition catalogue, Delaware Art Museum (Wilmington), 1975.

———. *Alfred Stieglitz and the American Avant-Garde.* Boston: Graphic Society, 1977.

Hunter, Sam. *Modern American Painting and Sculpture.* New York: Dell, 1959.

International Studio, 1916–1917.

284

Kahn, E. J. *Harvard*. New York: Norton, 1969.

Kazin, Alfred. *On Native Grounds*. New York: Harcourt Brace Jovanovich, 1942.

Kean, Randolph. "East Street Railways and the Development of Charlottesville," *The Magazine of Albemarle County History*, Vol. 33, 1975.

Kemler, Edgar. *The Irreverent Mr. Mencken*. Boston: Little, Brown, 1950.

Knight, Christopher. "On Native Ground: U.S. Modern," *Art in America*, October 1983, pp. 166–174.

————. "The 1916 Forum Exhibition and the Concept of an American Modernism," M.A. thesis, State University of New York at Binghamton, 1976.

Kogan, Herman. *The Great EB: The Story of the Encyclopaedia Britannica*. Chicago: University of Chicago Press, 1958.

Kreisworth, Martin. "The Will to Create: Faulkner's Apprenticeship and Willard Huntington Wright," *Arizona Quarterly*, Vol. 37, No. 2, Summer 1981, pp. 149–165.

Kuehl, John, and Jackson Bryer. *Dear Scott/Dear Max: The Fitzgerald–Perkins Correspondence*. New York: Scribners, 1971.

Levin, Gail. *Synchromism and American Color Abstraction, 1910–1925*. Exhibition catalogue, Whitney Museum and George Braziller, 1978.

Lisle, Laurie. *Portrait of an Artist: The Biography of Georgia O'Keeffe*. New York: Seaview Books, 1980.

Los Angeles Times, 1908–1913, 1920.

Lounsbery, Myron. "Against the American Game: The 'Strenuous' Life of Willard Huntington Wright," *Prospects*, Vol 5, 1980, pp. 507–555.

Lowe, Sue Davidson. *Alfred Stieglitz*. New York: Farrar, Straus & Giroux, 1983.

McWilliams, Carey. *The Southern California County*. New York: Duell, Sloane & Pearce, 1946.

Maltin, Leonard. *The Great Movie Shorts*. New York: Crown, 1972.

————. "Philo Vance at the Movies" in Jon Tuska (ed.), *Philo Vance: The Life and Times of S. S. Van Dine*, pp. 35–47.

Man Ray. *Self Portrait*. New York: McGraw-Hill, 1963.

Manchester, William. *Disturber of the Peace*. New York: Harper Brothers, 1950.

Mayfield, Sara. *The Constant Circle*. New York: Delacorte Press, 1968.

Moore, Ed. "Oneonta Past and Present" (5/2/61) in the Huntington Memorial Library local-history clipping file.

More, John Hammond. *Albemarle: Mr. Jefferson's County*. Charlottesville: University of Virginia Press, 1976.

Mott, Frank Luther. *A History of American Magazines*. Cambridge, Mass.: Harvard University Press, 1968.

Munson, Gorham. *The Awakening Twenties*. Baton Rouge: Louisiana State University Press, 1986.

New York Evening Mail, January–March 1914; 1917.

Nye, Russell. *The Unembarrassed Muse*. New York: Dial Press, 1970.

Paige, D. D. (ed.). *The Letters of Ezra Pound*. New York: Harcourt, Brace, 1950.

Paris, Barry. *Louise Brooks*. New York: Knopf, 1989.

Penzler, Otto. "Collecting Mystery Fiction: S. S. Van Dine," *The Armchair Detective*, Vol. 15, No. 4, pp. 350–356.

Photoplay, 1921–1922.

Pitts, Michael. *Famous Movie Detectives*. Methuen, N.J.: Scarecrow Press, 1979.

Pomeroy, Earl. *In Search of the Golden West: The Tourist in Western America*. New York: Knopf, 1957.

———. *The Pacific Slope*. New York: Knopf, 1965.

Pratt, George. *Spellbound in Darkness: A History of the Silent Film*. Greenwich, Conn.: New York Graphic Society, 1973.

Rascoe, Burton. *Before I Forget*. Garden City, N.Y.: Doubleday, Doran, 1937.

——— (ed.). *The Smart Set: An Anthology*. New York: Reynal and Hitchcock, 1934.

Read, Forrest (ed.). *Pound/Joyce: The Letters of Ezra Pound to James Joyce*. New York: New Directions, 1967.

Reid, B. L. *The Man from New York: John Quinn and His Friends*. New York: Oxford University Press, 1969.

Rewald, John. *Cézanne in America*. Princeton, N.J. : Princeton University Press, 1989.

Riggio, Thomas (ed.). *Theodore Dreiser: American Diaries: 1902–1926*. Philadelphia: University of Pennsylvania, 1983.

——— (ed.). *The Dreiser–Mencken Letters*. Philadelphia: University of Pennsylvania Press, 1986.

Rose, Barbara. *American Art Since 1900*. New York: Holt, Rinehart & Winston, 1975.

San Francisco Bulletin, 1919.

Scott, David. "The Art of Stanton Macdonald-Wright" (exhibition catalogue), The National Collection of Fine Arts, 1970.

Seligmann, Herbert. *Alfred Stieglitz Talking*. New Haven: Yale University Press, 1966.

Simonson, Lee. *Part of a Lifetime*. New York: Duell, Sloane & Pearce, 1943.

Sketchbook of Lynchburg, Virginia: Its People and Its Trade. Lynchburg: the Virginian Job Printing House, 1887.

The Smart Set, 1912–1914.

Smith, David R. "S. S. Van Dine at 20th-Century Fox" in Tuska (ed). *Philo Vance: The Life and Times of S. S. Van Dine*, pp. 48–58.

Starr, Kevin. *Americans and the California Dream: 1850–1915*. New York: Oxford University Press, 1973.

———. *Inventing the Dream: California Through the Progressive Era*. New York: Oxford University Press, 1985.

Stenerson, Douglas. *H. L. Mencken: Iconoclast from Baltimore*. Chicago: University of Chicago Press, 1971.

Storrs, Les. *Santa Monica: Portrait of a City Yesterday and Today.* Published by the Santa Monica Bank in commemoration of the Santa Monica Centennial, 1974.

Swanberg, W. A. *Dreiser.* New York: Scribners, 1965.

Terhune, Albert Payson. *To the Best of My Memory.* New York: Harper's, 1930.

Thayer, John Adams. *Astir.* Boston: Small, Maynard, 1910.

Town Topics, 1912–1914.

Tuska, Jon. *In Manors and Alleys: A Casebook on the American Detective Film.* New York: Greenwood Press, 1988.

———— (ed.). *Philo Vance: The Life and Times of S. S. Van Dine.* Bowling Green, Ohio: Bowling Green University Press (Popular Writers Series No. 1), 1971.

————. *The Detective in Hollywood.* New York: Doubleday, 1978.

Untermeyer, Louis. *Bygones.* New York: Harcourt, Brace & World, 1965.

Vacha, J. E. "When Wagner Was Verboten," *New York History,* April 1983, pp. 171–188.

Waters, Cecile. *Holsinger's Charlottesville.* Charlottesville, Virginia: Heblich, FT, Bates & Co., 1976.

Watson, Dori Boynton. "Stanton Macdonald-Wright," M.A. thesis, UCLA, 1956.

Webb, William. "Charlottesville and Albemarle County: 1865–1900," Ph.D. thesis, University of Virginia, 1955.

Weintraub, Stanley. *London Yankees.* New York: Harcourt Brace Jovanovich, 1979.

Wertheim, Frank Arthur. *The New York Little Renaissance.* New York University Press, 1976.

The West Coast Magazine, 1909–1912.

Wheelock, John (ed.). *Editor to Author: The Letters of Maxwell E. Perkins.* New York: Scribners, 1950.

Wilson, Edmund. "The All-Star Literary Vaudeville" in Loren Baritz (ed.), *The Culture of the Twenties.* New York: Bobbs Merrill, 1970.

Wood, James. *Magazines in the United States.* New York: Ronald Press, 1971.

BIBLIOGRAPHY OF W. H. WRIGHT'S BOOKS

Published under his own name:

Europe After 8:15 (with H. L. Mencken and George Jean Nathan). New York: John Lane, 1914.

What Nietzsche Taught. New York: Huebsch, 1915.

Modern Painting: Its Tendency and Meaning. New York: John Lane, 1915.

The Creative Will: Studies in the Philosophy and the Syntax of Aesthetics. New York: John Lane, 1916.

The Man of Promise. New York: John Lane, 1916.

The Forum Exhibition of Modern American Painters. Exhibition catalogue, Anderson Galleries, New York, March 1916.

The Great Modern French Stories: A Chronological Anthology. New York: Boni & Liveright, 1917.

Misinforming a Nation. New York: Huebsch, 1917.

Informing a Nation. New York: Dodd, Mead, 1917.

The Future of Painting. New York: Huebsch, 1923.

The Great Detective Stories: A Chronological Anthology. New York: Scribners, 1927.

Published under the name "S. S. Van Dine":

The Benson Murder Case. New York: Scribners, 1926.

The "Canary" Murder Case. New York: Scribners, 1927.

The Greene Murder Case. New York: Scribners, 1928.

The Bishop Murder Case. New York: Scribners, 1929.

The Scarab Murder Case. New York: Scribners, 1930.

The Kennel Murder Case. New York: Scribners, 1933.

The Dragon Murder Case. New York: Scribners, 1933.

The Casino Murder Case. New York: Scribners, 1934.

The Garden Murder Case. New York: Scribners, 1935.

The President's Mystery Story (with Rupert Hughes, Samuel Hopkins Adams, Anthony Abbot, Rita Weiman, and John Erskine). New York: Farrar & Rinehart, 1935.

Philo Vance Murder Cases. New York: Scribners, 1936.

The Kidnap Murder Case. New York: Scribners, 1936.

A Philo Vance Weekend. New York: Grosset & Dunlap, 1937.

The Gracie Allen Murder Case. New York: Scribners, 1938.

The Winter Murder Case. New York: Scribners, 1939.

INDEX

Philo Vance novels. *See also specific titles*
anthology of, 254–56
desire to discontinue, 203, 210, 214, 222–23, 234, 245
dictation of, 249
diminishing quality of, 231–33, 236–37, 249, 256, 261–63
elements of, 185–86, 216, 249–50
film versions of, 196, 204–8, 212–13, 233–34, 237–38, 240–44, 250, 256, 260–63, 269
income from, 181, 192–93, 196, 230–31, 240, 256
intricacy of plots, 185
love interest, 248
market for, 185, 191, 196–97
method of deduction, 185–86
parodies of, 213, 260
promotion of, 183–84, 188–89, 198, 200, 213, 214, 236, 254, 256, 257
reviews of, 184, 193–94, 199, 210, 215, 219, 236, 250
sales of, 184, 215, 236, 256
serialization of, 189–90, 195, 197, 201, 227, 240, 254, 257
social life and, 214
themes of, 216, 249–50
the Thirties and, 248, 253–54
titles of, 200–1
translations of, 197
the Twenties and, 188, 191–92
Photoplay, 161–63
Picabia, Francis, 68–69
Picasso, Pablo, 78
Poetry
in *Smart Set*, 12–13, 16–17, 29–30
Wright's, 45, 49
Poirot, Hercule, 173
Politics, pro-German, 109–11, 127, 131–35
Pollard, Percival, 54, 61, 66
Portrait of the Artist's Brother (S. Wright), 271
Portrait of S. S. Van Dine (S. Wright), 81
Pound, Ezra, 3, 16–17, 20, 25, 26, 29, 32, 217
Powell, William, 204, 206, 208, 211, 212, 233, 234, 237, 240, 256
Powwow Murder Case, The (Wright), 256, 258, 263
Prentice, William, 247
President's Mystery Story, The, 253

Quinn, John, 69

Racism, 183
Rascoe, Burton, 137, 235–36, 242, 243
Rathbone, Basil, 212, 214, 256
Ray, Man, 101, 149
Redman, Jeanne, 167–68, 209
Reedy, William Marion, 54, 126
Reedy's Mirror, 124, 127
Reinhardt, Max, 239, 246
Renoir, 82, 83
Rideout, Henry Milner, 56–57
Rinehart, Mary Roberts, 230

Roosevelt, Franklin D., 253
Rumely, Edward, 128–29, 134
Russell, Morgan, 18, 31, 34, 72–80, 86, 88, 154. *See also* Synchromism
exhibitions of, 83–85, 100–3, 271
goals of, 73–75
influences on, 73–75
personal characteristics of, 74
retrospective, 85, 271
Russell, Rosalind, 242, 244
Rubáiyát The (film), 152, 156
Ryerson, Florence, 205, 206, 211, 224, 241

St. Clair, Malcolm, 204–8
Salmon, André, 79
San Francisco, 143–47
San Francisco Bulletin, 143–45
Santa Monica, CA, 39–41
Saturday Review of Literature, The, 250–52
Sayers, Dorothy, 172–74, 230, 232
Scarab Murder Case, The (S. S. Van Dine), 213–16
Schallert, Edwin, 43
Schermerhorn, Claire. *See* Burke, Claire
Schnitzler, Arthur, 18, 22
Schulberg, B. P., 204, 205, 211
Screenwriting, 207, 221–22, 226
Scribners, 199, 257, 261. *See also* Perkins, Max
first Philo Vance novels and, 181
The Man of Promise and, 214, 217
Scribner's Magazine, 4, 7, 10, 189–90, 195, 197, 201
"Second, Child, The" (Wright), 67
Seldes, Gilbert, 219, 236, 251
Sexuality
planned book on, 112
as theme of works published in *Smart Set*, 11–15, 21, 23–26
Wright's, 42–43, 46
Simonson, Lee, 44, 45, 72
Sinclair, May, 17, 20, 27
Sinclair, Upton, 54, 64
Smart Set, The (magazine), 3–32, 87, 112
advertisers in, 23
"The American" series, 22–23, 28
anthology of, 235–36, 242–43
assessment of, 4
contoversial pieces published in, 11–15, 21–26
expenditures at, 30, 31
fiction published in, 10–12
firing of Wright, 30–32, 145
hiring of Wright, 12, 28, 66–67
"Los Angeles: The Chemically Pure," 7–10
Mencken and, 3–4, 6, 9, 14, 19–26, 28, 59, 62, 66, 112, 210, 235, 236, 242–43
1913 trip to Europe and, 15–20, 24–25, 28, 70, 76, 78, 86
office politics at, 4–5
"Owen Hatteras" column, 22, 24
payment of writers at, 12–13, 30, 31
plans for, 5–7, 22
poetry in, 12–13, 16–17, 29–30

293

294

JOHN LOUGHERY is the art critic for *The Hudson Review* and an English teacher at the Columbia Grammar and Preparatory School in New York City. His art, film, and book reviews have appeared in a variety of periodicals, including *Arts Magazine, Art Journal,* and *New Art Examiner.* He is currently working on a novel and on a biography of the painter John Sloan.